The Pursuit of God's Own Heart!

*A profile study of a worshiper: David,
whom God said is "a man after my own heart!"
And A look through the lens of David's life,
the meaning and purpose of the Christian life!*

JOHN E. LEON

ISBN 978-1-64140-372-6 (paperback)
ISBN 978-1-64140-374-0 (hardcover)
ISBN 978-1-64140-373-3 (digital)

Christian Faith Publishing, Inc.
832 Park Avenue
Meadville, PA 16335
www.christianfaithpublishing.com

Unless otherwise noted, The English Standard Version Study Bible by Crossway, 2008, was primary source cited.

Also, The Nelson Study Bible, New King James, by Thomas Nelson Publishers, 1997, and The New International Version, by Holman Bible Publishers, 1986.

Printed in the United States of America

David, the Lord declares to you that the Lord will make you a House!
—*2 Samuel 7:11*

Acknowledgments

To

The one, whose prayers initiated God's pursuit of my heart long before I would know her as my best friend and wife, my dear Patricia, for with her encouragement, confidence and critical insights, this work found completion; and ultimately to the Lord Jesus Christ who planted the seed deep within my soul, the compelling pursuit to know Him, for without Whom, such a book would not have been written...

"Indeed, I count everything as loss because of the surpassing worth of knowing Christ Jesus my Lord!" Phil. 3:8

Preface

I have never written a book before because I haven't had the desire—until now. Certainly, I did not plan to write this one. However, I believe the Lord had everything to do with the purpose and premise of this book. Have you ever had a creative concept for a project and it expanded far beyond your expectations?

Originally, this book evolved from a teaching series in our fellowship regarding the purpose and principles of worship. We began to study the life of a man well-known in all the Bible to be one of the individuals who really understood the dynamics of worshiping God—David. Since it is ascribed to David, at least by most scholars, as the author of 75 of the 150 psalms, the value of such a study would be unquestionable.[1] Also, David was historically a central figure in establishing various traditions of worship in the future life of Israel.

But there was another reason for this study. It had everything to do with the characterization given to him by God Himself. David was the only man in the Old Testament whom God described, "I sought and found, a man after My own heart." So this book takes us on a journey into the life of David, with the goal of discovering what God meant by such a description of a man who would become the greatest and most effective monarch in Israel's history.

The answer to the meaning and understanding of this characterization by God is progressively revealed in each chapter, contributing to the profile of such a man. Subsequently, as we travel through the narrative of David, we will soon realize God is telling a greater story—His Story—to each of us, which transcends all human history. It is known of which I like to describe as the *metanarrative* of God. It is God's grand narrative that is beyond, if you will, of David's narrative. And yet David's story contributes significantly to God's metanarrative, particularly with regard to the promise God makes David: "The Lord will make you a house." Therefore, we will discover David's life juxtaposes God's purpose and the building of this house that will fulfill God's promise to David. So, significant in importance is such a house, it is central to the metanarrative of God, because it was conceived by Him "before the foundation of the world" (Eph. 1:4–6).

We will realize also the reason this house parallels David's story is because it has everything to do with you and me. The house comprises people. It is the eternal family God desired and planned before all creation. This eternal family are all those devout followers of Jesus Christ. And just as God desired "a man after His own heart," God desires to have a people with the same passion and willingness to cultivate such character, as David realized in his own life. Therefore, one cannot discuss David without talking about prayer and the importance of such an activity in his life or worship and how it enabled him to cultivate an intimate relationship with God. We learn that one cannot ignore a foundational cornerstone of David's character, which is the most important Godly attribute but the least understood: humility. Further yet, when viewing David's life, unavoidable for discussion are such frequently misunderstood dynamics as repentance, reconciliation, holiness, and becoming a student of God, as David did. Ultimately, this book discusses the dynamic meaning and enriching purpose of the Christian life!

So we begin through the early years of David's life when he is first called by God to become the second king of Israel's monarchy, culminating with one of the most pivotal moments in David's life and in all of the Bible. It happens during the last ten years of his reign and became known as the Covenant of David or the Davidic Covenant.[2] A conversation occurs between God and David, initiated by David's desire to build God a house (Temple). Nathan, the Lord's prophet, gives David his blessing, believing it's a wonderful idea. However, later that night God speaks to Nathan in a vision, and David's plans are reversed by God. Instead, God tells David He is going to make him a "house," promising him this house will remain forever. The magnitude of God's promise to David is, as an understatement, the most overwhelming, unanticipated, undeserved, and shocking development David could have possibly experienced in his lifetime.

When David first responds to God's decision, he begins with three powerful words: "Who am I?" It is those words of humility that express an overflowing heart of gratitude to the God he loves and for all God has done for him throughout his life. And yet such a declaration has even broader meaning because it has a direct relationship to discovering what it means to have a heart after God's own heart. The question serves for many a greater meaning, as it always has, regarding one's purpose in life? Or where does one find their place in this world? Why does one exist and what is the meaning of this life?

As you travel with me on our journey through David's life, we will learn the answers to those questions—just as David did during his life—by discovering what exactly God meant when He said of David, "I have found a man after My own heart!" And, most importantly, the answer to the ultimate question, "Who am I?" will be realized by discovering the definition of what kind of "House" God did promise to build for David!

It is, therefore, my prayer that you will realize, just as I have, that having a heart after God's own heart is not just something the Lord desired of one man but it is His will for each of us. And that the greater personal message transcending David's' life will go far beyond the reach of mere information but will result in an inward transformation for you, leading you to fulfill His ultimate destination for your life. For as we know, God is worth no less!

Introduction

David has always been my favorite. For me, he's always been the most fascinating and intriguing of all the characters in the Old Testament. Perhaps it could be attributed to his pronounced paradox of human frailty and the deep spiritual aspiration to know God. There are certainly the definitive contrasts in which he could wield a sword ruthlessly like no other soldier but then be found unashamedly expressing his tears, openly, in intimate worship or dancing exuberantly, without his royal robes, before the Lord and all Israel to see his unbridled joy.

David was a man's man. He knew how to fight. His success as the greatest king in Israel's history indicates this reality. Just look at his record:

- Territorially, David expanded the boundaries of Israel from six thousand to sixty thousand square miles.[1]
- He established extensive trade routes that reached throughout the known ancient world. Therefore, unprecedented wealth came into the nation, from Phoenicia, Egypt, Damascus, Assyria, and Arabia!
- The old, longtime enemies of Israel that Joshua did not subdue were finally conquered: Philistia, Moab, Damascus,

Zobah (Arameans), Ammon, Amalek, and Edom were all brought under the subjugation of David's monarchy![2]

- David captured Jerusalem in 1004 BC, seven years after he began his reign in Hebron in 1011 BC.[3]
- And one of the most singular, momentous achievements was David uniting Israel and Judah under one monarch.[4]

There would be no other king comparable to the effectiveness of David's reign in all of Israel's history. But David, not only knew how to fight, he knew how to worship deeply. Half of the Psalms, which became the worship songs of Israel, were authored by David. Many of them reveal a tenderness and humility that is not always associated with military men. They also offer a tremendous insight into David's relationship to the Lord, reflecting the rare dynamic of knowing how to worship God "in spirit and truth" (John 4:23–24).

Another fascinating factor is that David has more scripture recorded regarding his life than all the other Old Testament figures. Both Abraham and Joseph have fourteen chapters. Jacob has eleven; and Elijah, ten chapters. David has seventy-five chapters in the Bible devoted to his story. There are forty-two such chapters in the two books of Samuel and 1 Kings. First and Second Chronicles add another twenty chapters while thirteen of the superscriptions in the book of Psalms directly relate to significant events in his narrative.[5] Further yet, the New Testament comprises fifty-eight citations regarding the Old Testament record of David's life.[6]

But there was something more, much more that captivated my interest regarding David. It was the divine inscription, if you will, that God used to "mark" David's relationship with Him. It was not what his family said of him or the nation he governed for forty years, but it was the description given to him by God Himself. This is what piqued my interest. The only man in all the Bible who God said,

"I have searched for and found a man after My own heart" (1 Sam. 13:14).

Such a characterization provokes personal questions: What does that really mean to have a heart after God? What did that look like? What does that involve and what are the traits of such a heart? But greater yet, how and why would God give such an inscription of a man who would later commit adultery, murder, and deception in a scandalous cover-up? After all, no one would dispute the reality, especially in today's culture, such a story would indeed be a captivating scandalous plot for any contemporary novelist!

But regardless of those seemingly inexplicable facts, God would not have given David such a characterization if it were not true. It is worth noting we cannot discover the authenticity of God's description of David if we ignore the glaring weaknesses and egregious missteps in his life. There are some lessons God desires for us to learn from this man. David was a sinner, just like you and me. So why would God distinguish him with such an inscription, if it were not true?

First, God spoke of such a man, long before David was born. Listen to the prophecy: *"And I will raise up for myself a faithful priest, who shall do according to what is in my heart and in my mind. And I will build him a sure house, and he shall go in and out before my anointed forever" (1 Sam. 2:35).* Here we recognize an important sign of the Davidic Covenant: "I will build him a sure house" (2 Sam. 7:11).

Secondly, this prophecy also gives us a leading indicator what it means to have "a heart after God's own heart." But let's not get ahead of ourselves despite the clue.

Thirdly, such a description serves a greater purpose from God's perspective in which He desires to capture our attention today by teaching us what it truly means to have a heart after His own heart. This generates a series of questions: What are the practical realities for every believer in cultivating such a level of intimacy with the Lord of creation? Is this possible for every individual, or is it just for a select few? Or is this level of relationship reserved only for David because of his "special" calling? These questions form the very pulse of this book, particularly against the backdrop of David's humanity regarding his obvious personal contradictions amid such an extraordinary divine characterization.

It is not by accident so much scripture is devoted to the life of David, but by divine design. God's inscription of David is not mere coincidence. Would not this divine description encapsulate God's greatest desire for you and me? Of course, it would, since this has been the eternal quest of God even before man's creation! Father-God is constantly searching, consistently seeking, and always desiring a man who is in pursuit of (after) His own heart!

It is therefore important for us to realize this "divine inscription," if you will, transcends God's personal commendation of one man's relationship to Him because it is an expressed desire of God's own heart for every believer to have such a relationship with Him. It is God's intentional purpose for us to learn and understand what it means to have a heart fully devoted to Him and thereby learn from the life of David. The apostle Paul states such an importance of learning from those in the "rearview mirror" of God's narrative ... *"For whatever was written in former days was written for our instruction, that through endurance and through the encouragement of the Scriptures we might have hope" (Rom. 15:4).*

So let us begin our own pursuit of learning and discovering what it means to have a heart after God's own heart. An inscription our Heavenly Father desires to write also on your heart and mine.

Prologue

The Invaluable Meaning of God's Word

L et's face it. The Bible is the most complex and comprehensive book ever written. And why shouldn't it be, since the Author surpasses the most brilliant human mind that has ever existed. So let me offer a brief insight regarding the interpretation of God's Word.

Since this book is about David's life, understanding the context during the time he lived is essential. The context for a biblical account is vitally important. We must therefore consider an important term known as *exegesis*. This refers to the process of interpreting Scripture. It is especially important in this book because there are over four hundred scriptures cited that are germane to the unpacking of God's inscription of David's life. The exegesis of Scripture involves three major underpinnings: the historical, literary, and theological analysis of the biblical text. These three pillars complement each other, producing a "conversation with the reader, a conversation about texts and their contexts, particular words, their meaning, and the claims others have made about them."[1] Establishing the context of a certain scriptural account will enhance our conversation and in particular provide significant insights regarding the nature of God's relationship with David. In this way we will better understand the essence of God's character.

The Historical Context

After the death of Joshua, there was a leadership vacuum in the nation of Israel. The nation wanted a king to lead them. So through the first Old Testament prophet Samuel, God directs him to anoint Saul as the first king of Israel. The establishment of the monarchy of Israel has begun.

Samuel was mentored from childhood by Eli, the high priest at the time. Eli also had two sons who served as priests in the Temple but were corrupt because of their sexual immorality, as well as their contempt for the sacrificial offerings of the Lord (1 Sam. 2:17). Eli's sons were consuming the best portions of meat the people were bringing to be offered to God as their sacrifice of worship. Scripture informs us the spiritual malady the sons suffered is that they served the Lord in the Temple but "they did not know the Lord" (1 Sam. 2:12).

As a result of this grave error, Eli was viewed by God as culpable in his sacred position as the high priest of the Temple, and as their father, since he was negligent in correcting his sons' behavior, resulted in the following indictment by God: *"I promised that your house and the house of your father should go in and out before Me forever,' but now the Lord declares: 'Far be it from Me, for those who honor Me I will honor, and those who despise Me shall be lightly esteemed. Behold, the days are coming when I will cut off your strength and the strength of your father's house, so that there will not be an old man in your house"* (1 Sam. 2:30–31).

This background is shared primarily to underscore the importance of this preeminent truth. Not only is it the dominant theme of the entire history of the monarchy of Israel, it pervades the narrative of David. We will be visiting this all-important principle throughout this book.

Saul had a charismatic stature being the "most handsome and the tallest man in all of Israel" (1 Sam. 9:2). But Saul's demise was attributed to his arrogance and obstinate attitude toward the Lord.

King Saul was preparing for a major battle with Israel's arch enemy, the Philistines. The sacred protocol for Israel was to offer a sacrifice before every battle and ask God's provision for victory. Samuel had not yet arrived. Due to Saul's fear of losing his army, since the Philistines overwhelmingly outnumbered the Israelites, the king preempted Samuel's duty and offered the sacrifice that was reserved only for the high priest to perform.

Saul had usurped Samuel's God-given position. God pronounced judgment on Saul declaring, *"You have done foolishly. You have not kept the command of the Lord your God, with which He commanded you. For then the Lord would have established your kingdom over Israel forever. But now your kingdom shall not continue. The Lord has sought a man after His own heart, and the Lord has commanded him to be prince over His people, because you have not kept what the Lord commanded you" (1 Sam. 13:13–14).*

We see two different men, with two different positions, who failed in their responsibilities to the Lord and incurred similar fates for the exact same reason. Eli was told his household of priests would not continue to serve in God's Temple in the future, which was a humiliating blow during ancient times not to have an ancestry to carry on your work as well as the legacy of one's name.

For Saul, it meant his rule would be ineffective and he would not have a ruling dynasty to carry on his name. But the cause for the failure of both men is the same. And this is the first lesson we must learn—these men did not value the importance to "honor" God first and foremost in their lives.

So God reveals to Samuel that He has been on a search for "A man after my own heart." Now it's important to consider the adverb *after*. The fundamental meaning of this word refers to "following in time or place." But the grammatical structure of the sentence and the usage of the word implies "to obtain, to seize, or to pursue." God is announcing to Samuel, He has found "a man in pursuit of knowing Me!"

This is our introduction to David. As we begin our journey with David, we must not lose sight of the all-important principle that can be attributed to David's incomparable and effective reign as the second king of Israel. God did *not* say, "I have searched for a military genius or a great athletic warrior or a dynamic administrator," although David became all those things. God said, "He searched for a man after my own heart." And the corollary to such "a find" would be realized in David, of that which a high priest and a king would not do—honor God with his whole heart!

A final thought. God is omniscient, meaning He knows the past, present, and future. I don't believe God was saying to Samuel at the time, "I have found a man who has arrived!" But rather God knew (indicated by His prophecy before David's birth) David would someday truly, fully apprehend the meaningful and purposeful identity He ascribed to him … "For I already know his heart is in pursuit of Mine, as he sings to Me, while tending sheep in the pasture fields of Bethlehem!"

CHAPTER 1

The Divine Pursuit
of David!

The Lord has sought out a man after His own heart, and the
Lord has commanded him to be prince over His people!
—1 Samuel 13:14

God let Samuel know He had "searched for a man after His own heart" (1 Sam. 13:14), and he was to be found in the town of Bethlehem. God sends the reluctant Samuel to call on a dad by the name of Jesse, who is the father of eight sons. It is quite a profound scene because everyone is filled with fear for different reasons. Samuel is fearful for his life should Saul hear of him anointing a new king while he is still on the throne. And a personal visit from God's prophet naturally induced fear in the hearts of the residents because such a visitation was not the norm.

The Lord relieved Samuel's fear by directing him to lead the people in a sacrifice to disguise his motive for the visit. Samuel reassured the people he came in peace to worship the Lord with them. After the time of worship, Samuel began his "interviews" for the right candidate beginning with the oldest, Eliab (a name to remember), then Abinadab. Next was Shammah, until Samuel had reviewed all seven sons and informed Jesse, "The Lord has not chosen these." Samuel then inquired, "Are all your sons here?" Jesse replied, "There remains yet the youngest, but he is keeping the sheep!" Samuel then instructed Jesse to bring him in from the field. As soon as David arrived, God spoke to Samuel. "Arise, anoint him, for this is he."

Now let's not move too quickly over this decisive moment—this God moment—when God discloses, "This is he!" I can't help but wonder how much God longed for this moment to introduce Himself in a real tangible way to this young shepherd boy who was learning to sing songs of worship to Him while occupied with the responsibility of attending the sheep for his family. For we are given the background for this moment in which God tells Samuel, "I have sought…for a man after My own heart!"

Although we do not know how long God commenced such a search, we can glean from the Hebrew meaning for the word *sought*. It does mean "desired." God waited patiently for the right heart with the right man, meaning it could not be just any man. God had desired for a man who would lead His people "with a heart after His own heart."

This tells us two things about the nature of God's heart for people. First, God wanted such a man after His own heart because of His love for Israel. God desired a man who would represent His own heart accurately and authentically. He did not want another king who would abuse the people or his power due to self-interests.

The second aspect reveals how God desires for the individual heart to know and experience Him. Such knowledge could only be given to a man who would become interested in the Lord and His will. Remember this truth, for this thematic strand is woven through-out this book—it is that prominent.

This was a long-awaited moment because God had pursued such a man; and when the Lord states, "This is he," God is saying to

Samuel, "I have found him! He is the one…he's the man…he is the right man for My purpose for Israel!"

Now can you imagine the powerful scene for this family and prophet and their emotions regarding such an announcement? What do you think Samuel's reaction was to the news? Can we understand how relieved and excited Samuel must have been that God had finally revealed the next king of Israel to him? After all, God had already informed Samuel the next king would be chosen from the "sons of Jesse" (1 Sam. 16:1) and David was the last son. But not only that, based on appearance and stature, he would be the least qualified, wouldn't he? For during ancient times, the eldest son was given the most esteem and respect in the family. David was the youngest son, probably about thirteen to fourteen years of age at the time, and he did not even qualify to enlist in the military, which was twenty years of age to be eligible (Num. 1:3).

Also, being a shepherd was considered one of the most menial, lower-class occupations one could possibly have. It was not a very attractive or lucrative job and could be very dangerous work due to wild predators or thieves. David did not possess the stature for ruling a nation.

And what about the dad's response? Yes, probably much pride, but probably some apprehension on how it could affect his family. And how about the brothers? They were probably confused, disappointed, and some of them jealous that their younger brother was chosen over them, which would be revealed later during a crisis.

Anointed to Serve

And then there was David. What were his thoughts when he first heard those words from the prophet's lips, "God has chosen you to be the next king of Israel!" First of all, when David arrived from the field, dirty and smelly, having been with sheep, I'm sure he was very nervous to see the prophet of God visiting with his family. He had to sense something was up. "What would warrant such a visit from this godly man?"

Of course, David was not disappointed considering what happened next in this scene, for Scripture gives us insight into David's thoughts. Samuel took the horn of oil and anointed David in the midst of his brothers, and we are told, "The Spirit of the Lord rushed upon David from that day forward" (1 Sam. 16:13, ESV).

David could not have been more bewildered, awestruck, and overwhelmed. He had just had a powerful encounter with the Lord! Based on the Hebrew language of this scripture, the word *rush* indicates the Spirit came upon him with a "forceful effect." This is later affirmed in the words he expressed in one of his psalms: "*You hem me in, behind and before, and lay your hand upon me. Such knowledge is too wonderful for me, it is high; I cannot attain it*" (Ps. 139:5–6).

According to this account, in David's own words, this encounter was too much for him to explain, let alone understand. It was very overwhelming for David to experience the physical "touch" of God's Holy Spirit. It also indicates when David was encased by the Holy Spirit, as he described, he was overcome with astonishment, joy, gratitude, and amazement with God's Presence all over his entire being. But most importantly, David clearly knew he had been physically affected by the power of God's Spirit. God had personally affirmed the symbolism of the actual anointing with oil by showing up through His Spirit; and everyone present knew something extraordinary happened—Samuel, David's dad Jesse, all his brothers, his entire family, and, most certainly, David.

God especially wanted David to know He had shown up in his life in a dramatic way. God wanted David to know, through this encounter, it was by God's own initiative he had been chosen for God's divine purpose, as well as for his family to know this reality too. David, more than anyone, needed to become aware he had nothing to do with God' decision to appoint him the next king of Israel. It was about a greater purpose and God's design, which transcended the personal limitations of one young shepherd boy.

This was a moment about God and His sovereign plan for one man's life. It was about that all-important, indescribable, unfathomable attribute of God's own heart, which is called grace. The Greek word for grace is *charis*, which means gift or favor.[1] God was giving Himself to David through His Spirit. David would never again be alone. What a gift!

A well-known definition of God's grace is "unmerited favor." David could not qualify based on his resume. David could not earn the position. But I also like a more expanded definition by Dr. Dallas Willard as he describes this great attribute known as God's grace or favor: "Grace is God acting in our lives to accomplish what we cannot accomplish on our own!"[2]

This was an important foundation God established for David's life. David needed to learn early, if he was to be effective and able to avoid the missteps of his predecessor, the importance of relying upon God would be imperative, so as to do what his human limitations would not allow him to do. God chose David to be the next king, not David. David's life would not be the same, even though he would return to the family task of tending the sheep, for his calling by God would inevitably be tested. In the meantime, everyone present knew this incident must remain top secret because during these formative years of David, Saul would still remain king!

A Major Test!

Every calling or word from God will always go through a major test regarding one's faith. Did God really speak to me? Did God choose me to do a specific work for Him? Is this really my purpose in life? Everyone will experience such a test because it is God's way of preparing one for the work they are called to do.

Many people, including the nonreligious, are familiar with the story of David and Goliath. Consider athletic events in which the underdog is pitted against the overwhelming favorite. The matchup is characterized by sports journalists, metaphorically, as "David versus Goliath."

This was David's first major test since his calling by God and the anointing by Samuel. Several years have passed since that experience, and he is now about sixteen to seventeen years of age. Now I would like us to focus on the dynamics that tested David's calling and virtually put David, not only on Saul's radar screen but all of Israel, as well as all of the nation's enemies. The test was *not* primarily in regard to the intimidating size of Goliath (almost ten feet tall) and his powerful weaponry, though the confrontation was a factor in shaping David's character. The real test were the attitudes and "words" of David's family, friends, and foe. How would David respond in the midst of suspicion and skepticism? So let's view the scene.

The Philistines had gathered their army for a major confrontation with Saul and Israel's army. As was the custom in ancient times, the challenge involved two men, one each from the opposing armies, to fight the other to the death, with the winner subjugating the losing army to their rule! For forty days (2 Sam. 17:16), Goliath mockingly pranced back and forth in the valley of Elah, belting out his toxic, hate-filled invitation for any Israelite to accept his challenge to the duel of death. But no one accepted because "Saul and all of Israel were afraid" (2 Sam. 17:11). One day Jesse called for David from the field. Yes, the future king of Israel, still tending sheep, and was now sent by Dad with food to take to his three older brothers who were on the frontline of the battle. David arrives on day 41 and is in the trenches to distribute the food for his brothers. Suddenly Goliath appears and ensues with his typical mocking and defiant challenge. David is pro-voked with anger and says, "What shall be done for the man who kills this Philistine and takes away the reproach from Israel? For who is this uncircumcised Philistine, that he should defy the armies of the living God?" (1 Sam. 17:26). Let me offer my own translation: "Who is this guy? Where did he come from, and who does he think he is defying our God?" But someone overheard David's righteous indig-nation, and that someone was Eliab, David's oldest brother.

Israel is on the threshold of facing her greatest battle, but in the trenches a family battle becomes priority as Eliab lashes out at his youngest brother with a stinging indictment: "Why have you come down? And with whom have you left those few sheep in the wilder-ness? I know your presumption and the evil of your heart, for you have come down to see the battle."

But David responds with a normal sibling reaction to an elder brother: "What have I done now? Was it not a word?" David natu-rally wants to defend himself against the attempt by his older brother to embarrass him. Eliab not only questions David's motivation for being on the battlefield—unaware he was sent on a mission by his dad for the benefit of he and his brothers—but let David know he was not qualified to be on the battlefield. Eliab subsequently felt compelled to offer David an exclamation mark to his diatribe by tell-ing him in no uncertain terms where David was most qualified to be in attendance—back at the ranch, taking care of the sheep! Needless to say, it was a humiliating blow for the shepherd boy in front of the army of Israel!

Nevertheless, David was undeterred because this incident was soon reported to Saul, causing the king to send for the young lad. Now David had already been introduced to Saul because he played his lyre for Saul and had become Saul's armor-bearer. It is recorded that "Saul loved him greatly."

David had developed a friendship with the king, as well as with members of the royal court. David respectfully made his case before Saul: "Let no man's heart fail because of him (Goliath). Your servant will go and fight with this Philistine." Saul responded, "You are not able...for you are but a youth, and he (Goliath) has been a man of war from his youth."

But David, even though he felt misunderstood by his brothers and his king, persisted as he politely offered his resume: "Your servant used to keep sheep for his father. And when there came a lion, or a bear, and took a lamb from the flock, I went after him and struck him and delivered it out of his mouth...Your servant has struck down both lions and bears, and this uncircumcised Philistine shall be like one of them, for he has defied the armies of the living God" (1 Sam. 17:32–36). Finally, Saul relented, giving David his blessing.

David's Confidence in God

Now, as David walked onto the battlefield, he was only equipped with five smooth stones and his sling. Can you imagine what his brothers must have thought when they saw him going up against this giant warrior in the open valley? What was Saul's thoughts and the entire army of Israel as they watched in utter disbelief? David was the youngest, the most inexperienced, ill-equipped soldier that day. The future of the nation rested on his young shoulders in this winner-takes-all battle, giving Israel and Saul more reason to be fearful of the outcome!

But David had something more, something much more. He had the Spirit of the living God of Israel with him. And he knew it. As soon as Goliath realized who his opponent was—a kid with a sling—it says Goliath "disdained him," while the expletives poured out toward David as the large warrior cursed him and let David know he was not a worthy opponent. But David then gave a brief response to Goliath, "You come to me with a sword, and with a spear and with a javelin, but I come to you in the Name of the Lord of hosts, the God of the armies of Israel, whom you have defied" (vv. 42–45).

Then, with one stone from his sling, David became the hero of Israel. But for David this was the real test: How many people, who were supposed to be on David's side, actually believed he could win the battle? David's family had *dismissed* him. David's friends, including his king, *disqualified* him. And of course, his foe naturally *disdained* him because David was not a worthy combatant.

Eliab in his jealous anger questioned David's motive falsely, accusing him, and then humiliated him. All King Saul offered him for encouragement was that "he was not able to do the job because he was too young and inexperienced" (v. 33). And, of course, what else could one expect from the enemy, as Goliath mockingly declared David to be incompetent since he did not even measure up to the appearance of a soldier due to his youth and was not properly equipped for battle, as the giant of a man cursed his very existence!

This was the real test for David, rather than the physical confrontation itself, as far as God was concerned. The onslaught of words that diminished and devalued David, especially from the people who were supposed to be on his side supporting him, was the defining moment for David. Would David agree with his critics and capitulate to their claims, or would he stand his ground maintaining his confidence in the Lord and fight? Would he be filled with fear and flee because of these voices of doom? Or would he listen to a *voice* of faith and fight? You see, friend, the power of words cannot be overstated, because the Bible states, "Death and life are in the power of the tongue" (Prov. 18:21).

Let's look more closely at how David responds to these "voices of death," because we will get a glimpse of a man whose heart is in pursuit of God's heart. First of all, when Eliab falsely accuses David's motive and then insults him, what is his response? Not much. He does not spend time defending himself, his motive, or his occupation.

Now consider how he approaches his friend, the king of Israel. David is careful in making sure he does not disrespect his king. You see, David has quickly learned this "standoff" has been going on for forty days and no one has been willing to take the challenge from Goliath, Israel's enemy. Not one—not the army, not the royal court, not even the king.

Subsequently, David's first words to Saul and the royal court are words of comfort, reassurance, and hope. There is not any implied criticism as he offers his king, "Let no man's heart fail because of Goliath...Your servant will fight him!" David was simply saying, "Don't worry, King, I will take care of Goliath!" This young man is simply wanting to offer encouragement and reassurance to the king he loved and wanted to serve!

As we get a more crystallized glimpse into David's heart through this test, we hear a very important self-description: "Your *servant...* will fight him!" That's how David sees himself: a servant, but just not any servant, He is the king's servant! And after Saul reluctantly gave his blessing to David, the young teenager, the servant of the king is going off to fight the greatest battle of his life.

David, dressed only in his shepherd gear, without armor, no shield, no sword, no spear, marches into battle but with the heart of a shepherd. For you see, David was protecting his flock that day in the valley of Elah. Though the people were not yet his to rule, David did want to lay down his life for them, if necessary, in order to protect them. So, without much support behind him (people believing in him), David was committed to protecting his family, his friends, his king, and a nation, no matter the personal cost. David was willing to sacrifice his life to do it. David was learning what it meant to have the heart of a true shepherd.

But there was also something more that drove David to engage this giant of a warrior. As David quickly looked in the brook for just the "right smooth stones" for his arsenal (17:40), I believe he was listening to that still, small voice that encouraged and gave him a stilled confidence that day: "Thank you, David, for desiring to defend My Name and people. Thank you, David, for wanting to *Honor* Me by risking your life. And now, just as I was with you when 'we' killed the bear and lion, so I am with you now. I will never leave you or give up on you, especially when you are depending upon Me. David, let's do this!" David did his part by trusting God to do what he could not do! This, my friend, is the grace of God in action!

Thus, we discover, the first and most important attribute of David's heart toward God. David desires to *honor* God even at great personal cost through the willingness to risk his own life for God's greater purpose. When one is willing to honor God like this, God's grace will always enable and sustain such a commitment.

Now it is important to understand, one cannot give such devotion to God without an attitude of humility. It is through this ordeal, we realize also one of the most important attributes of David's heart: humility. Over the years during my journey with the Lord—based on personal observation and experience—I have framed what I tend to believe to be the essence of humility. This godly attribute is further delineated in chapter 12, but for now let me share with you a personal definition formed from God's Word: *It is the personal acknowledgement, through daily practice, that one is nothing without God—inadequate and incomplete in life without being fully dependent upon God by trusting Him to accomplish what only He can do in one's life!*

Through David's own words, he echoes this dynamic in one of his psalms ... *"I say to the Lord, 'You are my Lord; I have no good apart from you!'"* *(Ps. 16:2)*. David had already begun to discover in his young life that he was *incomplete* without God and, therefore, the only way he could be adequate or effective in life was by becoming fully dependent upon God through trusting Him to accomplish what only God could do in his life! Through this test, David discovers the importance of humility.

But before we can go any further we must understand the word *test* in the context of spiritual growth. It is God who "tests" and the enemy of our soul who "tempts." And there is a big difference. Temptation is always about sin. God has nothing to do with temptation. But when God tests, it is for the importance of learning the lesson God desires for us to learn about Him, as well as about ourselves. The "test" is always about character formation. David declares this truth in one of his psalms he recorded: "Search me, O God, and know my heart! Try me and know my thoughts! And see if there be any grievous way in me, and lead me in the way everlasting" (Ps. 139:23–24). David is saying, "Try me (test me) and show me what is truly in my heart since you, O Lord, are the only one who knows the human heart."

God introduced this test to David to teach him humility by being fully dependent upon God to do what David could not do! This Godly attribute is to be a central piece of his character in preparing him to be God's shepherd of His people. We then see God cultivating a true shepherd's heart in David through this major challenge early in David's life. David's love for his family, his people, his king, and, most importantly, the Lord compelled him to be willing to even sacrifice his life, if it meant doing so. The real miracle was that he did it against a background of criticism, skepticism, and disbelief. Because rather than listen to the voices that said "You can't," David preferred to listen to the One Voice who told him "We can!" David was not alone!

Now we must understand this vitally important and ultimate eternal truth that produced this momentous victory, not only for King Saul and Israel but especially for this young teenage shepherd boy. David succeeded because of God's pursuit of David. In other words, it was by God's initiative and the Lord showing up in David's life—anointing him with His Holy Spirit—that caused David to win the battle. David won because of divine pursuit. Without God's Spirit, David would have been overwhelmed by the odds and certainly would have experienced inevitable defeat. The stakes were high, and the salvation of an entire nation rested upon the shoulders of one very young man, a shepherd boy.

So David's defeat of Goliath is due to the divine pursuit of God. God introduced Himself to David by making the first move. Then God introduced a major test into David's life for all Israel to see by creating an opportunity for David to become the pursuer and not the pursued.

The word *test* is intentional and introduced because of the fundamental importance that is not only significant to the context of this scene in David's life, but also the prevalent emphasis it has to do with the Christian life throughout Scripture. It is a foundational reality in the life of the believer. It is an invaluable instrument used by God to fashion and form His character in those who desire to be His students.

Therefore, God provides tests periodically in our daily lives to help us grow in our walk with Him and so that we will arrive to our ultimate destination He established before we even existed. Invariably, such tests teach us something about ourselves—our heart, God's heart, particularly in our relationship with Him. This is a pervasive principle throughout God's Word. Listen to these words of David: "I bless the Lord who gives me counsel; in the night also my heart instructs me" (Ps. 16:7). Elsewhere, he stated similarly, "You have tried my heart, you have visited me by night, you have tested me, and you will find nothing" (Ps. 17:3). Personally then, I like to refer to our world as God's classroom in which He is constantly teaching those who desire to be His student and are wanting to know Him so as to fulfill the very purpose God has for their life.

This was true of David's life. Goliath was David's first major test God wanted to introduce to him for the purpose of training. David needed to learn early the importance of pursuing the heart of God by becoming fully dependent upon Him, especially if he was going to be an effective ruler of Israel. David's pursuit of God's own heart was a result of God's pursuit of David. And more importantly, David responded to God's overture with a heart of humility—through complete trust and full dependency upon the Lord.

It was this kind of heart God was searching for, as David did well in his first major test. David was willing to honor the Lord no matter the personal cost involved, and he did it with humility—fully dependent in trusting God to do in him what he could never do alone! And he was willing to face the challenge despite the cynics.

Through this major confrontation with Israel's enemy, God was establishing an important foundation early in David's life. A vital lesson learned, for overnight he became the celebrated hero of Israel. But this was just the beginning of teaching David in the grand class-room of God's world.

When the applause would gradually diminish, this same hero would soon become a fugitive for the next ten years throughout Israel before he would become king. For God had only just begun fash-ioning and forming this young man's heart. There would be other important lessons to learn on the way to the throne. The young David would now face the greatest challenges of his life as he would again be pursued but this time by a treacherous enemy who sought to destroy him. It would be a time of great anxiety, confusion, and chaos. And so more than ever, as he is pursued like an animal in the wilderness, David would find himself in constant pursuit of God's own heart, as he completely learned to trust and depend upon God to take him to the very destiny for which he was created—a shepherd of God's people!

....

CHAPTER 2

The Unique and Unexpected Friend!

A friend loves at all times, and a brother is born for adversity.
—Proverbs 17:17

With the monumental victory over Goliath behind him, David immediately became the celebrated hero of Israel. And why wouldn't he? The Israelite army had just witnessed a great miracle in which an inexperienced young teenager had slain a powerful veteran of war. Consequently, David was welcomed into Saul's royal court, of which it was said, "And Saul loved him greatly, and he became his armor-bearer" (1 Sam. 16:21).

Additionally, since David was also talented with a musical instrument known as a lyre, he occasionally played for Saul, producing a calming effect, particularly when the king was feeling agitated.

So for the next couple of years, David served in the royal court. Saul assigns him to a position of military leadership, even though David does not meet the qualifying age of twenty to serve in the army. However, this act by Saul is met with approval of the people and the royal court, which also includes Saul's eldest son, Jonathan, the heir to the throne of Israel.

Jonathan's Initiative

It's at this time a unique bond of friendship is born between Jonathan and David. It is said, "Jonathan made a covenant with David, because he loved him as his own soul" (1 Sam. 18:3). Then in a deeply meaningful gesture to constitute this "covenant of friendship" and in demonstration of his genuine unconditional commitment, the heir-apparent to the throne of Israel does something extraordinary. Jonathan removes his robe, his armor, and even his sword, and gives it to David for his personal use (1 Sam. 18:4–5). Jonathan was a prince of Israel. His clothes and armor would signify royalty intended for such a position.

A couple of things stand out by this act of Jonathan. With David wearing the prince's robe, it would signal to the men David led that he was valued by the royal court. This would designate David with a distinction that he was no ordinary leader but was greatly respected, personally, by the prince of Israel.

Secondly, for the prince of Israel to give away such significant possessions was an extraordinary act of selfless devotion to David, as well as a certain reversal of protocol. Since Jonathan was a prince, he had rank and position over David. David was a subordinate in the king's army. But here we have this remarkable picture. Rather than David, it is the prince who is offering his unconditional commitment and loyalty to David. It is royalty who offers loyalty! It is the ruler who honors the servant!

Why does this occur? Does Jonathan know the "secret" about Samuel's anointing of David? It is highly improbable Samuel would have told Jonathan since he was the heir to the throne and the potential for an adverse reaction to such news. Though Scripture does not inform us, based on Jonathan's atypical actions, we can sense one of two things regarding the development of this unique friendship. Either Jonathan was aware of David's destiny or God was involved in the introduction of such a friendship. Based on the pivotal turn of events in David's immediate future, I'm compelled to believe the "God factor" was central in giving to David such a marvelous friendship that he would need in the desperate circumstances he would soon find himself.

In addition to David's need for a true friend, another indicator pointing directly to God's involvement is the rare attribute found in leadership, particularly in a prince of Israel: humility! Therefore, we will soon discover God's purpose for this friendship while an assault from hell breaks out in David's life. This friendship had God's fingerprints all over it! Yes, indeed, it is just like Him!

Saul's Fear-Fed Pride!

It's important to underscore that Jonathan's offer of friendship occurred during the peak of David's popularity. Saul had sent the "new celebrity" of Israel out on many military excursions against Israel's arch enemy, the Philistines, and it is recorded: "David went out and was successful wherever Saul sent him, so that Saul set him over the men of war" (1 Sam. 18:5).

Subsequently, when Saul would visit various cities throughout Israel, the women would greet their king with songs, celebrating Israel's victories with the following acclaims: "Saul has struck down his thousands, and David his ten thousands" (1 Sam. 18:7). This enraged the insecure Saul. He was filled with jealousy and fear as he declared, "They have ascribed to David ten thousands, and to me they have ascribed thousands, and what more can he have but the kingdom?" (1 Sam. 18:8).

Saul became fearful of losing his position and status in life because he felt threatened by the military successes of David. But it also went much deeper than that for Saul as Scripture informs us what he did to remedy the situation:

> *Saul was afraid of David because the Lord was with him, but had departed from Saul. So Saul removed him from his presence and made him a commander of a thousand. And he (David) went out and came in before the people. And David had success in all his undertakings, for the Lord was with him. And when Saul saw that he had great success, he stood in fearful awe of him. But all Israel and Judah loved David, for he went out and came in before them. (1 Sam. 18:12–16)*

It's important we take a moment to ponder the dramatic and radical change that occurs in Saul's personality relative to David. Let's face it, fear is a powerful prescription for self-destruction. Saul remembered the indictment he received from God's prophet Samuel regarding his future: "The Lord has torn the kingdom of Israel from you this day and has given it to a neighbor of yours, who is better than you" (1 Sam. 15:28). This explains the background for the irrational behavior Saul would soon exhibit toward David. For Saul knew his hold on power would eventually wane. Not only did he fear that prospect, but the reality in which someone would take his place who would be more effective than his rulership. This is the meaning of his acknowledgment of David's success as the scriptural passage enunciates, "Saul was afraid of David because the Lord was with him, but had departed from Saul."

The naked, cold, and frightening realization for Saul was not only the fact God's Spirit had left him, but God's Spirit was with David. Trust me, Saul knew the difference. Saul knew the distinction of experiencing God's Presence in his life, as well as knowing the tormenting absence of God working in his life. And now Saul recognizes God's Spirit is with David, causing him to acknowledge the sole reason for David's military victories—God is with David!

Saul cannot accept this new reality, and consequently, he conspires to rid himself of this threat to his rule by removing David from the royal court and then sending him on more dangerous battle missions with the hope David will be killed on the battlefield (1 Sam. 18:26). But this plot failed because as David engaged the Philistines in more battles, he only gained more victories and admiration throughout Israel. No doubt, God was with David!

Jonathan's Protection of David!

As a result Saul became more brazen in his plan to eliminate this threat to his throne by discussing with his royal court, including his eldest son, Jonathan, his desire to have David murdered (1 Sam. 19:1). Now we begin to see the unveiling of God's purpose in the friendship between the prince and David through the initial reaction of Jonathan to this heart-wrenching news.

The account states Jonathan immediately tells David of his father's diabolical plot. His motivation is based on what I would describe as the character attributes that forge a friendship found in the selfless love of God. It is such characteristics that comprise the "mark" of a true friendship. And the first dynamic of this friendship is given to us right away in the first verse when Jonathan is told of his father's plan for David: "Jonathan *delighted* much in David" (1 Sam. 19:1).

The word *delighted* has various meanings: pleased, esteemed, valued, or enjoyed! We can conclude Jonathan enjoyed and was very pleased with the successes of David. Isn't this an important characteristic of a true friend? A true friend delights or enjoys the successful achievements of their friend. Remember, Jonathan is the heir-apparent to the throne; and unlike his father, Jonathan is not threatened by the successes of David, but rather is pleased and happy for him. What a "gift" God has given to David at this perilous time in his life!

The second attribute is, a true friend *defends* in times of testing and trouble. The Bible qualifies this important truth further: "A friend loves at all times, and a brother is born for adversity" (Prov. 17:17). However, too often when an individual is encountering adversity with clouds of confusion and chaos swirling around, whether it is self-induced or not, the person's friends take a hiatus and typically are missing in action. When a friend is most needed, for whatever reason, they are absent. And often, self-protective measures are the motivation so as to avoid association with the discomfort, dissension, conflict, or controversy. But not Jonathan, who finds himself in the most compromised and controversial position of anyone in this evolving dramatic scene in his willingness to confront his father, the king:

> *And Jonathan spoke well of David, because he has not sinned against you, and because his deeds have brought good to you. For he took his life in his hand and he struck down the Philistine, and the Lord worked a great salvation for all Israel. You saw it, and rejoiced. Why then will you sin against innocent blood by killing David without cause? (1 Sam. 19:4–5)*

Jonathan proved the weight of his words and the worth of the covenant he made with David by challenging his father. We must keep in mind during ancient times kings did not hesitate in executing their sons at the slightest inkling of betrayal or the thought of treason. Jonathan was willing to stand on the side of justice and advocate for the best interests and well-being of his friend. But he was also acting in the best interests of his father, attempting to protect him from himself. Committing murder and shedding innocent blood was a gross violation of God's commandment.

The result of this initial confrontation by Jonathan is the reassurance from his father that he will not have David killed, and as an overture to validate the promise, Saul reinstates him into the royal court. But the promise is short-lived because one evening while David is playing his lyre for the king, Saul hurls his spear at David, barely missing his target, and David quickly escaping.

As the dramatic instability of Saul escalates, the demands on Jonathan's friendship with David intensifies. But isn't that true of any relationship, whether it is a spouse, family member or friend who is in trouble? When someone is hurting or in desperate circumstances, our depth and degree of commitment will always be tested. Jonathan must somehow reach out to his friend and offer him some kind of consolation or hope in the midst of David's confusion and bewilderment. So they meet in secret, and we are given a further "window" into their friendship with the following exchange as David begins with his inquiries of Jonathan:

> *"What have I done? What is my guilt? And what is my sin before your father, that he seeks my life?" And he (Jonathan) said to him, "Far from it! You shall not die. Behold, my father does nothing either great or small without disclosing it to me. And why should my father hide this from me? It is not so." But David vowed again, saying, "Your father knows well that I have found favor in your eyes, and he thinks, 'Do not let Jonathan know this, lest he be grieved.' But truly, as the Lord lives and as your soul lives, there is but a step between me and*

death." Then Jonathan said to David, "Whatever
you say, I will do for you!" (1Sam. 20: 1–4)

Simply amazing, isn't it? Who wouldn't want a friend capable of such an unconditional commitment? "Whatever you say, I will do for you!" Jonathan is saying, "Whatever you want me to do…whatever you need from me, I will do it for you, David!" Again, what is so remarkable about this type of commitment is that it is coming from a prince of Israel to a subordinate! Only God could be involved, which we will discuss more a little later!

This meeting between the two of them concludes with a plan to discover what Saul's real intentions are as well as his motive. It was the time of a festival, which lasted several days, and all of the royal court was expected to be in attendance. For someone to be invited and not to attend the king's table was the highest insult to the king.

Consequently, David devised an excuse that "his family needed him in Bethlehem." They both were hoping this would flush out Saul's genuine intentions because of David's absence. They then mutually agreed on a signal from Jonathan in a distant field from the palace, indicating whether or not it was safe for David to return to the royal court.

On the first day Saul said nothing about David's absence. But the second day was intolerable for the king as he inquired of Jonathan as to David's whereabouts. Jonathan gave the explanation David told him to share with his father when asked. But Saul was not buying it as he became angry with his son:

> *"You son of a perverse, rebellious woman, do I not*
> *know that you have chosen the son of Jesse to your*
> *own shame, and to the shame of your mother's*
> *nakedness? For as long as the son of Jesse lives on*
> *the earth, neither you nor your kingdom shall be*

established. Therefore send and bring him to me, for he shall surely die!" Then Jonathan answered Saul, his father, "Why should he be put to death? What has he done?" But Saul hurled his spear at him to strike him. So Jonathan knew that his father was determined to put David to death. And Jonathan rose from the table in fierce anger and ate no food the second day of the month, for he was grieved for David, because his father had disgraced him.

Saul blames his son for David's absence from the festival because Jonathan approved it. Then he becomes more enraged when Jonathan confronts him, resulting in Saul hurling the spear at his son and barely missing him. This brings us to the third dynamic: a true friend is *devoted* no matter the personal cost!

Jonathan was angry because he had been publicly humiliated in front of the royal court, which comprised his peers as well as his subjects. Further yet, what was most "disgraceful" for Jonathan was this incident revealed he no longer had influence with his dad as he previously had when it came to David. Do we know how painful it must have felt for Jonathan to lose credibility with the royal leadership of Israel? He must have known this would impact his effectiveness as a leader.

And then for his father to attempt to seriously injure him with the spear? Despite the personal disgrace and the attempt by his father to do him physical harm, Jonathan would not relent from his commitment to David. Jonathan would not retreat from doing or saying the right thing when it came to his friend, the next king of Israel. Even if his devotion to David would cost him his life, Jonathan was going to remain loyal to him. It goes without saying, we could use such devotion and commitment in our relationships today, couldn't we?

David Must Say Farewell to Family and Friend!

We are now allowed to view a profound scene with divine implications as the very next day Jonathan "keeps his appointment with David" (1 Sam. 20:35) to let him know the outcome of their plan. The plan had worked as it exposed the true intentions of Saul. Saul would spare nothing to ensure his eldest son would ascend to the throne of Israel, which meant David would need to be put to death at whatever cost.

Jonathan then gave the signal in the field where David was waiting. Both knew the implications of the preplanned signal, for it meant David's life was in jeopardy. It would mean David would need to flee the area and move his parents from nearby Bethlehem to safety in Moab, where his great-grandmother, Ruth, was originally from (1 Sam. 22:3).

When Jonathan signaled with the arrows, David understood what he now must do. Let's view the scene as David moves from behind the rocks toward Jonathan:

> *David rose from beside the stone heap and fell on
> his face to the ground and bowed three times. And
> they kissed one another and wept with one another,
> David weeping the most. Then Jonathan said to
> David, "Go in peace, because we have sworn both
> of us in the name of the Lord, saying, The Lord
> shall be between me and you, and between my
> offspring and your offspring, forever." And he rose*

*and departed, and Jonathan went into the city. (1
Sam. 20:41–42)*

This powerful scene underscores the depth of loyalty, commitment, and selfless love between these two close friends. Both of
them fully understood what must now happen and sense this is their
farewell meeting. David must depart from this area for the sake of
his own well-being and survival. David appears to be broken and
devastated, not simply because he knows he must flee for his life but
because of the demonstration of Jonathan's proven devotion to him.
Jonathan is willing to even risk his own life in order to protect and
preserve David's life.

Unconditional Love

In fact, Jonathan, as he bids David good-bye, reiterates the
extraordinary covenant between them, as if to remind David, no
matter what the future holds there will always be between them—a
faithful, selfless commitment, and loyalty to each other!

This friendship is a window into the selfless love and commitment God has toward anyone who desires to have a relationship with
Him. It was God who introduced this loyal friend into David's life.
And there was a larger divine purpose surpassing the practical benefits of protecting David's life.

Unfortunately, there are those who would twist or distort this
relationship into something other than a very close, divine-ordained
friendship. For it would be ten years later when David learns about
the death of Jonathan on the battlefield and laments the tragic loss
of his dear friend with these heartrending words: "Jonathan lies slain
on your high places. I am distressed for you, my brother Jonathan;

very pleasant have you been to me; your love surpassing the love of women" (2 Sam. 1:26).

Understandably, especially in today's contemporary culture, the characterization regarding the mutual love of their friendship—"surpassing the love of women"—has created egregious misconceptions. One of the most important rules regarding the interpretation of Scripture is context—a prominent principle that is applied in the guidelines of solid exegesis (Scripture interpretation). The historical context involving ancient customs is important in order to understand David's lament.

During ancient times, women were selected or "given in" marriage through a patriarchal system. This was even more amplified among royalty in which marriages were "arranged" for political purpose or power (alliances). This meant the woman did not have a voice in the matter. Very often it was about cultural tradition or political advantage, but not necessarily love. Certainly, at the least, the free will of the woman was not involved in the arrangement and subsequently was often given a consideration equal to that of a negotiated piece of property in the matter of marriage.

It is from such context, David's comparison of Jonathan's love for him is his personal declaration that Jonathan's love, devotion, and friendship was of itself voluntary!

The weight of such a statement cannot be fully understood without considering the personal context of Jonathan. Jonathan was a prince. He was a man of position and power. And most importantly, he was the rightful heir to the throne. If Jonathan didn't have the right heart and felt threatened by David, he had the power to eliminate the "problem." But Jonathan had a great heart, according to David's perspective. For Jonathan *chose* to be his friend. He didn't have to do that. It was entirely by Jonathan's own volition. Jonathan initiated the covenant between them. Jonathan chose to be committed to David, no matter the personal cost or how unpopular it would make him among the royal court. Ultimately, Jonathan had the power and complete freedom in choosing to serve David's interests, even at his own personal expense, causing David to acknowledge such devotion was an extraordinary love beyond normal human capacity.

This leads us to the fourth godly attribute regarding this friendship. It is now several years after David departed from the area in flight for his life. He has been running from city to city and hiding out in various caves throughout the Judean wilderness. But Saul is so ruthless and bent on capturing and killing David, he eventually makes a statement to anyone in Israel who would harbor or provide assistance to the fugitive. He killed the high priest Ahimelech and eighty-five priests for giving food and refuge to David at the city of Nob (1 Sam. 22:18–19).

Saul is now in hot pursuit of David with three thousand elite soldiers of his army, and it is in the vicinity of Ziph, a city about five miles south of Hebron, where David encounters Jonathan for the last time:

> *And Jonathan, Saul's son, rose and went to David at Horesh, and strengthened his hand in God. And he said to him, "Do not fear, for the hand of Saul my father shall not find you. You shall be king over Israel, and I shall be next to you. Saul my father also knows this." (1 Sam. 23:16–18)*

Can you see the fourth attribute of Jonathan in his statement to David? Jonathan is *dedicated* to the interests of God! In his statement, Jonathan is reiterating God's will for David's life. We are not told how Jonathan found out, but based on this declaration by Jonathan, he discovered God's plan and purpose for David's life. David was to be the next king of Israel, and Jonathan was dedicated to doing everything possible to ensure David fulfills his God-given destiny!

In the last recorded exchange between David and him, Jonathan is basically stating, "Don't worry, my dear friend, my dad is not going to win this battle. My dad is not going to find you, let alone kill you, as long as I have anything to say about it. So, don't worry, David. It might not look very good right now, but someday you are going to be king of Israel, and I will be right by your side, supporting and encouraging you!" Can you see a picture of God's selfless love in the friendship of Jonathan? Indeed, it is the heart of a servant, and yet he is a prince of Israel.

We are told the very reason for this final encounter between the two of them is so Jonathan could "strengthen his hand (David) in God." To *strengthen* means to "encourage," "reaffirming support" for the person. You see, Jonathan is doing God's work by encouraging David not to lose hope or to give up on his future, no matter how dire the circumstances may appear. And what Jonathan does not realize is this time will prove to be the last moment he will see David as he bids him farewell by reaffirming God's promise to David, "You shall be king over Israel!" And then Jonathan went home.

Attributes of True Friendship!

It's just like God to give David a friend who would be dedicated to his personal well-being, as well as to God's own interests and His purposes for a person's life. But it is also just like Him to have a greater purpose in providing such a friendship for David. Certainly, Jonathan fulfilled the basic quality attributes of a true friendship. Jonathan *delighted* in the marvelous and heroic exploits of David, for it was that mutual interest in which both desired to honor God with their lives that caused "their souls to be knit together" (1 Sam. 18:1). This made it easy for Jonathan to be willing to *defend* David despite the political controversies and repercussions that would inexplicably result.

Further yet, Jonathan was so *devoted* to his friend, he was willing to sacrifice his own interests, even if it meant losing his life in order to preserve David's life. Such devotion was also reflected in the unfathomable depth and degree of being *dedicated* to the interests of God, exemplified by Jonathan's unwavering commitment to invest all his resources possible in order to see God's destiny fulfilled in David's life, even if his own life is compromised!

Such are the extraordinary qualities God gave to David in the form of Jonathan. It was an expression of friendship, reflected through unconditional covenant by a prince of Israel and the heir to the throne. And for what ultimate defining purpose did God give such a "gift" to David?

Yes, it is true Jonathan was God's gift to David at a time when he needed a friend, but not just any kind of friend. For you see, Jonathan is a prototype of Jesus Christ. Jonathan embodied many of the attributes that epitomized what it meant to be a "servant." Jonathan was God's chosen model for His classroom laboratory in order to prepare David to rule Israel. Father-God was using the man who was the rightful heir to the throne to teach David what it meant to have the heart of a servant.

For God did not merely want a king. He wanted someone who would be like a shepherd that would lead God's flock. God desired a person who would love the people of Israel, as God loved them. God wanted a man who would represent God's heart to the people, accurately and authentically. God wanted a man who would not rule from a selfish, ambitious, hubris position like his predecessor, but one who would serve the people selflessly.

When David slew Goliath, he was about seventeen years of age at the time, while Jonathan, being the eldest son of Saul, was in his mid-thirties. So Jonathan being twice the age of David had years of leadership experience, militarily and politically, which would bene-fit the young and future king of Israel. And although the practical dynamics comprising the fundamental necessities of ruling effec-tively were vitally important, teaching David what it meant to have a heart of a servant was the preeminent priority God wanted David to cultivate through this friendship.

Who could possibly be a better teacher or mentor for David than an heir to the throne? Jonathan had the position of power, but grace was offered to David through his hand of friendship. Jonathan had the position to rule, but humility compels him to give it up to serve David, who is his student. Jonathan has a status of wealth and influence but is willing to invest it all in David. And if that is not enough, the rightful heir to the throne, motivated by his love for David, impels him to be willing to sacrifice not only his inheritance to reign, but his very life, if necessary, in order for David to rule and live!

This is why one should view Jonathan as a prototype of Jesus. He personifies the characterization by the New Testament writer describing the attributes of the Incarnate Jesus: "Who, though He was in the form of God did not count equality with God a thing to be grasped, but made Himself nothing, taking the form of a servant, being born in the likeness of men. And being found in human form, He humbled Himself by becoming obedient to the point of death, even death on a cross" (Phil. 2:6–8).

As previously emphasized at the beginning of this book, this writer believes God's divine search "for a man after My own heart" was founded upon the ultimate outcome of David's season of preparation during his flight as a fugitive throughout the desert. God knew He would have to teach and prepare David for rulership, which explains why David would not ascend to the throne for the next thirteen years of his life, but instead would be on the constant run in the Judean wilderness. God was teaching David, through his friend Jonathan, what His own heart was like. Jonathan was a mirror of God's heart. Jonathan was full of grace, faithfulness, gentleness, goodness, patience, kindness, joy, mercy, humility, and love toward David. Today, we know those attributes as the "fruit of the Spirit" (Gal. 5:22–23).

God gave David a model to follow and learn from, while God was fashioning and forming: "a man after My own heart." A man who would have the heart of a shepherd, a heart willing to serve the people of Israel with a single-minded devotion and commitment. Such a man encapsulates the words that echo through eternity of Another: "Greater love has no one than this, that someone lay down his life for his friends" (John 15:13).

God gave such a friend to David to prepare him to be the shepherd of His people someday. Indeed, a true friend who taught him how to serve—Jonathan, a prince of Israel!

CHAPTER 3

A Season of Preparation!

Make me to know your ways, O Lord; teach me your paths. Lead me
in your truth and teach me, for you are the God of my salvation.
—Psalm 25:4–5

D avid was about twenty years old when he and Jonathan realized his need to leave the area if David was to survive the murderous schemes of Saul. Although David didn't know it at the time, this meant the next ten years of his life would be lived as a fugitive—a hunted man constantly searching for ways to merely survive. While he wandered in the wilderness of Israel, he had to wonder about his future. What had happened to his destiny? Would he really become the next king of Israel as God had promised?

The questions and self-doubts had to linger, considering his dire circumstances in which he found himself. Had he heard right or did the prophet Samuel make a big mistake? After all, he was eating like a scavenger and being hunted like a wild animal. How was he going to become the next king of Israel, when even the people were so loyal to Saul? For David, there appeared to be no safe place to hide since even two different tribes of Israelites where he had stayed overnight had also betrayed his whereabouts to Saul.

What David did not realize and understand was that, which he was currently experiencing would become known as God's "season of preparation." This was God's method for fashioning and forming a leader as evidenced in the lives of others, such as Moses, Joseph, and Elijah, to name a few. Every person who would be used by God for a leadership role would always have such a "season" in which God prepared the leader for their God-ordained purpose.

Moses spent forty years in the wilderness shepherding sheep (sound familiar) before God called him to lead the Israelites out of slavery at the age of eighty. Joseph experienced about thirteen years of preparation since he first had his "dream of being a ruler." Much of it was spent in an Egyptian prison prior to ascending the second most powerful position in all of Egypt. And after predicting a severe drought in Israel to King Ahab, a worshiper of Baal, Elijah spent a good part of three years in the desert alone with God, before his famous confrontation with the 450 priests of Baal on Mt. Carmel.

Now this was David's season of preparation. David had some issues that required God's attendance. God was preparing David during this season, getting him ready to rule because this time He wanted a leader who would govern His people with a heart after His own heart! We need to remember the preeminent truth God would be teaching David, which He first spoke to the godly prophet in establishing Israel's monarchy: "*For those who honor Me I will honor*" (1 Sam. 2:30). For that is the kind of heart God was searching for and found in the next king of Israel! But David still required God's "refining attendance" regarding the condition of his heart as it is underscored in an incident in the Judean wilderness.

A Friend of Saul, a Foe of David!

A common practice in Israel during this time was wealthy landowners hiring a group of men to protect their shepherds and flocks from wild predators or thieves while the herds were grazing in the field. There was one such landowner known as Nabal. Scripture tells us, "He was very rich; he had three thousand sheep and a thousand goats," and his wife's name was Abigail (1 Sam. 25:2). We are also informed of both their characters in which Nabal is described as "harsh and badly behaved" and Abigail as "discerning and beautiful."

David and his men had volunteered their services by providing such protection for several months. He soon learned Nabal was shearing his sheep in Carmel. This was a traditional indicator it was "payday." It also would be a festive occasion to celebrate, as well as the time to compensate all the servants who had worked hard in producing the harvest. David subsequently sent "ten young men to inquire in his name" regarding compensation for the "services he and his men had provided for months" (1 Sam. 25:5–8). However, this would prove to be a pivotal and much needed "teaching" moment for David as Scripture gives us the following account of Nabal's response to the request and the subsequent reaction of David to the bad news from Nabal:

> *And Nabal answered David's servants, "Who is David? Who is the son of Jesse? There are many servants these days who are breaking away from their masters. Shall I take my bread and my water and my meat that I have killed for my shearers and give it to men who come from I do not know where?" So David's young men turned away and came back and told him all this. And David said to his men, "Every man strap on his sword!" And every man*

of them strapped on his sword. David strapped on his sword. And about four hundred men went up after David, while two hundred remained with the baggage. (1 Sam. 25:9–13)

Certainly, Nabal is living up to his reputation of "being harsh and badly behaved" as he enunciates "my" when referring to his property four times in one sentence! But we should not be surprised since the Hebrew word for his name means "foolish or boorish." To be labeled a "fool" would mean he lived as "if there was no God and a self-absorbed lifestyle." This corresponds to his behavior being described as "harsh," meaning he was demanding, deceptive, and unfair in his business practices.

This explains his highly insolent dismissal of David's request while also giving perspective to David's enraged response, "Men get your swords, we've got some killing to do!" For David swore to his devoted men, "Surely in vain have I guarded all that this fellow (Nabal) has in the wilderness, so that nothing was missed of all that belonged to him, and he has returned me evil for good. God do so to the enemies of David and more also, if by morning I leave so much as one male of all who belong to him!" (1 Sam. 25:21–22). Indeed, David is very angry and bent on spilling the blood of Nabal's entire household.

While David is in pursuit for what he believes is rightfully his due compensation, as well as seeking vindication for the humiliation he has suffered at the hands of the wealthy land-owner, Nabal's wife, Abigail, learns of the incident through one of her servants:

Behold, David sent messengers out of the wilderness to greet our master, and he railed at them. Yet the men were very good to us, and we suffered no harm, and we did not miss anything when we

were in the fields, as long as we went with them.
They were a wall to us both by night and by day,
all the while we were with them keeping the sheep.
Now therefore know this and consider what you
should do, for harm is determined against our
master and against all his house, and he is such
a worthless man that one cannot speak to him. (1
Sam. 25:14–17)

Even the servants knew their boss and did not have a high opinion of him since they considered him a "worthless man" and one so self-absorbed, he was incapable of listening to moral reason. But more importantly, as a good servant should be, this servant was greatly concerned for the well-being and safety of the entire household that included Abigail, evidenced by the belief, "harm" is going to come their way because of their master's unreasonable selfishness.

Abigail: A Mediator of God!

The apprehension expressed by the servant did not fall on deaf ears as Abigail sprang into action. She compiled "two hundred loaves of bread, five sheep (already cooked), and two hundred cakes of figs, wine, bags of grain, and a hundred clusters of raisins." Then she instructed her servants "to go on before her and that she would be right behind them" as they traveled to intercept David with these supplies.

Abigail and her servants soon encounter David and his men. In my opinion, it is one of the most profound and poignant scenes of divine intervention in the Bible, as she not only pleads for her life and family but also for David's well-being. Let's listen in as she falls prostrate before David:

On me alone, my lord, be the guilt. Please let your servant speak in your ears, and hear the words of your servant. Let not my lord regard this worthless fellow, Nabal, for as his name is, so is he. Nabal is his name, and folly is with him. But I your servant did not see the young men of my lord, whom you sent. Now then, my lord, as the Lord lives, and as your soul lives, because the Lord has restrained you from bloodguilt and from saving with your own hand, now then let your enemies and those who seek to do evil to my lord be as Nabal. And now let this present that your servant has brought to my lord be given to the young men who follow my lord. Please forgive the trespass of your servant. For the Lord will certainly make my lord a sure house, because my lord is fighting the battles of the Lord, and evil shall not be found in you so long as you live. If men rise up to pursue you and to seek your life, the life of my lord shall be bound in the bundle of the living in the care of the Lord your God. And the lives of your enemies He shall sling out as from the hollow of a sling. And when the Lord has done to my lord according to all the good that He has spoken concerning you and has appointed you prince over Israel, my lord shall have no cause of grief or pangs of conscience for having shed blood without cause or for my lord working salvation himself. And when the Lord has dealt well with my lord, then remember your servant. (1 Sam. 25:23–31)

Quite an intervention, right? Do you see God's "fingerprint" all over this encounter? But before we discuss the dynamics of this divine intervention in David's life, let's take a look at David's "heart issues" reflected in his initial reaction to the bad news given by his men. There are four adjectives or verbs that describe his disposition and are amplified through this incident, all of them beginning with the letter *I*—impetuous, independent, invokes, and inquire.

Let's consider the first adjective. *Impetuous* is defined by Webster's dictionary as "acting or done quickly and without thought; controlled by emotion rather than thought; marked by impulsive vehemence or passion, marked by force and violence of movement or action."

This certainly describes David's reaction as he is impulsive due to much anger and is enraged to the extent of shedding innocent blood. But we must go further and ask why? David was greatly insulted by Nabal, for it was Nabal who said, "Who is David? Who is the son of Jesse?" Remember it wasn't that long ago David slew Goliath. His fame spread throughout all of Israel because of the decisive victory over the Philistines. Nabal knows who David is because he is familiar with his family. But Nabal's statement more than implies, "David is not worth my time. David does not matter to me. He is a non-issue!"

We can all identify with being discarded or disqualified. And it hurts greatly because we were created in God's image. All of us instinctively desire for our lives to matter, and when we are told we don't, we can react like David. He is humiliated publicly and in front of his men, and he acts impulsively with rage to right the injustice.

The second characteristic of David is he acted *independently*. David did not consult or confer with anyone. He did not seek another's advice regarding his decision. He was immediate in his actions, and this is typical when it involves personal mistreatment or injustice when incurred.

Let's not forget what Nabal's servants said to Abigail, "David's men were very good to us, we suffered no harm, and we did not lose any sheep when we were in the fields, as long as we went with them." David knows what service he provided Nabal because David had learned early as a young shepherd boy in his walk with God to be committed to excellence, particularly during his military exploits. But now Nabal had devalued David's work, and therefore, Nabal was going to pay for the humiliating mistreatment he had subjected David.

The third action of David is he *invokes* God's name on his plans to annihilate Nabal's entire household. Listen to his declaration: "God do so to the enemies of David and more also, if by morning I leave so much as one male of all who belong to him" (1 Sam. 25:22). Isn't that just like many of us today, we predetermine our plans or agenda for ministry and rubber stamp God's name all over it. Even without consulting Him. And then when our plans or our vision of ministry crash, we blame God and everyone else for that matter!

Subsequently, this third characteristic as well as all the previous dynamics is directly correlated to the fourth principle which is *inquired*. David had developed the pattern of always having "inquired before the Lord" regarding his actions and directions he should undertake. But this time it was a glaring negligence in his life. Now God had to send someone to intervene on His behalf to protect David from himself—that is, if he wanted to become the next king of Israel.

As Abigail intercepts David and his men, she gets off the donkey and falls prostrate on the ground, beginning her address to David with a heart of humility by taking the blame for her husband's foolish travesty. She is a "picture" of Christ by assuming the role of mediator and advocating for David's well-being as she implores David to listen to her. "God is keeping you from making a big mistake by taking things into your own hands and shedding innocent blood." Let's not forget when we are introduced to Abigail she is described as "discerning." Abigail's discernment is godly wisdom as she tells David, "You don't want to do this evil deed, of shedding innocent blood!" Abigail has underscored the greatest evil David would be committing—taking things into his own hands! This is what is meant when she says, "Because the Lord has restrained you from blood guilt and *from saving with your own hand.*"

To be able to see this scene more clearly, we must get a fuller context of Abigail's intervention. Similar to Jonathan, she is also a prototype of Jesus. Like many nations during ancient times, Israel was a very patriarchal society in which women were treated as "lower class" citizens, and because of such a cultural mind-set, women were most vulnerable to mistreatment and disrespect. In essence, for the most part a woman lacked credibility in Israel. So here you have the wife of the man who blatantly humiliated David, appearing before him prostrate on the ground, willing to sacrifice her life for her family and servants, as well as looking out for David's welfare. Abigail has the heart of a servant in which she is willing to risk everything to redeem the situation, to right the wrong, to speak truth no matter the cost, even if it means losing her own life. And what is the truth she so desperately wants David, the future king of Israel to know?

Well, I believe it can be summed up in one sentence as she humbly implores him, "David, you are better than this, for God has a greater purpose for your life!" All her concerns are encapsulated in that statement as she speaks prophetically to him regarding his present and future circumstances, which will be determined by how he responds to her overture as she summarizes the possible ramifications for his life:

- You don't want to work this problem out in your own way (vv. 26, 31).
- You don't want to shed innocent blood (vv. 26, 31).

- Please forgive those who transgressed against you and receive these gifts (v. 28).
- You are the Lord's servant doing His work, therefore guard your heart (v. 28).
- God will make you a sure house (v. 28).
- Know you'll be protected from your enemies by God who cares deeply for you (v. 29).
- You will soon be king over Israel and you want a clear conscience when you reign over God's people (vv. 30–31).
- And remember your servant when the Lord blesses you (v. 31).

Wow! Indeed, a profound message to convey to this powerful warrior of Israel. What courage and strength Abigail demonstrated to David, a future king, not knowing how he will respond. This is extraordinary because David is not yet the king, but her message conveys a confidence within her that she knows someday he soon will arrive to his God-ordained destiny.

Abigail should be seen as an intercessor sent by God for this critical moment in David's life. She does not parse words or dilute her desperate message to David, so there is no room for misunderstanding. Not only that, Abigail expresses words of truth that oppose or contradict the very intentions of a man enraged with anger and bent on vengeance. She is not speaking to David what he wants to hear, and she is willing to tell him the truth regardless of the personal cost to herself.

Consequently, Abigail wants David to turn around from the path he is traveling on which leads to bloodshed and destruction to the path God has ordained for him. Abigail is not only warning David of what not to do, but what the future benefits would be if he did the right thing, one of which is God would establish him as king and "make him a sure house." This verse actually means a kingdom and reign that will be very effective. In effect, Abigail is declaring God's destiny for David: "David you are better than this. You need to see yourself as God sees you. You are the future king of Israel, and some day you will soon be ruling over these same people you want to kill!" She is looking out for David's reputation and future interests.

Abigail has the best interests and well-being of David in mind because she is revealing God's heart for David in this matter, but it still remains his decision. This is another pivotal moment in the young life of David. It is his greatest test yet; therefore, how will he respond to the pleas of this courageous Israelite woman?

David's Teachable Lesson Learned

David offers his initial response to the apprehensive Abigail: "Blessed be the Lord, the God of Israel, who sent you this day to meet me! Blessed be your discretion, and blessed be you, who have kept me this day from bloodguilt and from working salvation with my own hand!" (1 Sam. 25:32–33).

How relieved Abigail must have felt to hear those initial words from David: "You are a blessing to me sent directly from the Lord!" Even through the blinding rage of hatred and contempt, David is yet able to see God's handprint stamped all over Abigail's message of warning and exhortation to him. And he says as much by telling her, "You have kept me from making a horrific mistake by shedding innocent blood and working out my own salvation in my own way... and it is the Lord who has restrained me from hurting you...!"

David, therefore, attributes the intervention of Abigail as no less than God's gracious visitation to him through her. In the same way God spoke through Jonathan, David knows God is teaching him some important lessons through Abigail, the very nature of God's own heart!

Divine Redemption for David and a New Wife!

Abigail returned home afterwards to find her drunken husband, Nabal, partying and celebrating the harvest. The next day Abigail informs him what she had done for David. Based on the account in Scripture, it appears Nabal had a stroke and died ten days later. David hears the news and invites Abigail to become his wife. What an outcome! All this occurs because Abigail was willing to risk everything in order to right a wrong, and David being teachable by changing his wrongful course of action! There is always a better resolution to a problem when we depend on God for the answer rather than trying to "work out our own salvation!"

As we know the theme of this chapter refers to how God works in our lives during "seasons of preparation" in order to achieve His greater purpose in our lives. During the ten years of being a fugitive and merely trying to survive, God uses various methods and means to transform David's heart so that he will be well-prepared to rule Israel at God's appointed time. We must therefore understand that God's destiny for David was more than simply to be a king of Israel. God desired David to have the heart of a shepherd—a heart fashioned and formed after His heart. A shepherd, if one is really a true shepherd, is most interested in providing for the flock's well-being, which includes protection. Consequently, God wanted a shepherd-king who would rule, not from self-interests or personal ambition. God wanted a man who would rule Israel with a servant's heart, reflecting the heart of God. Unlike Saul, God wanted the next king to mirror His heart, modeling with authenticity the will and the very nature of God's own heart for the people to know and follow!

David discovered he could not afford to make the kind of misstep he almost made by reacting impetuously and independently. The potential result would have led to the tragedy of shedding innocent blood and causing an irreparable division among the very people he would someday lead.

Through this ordeal, the vital lesson God was teaching David was the invaluable priority and significance of prayer. It was imperative David learn the importance of developing a lifestyle of prayer, the primary method God uses to fashion a heart after His heart. It is God's primary method because prayer is an expressed dependence upon Him. To take the time to seek the Lord is a personal acknowledgment that one needs Him, and such a surrendered heart requires humility. This was an additional "piece" God was adding to David's leadership acumen in preparation for the throne.

Now many of you may already be familiar with the biblical concept of God using "seasons of preparation" to equip you for that which God has called you to do. Or perhaps you are like many young believers who have just discovered this principle for the first time. Perhaps you have been asking, "Why the struggle and why am I wandering in the wilderness, seemingly waiting for so long, and yet wanting to discover God's purpose for my life?"

Dear child of God, know this: you are not alone. Every believer, every pastor, every leader goes through a season of preparation. And though it is challenging and, yes, at times very painful, the ultimate destiny God is preparing you to fulfill will be well worth the price. This dynamic truth is underscored by God's word to encourage us to trust Him during such seasons in our lives: "But now, O Lord, you are our Father; we are the clay, and you are our potter; we are all the work of your hand" (Isa. 64:8).

Now let us discover the purpose and meaning of the primary method the Potter uses to fashion and form the kind of heart that will most effectively serve Him and therefore fulfill our Father's will in our lives through this God-ordained method known as prayer!

CHAPTER 4
....

The Pursuit of God's Heart: A Pathway of Prayer!

I am the Vine; you are the branches. Whoever abides
in Me and I in him, he it is that bears much fruit,
for apart from Me you can do nothing
—Jesus, in John 15:5

As we have learned from David's recent ordeal, there was a major malady that contributed to David's potential incursion on a pathway of bloody and unnecessary destruction of human life. David did not "inquire before the Lord"—a common idiom in ancient times referring simply to prayer. David simply had not prayed. However, this incident was the exception and not the rule in David's life. David was a man of prayer. Scripture reveals he had developed a pattern of seeking the Lord throughout his life.

Usually when David faced a life challenge, David sought the Lord. For example, there was an incident when David and his men were away fighting the Philistines. The Amalekites raided the village (Ziklag) where his men and their families lived, burning it to the ground and carrying off their wives and children. Scripture informs us the first thing David did: "But David strengthened himself in the Lord his God. And David inquired of the Lord, "Shall I pursue after this band? Shall I overtake them?" (1 Sam. 30:6–8).

God answered and told him to "pursue" because he would be successful in rescuing their families. He was successful because David was dependent upon God's guidance and direction, resultant in God revealing His will for David's situation.

Although a rare occasion for David to neglect the importance of prayer in his life, nevertheless, the value of prayer could not be ignored in importance to the potential debacle that ensued with regard to Nabal.

This truth is further accentuated by the abysmal failure of Saul's reign in which prayer and its deficiency is directly attributed to Saul's ineffectiveness, as Scripture records: *"So Saul died for his breach of faith. He broke faith with the Lord in that he did not keep the command of the Lord, and also consulted a medium, seeking guidance. He did not seek guidance from the Lord" (1 Chron. 10:13–14).* Tragically, not only did Saul neglect prayer with the Lord, he used "other resources," which was a form of idolatry. This is what is meant when it says that Saul "died for his breach of faith with the Lord."

The charismatic theologian, Dr. Gordon Fee, offers a profound statement regarding such a spiritual malady: "Prayerlessness is practical atheism."[1] One could conclude that Saul died due to his prayerlessness! No, I'm not saying Saul was an atheist, because he did believe in God. But he acted as if he were an atheist. Based on his self-destructive outcome (committed suicide on the battlefield), he seemingly did not put "legs" to his faith. And since the deficiency of seeking God was David's misstep regarding Nabal, it is vital for us to take a look at this dynamic spiritual gift from God that is central to cultivating a heart after God's own heart!

It is for this singular reason alone the subject cannot be ignored. Though I do not purport to be an expert on prayer, however, I continue to be a student of this dynamic spiritual power found in fellowship with God. Subsequently, I find myself constantly hungry in deepening this personal expression of conversation with Father-God. It is only because of His grace, I have experienced some dramatic answers to prayer. So because of this important subject, I know the Lord desires to have a discussion with you regarding this powerful discipline, sharing with you in this chapter some important and invaluable principles He has taught me regarding this sacred gift called prayer!

Prayer is something a lot of people talk about doing, but too few do anything about! Throughout my years of ministry, I have discovered a myriad of factors that contribute to the spiritual malady of prayerlessness in the Body of Christ: The busyness of life. It is apparently boring for some. People also feel their prayers are ineffective or believing one is not good enough or qualified, to name a few. It is this student's belief much of prayerlessness can be attributed to these symptoms, but I believe it is for the most part due to a lack of understanding regarding the integral meaning and foundational purpose it has in our walk with God.

The God-Filter!

This lack of understanding is only the genesis regarding prayerlessness. It also is largely determined by a distorted view of God. Brad Young, a theologian, offers this profound insight: "The problem with prayer is God."[2] Professor Young is underscoring that one's view of God and His character is an obstacle in knowing how to pray.

I've developed a phrase that is important to describe as well as to learn and recognize, that is, if you are genuinely interested in the individual's unique and distinct narrative regarding their belief in God or the lack of it. The phrase is known as *the God-filter!* It refers to how we view God, which has been formed and framed by our early life experiences and of which the effects are commonly negative. Unfortunately, some of these experiences were based on the limited contributions from other "believers." David Kinnaman shares some insights in this regard based on survey data collected from the well-known George Barna Group:

> We discovered that one-fifth of all outsiders, regardless of age admitted "they have had a bad experience in a church or with a Christian that gave them a negative image of Jesus Christ." This represents nearly fifty million adult residents of this country—including about nine million young outsiders—who admit they have significant emotional or spiritual baggage from past experiences with so-called Christ followers.[3]

Of course, this is a tragic commentary for the Church, but it is only one factor contributing to the God-filter, because there are others. Typically, the God-filter is subsequently responsible for blurring the God-ordained purpose of prayer with personal statements of beliefs or false assumptions, such as "My prayers don't make a difference, because God doesn't seem to answer!" "I'm not able to hear God's voice like others do, probably because I'm not worthy or qualified!" Or other attitudes, such as "God has always been distant to me—I don't seem to connect;" "I don't believe I can influence God, so why pray? After all, what's the point, God is going to do what He wants to do—He doesn't really need me to advise Him!"

These negative, paralyzing thoughts about prayer are amplified by A. W. Tozer's powerful and incisive truth: "What a man thinks of

God is the most important thing about him and will determine the whole course of his life!"[4] Essentially, if one is going to have a good, effective prayer life, it starts with a veracity and clear understanding of God's heart and purpose regarding this gift of conversing with Him.

A Relational, Dependent Faith!

It is from this premise we should discover the importance of faith as the starting point or entrance to connecting with God in prayer. God's Word reminds us of this truth as it declares, "And without faith it is impossible to please Him, for whoever would *draw near* to God must believe that He exists and that He rewards those who seek Him" (Heb. 11:6).

There is much to be said about faith since it is central to our journey of the Christian life, and because there is much misunderstanding regarding its definition. However, time and space does not afford the attention this subject requires, but I would like to offer what I have come to know as the definitive essence of faith, particularly in how it applies to the context of prayer. Most of us are aware of what is thought to be the definition of faith: "Faith is the substance of things hoped for, the evidence of things unseen" (Heb. 11:1). Or another Scripture, which serves as a corollary in many sermons: "So, faith comes from hearing, and hearing through the word of Christ" (Rom. 10:17). For me, that describes the function and progressive development of faith, rather than defining it. I have come to learn that in order to understand what faith is, one has to be able to realize the ontology or the nature of faith, since faith is embedded in relationship! Yes, faith is about relationship! The writer of Hebrews says as much just a few more verses beyond in chapter 12, verse 2: "Looking to Jesus, the founder and perfecter of our faith." So if we examine again Hebrews 11:6, we learn that faith is about drawing near to Him, first, believing He exists and then trusting "He will reward those who seek Him." Our reward is He shows up by His presence and in His response to our prayers. Faith is about a relationship in which we get to "know" the Originator (Author and Finisher) of our faith. Faith has everything to do with knowledge, and that knowledge is based on a relationship with God.

Tozer qualifies this spiritual truth regarding the characterization of faith: "Faith is the least self-regarding of the virtues. It is by its very nature scarcely conscious of its own existence. Like the eye which sees everything in front of it and never sees itself, faith is occupied with the Object upon which it rests and pays no attention to itself at all."[5]

This, of course, contradicts a prominent strain within the Church-at-large of emphasizing a faith that is focused on itself, resultant in "faith" becoming the object of our faith! In other words, sometimes when a person has prayed for another person's healing and the person does not get healed, the reason given is due to the "person's lack of faith," causing the person who has the physical condition to become inwardly focused on themselves and their lack of faith. Tragically, the focal point becomes the individual, along with the mind-set, "What is wrong with me!"

Anything that transfers us from the proper focus of the worthwhile Object of our faith to one's self is unfortunately and perhaps unintentionally putting the responsibility for the remedy on one's own human effort. Anytime we divert from an "upward movement" or focus on God to an intrinsic movement of "looking within ourselves," we are distorting the essence of faith.

More than ever, this definition of faith is underscored by Jesus's own words in John 15:5, through His illustration of the Vine-branch metaphor as He states, "I am the Vine; you are the branches. Whoever abides in Me and I in him, he it is that bears much fruit, for apart from Me you can do nothing." Jesus is stating throughout John 15 how one's prayers can be answered. It is based on the intimacy of an abiding relationship with Jesus. This is why Jesus states unequivocally, "Apart from Me you can do nothing." The *branch* must stay connected to the *Vine*, for it is through the sustaining intimate life of the Author and Finisher of our faith, we will be able to bear fruit.

It is through this intimate abiding relationship with Jesus, for which He later says, "So that whatever you ask the Father in My name, He may give it to you" (John 15:17). This is what almost got David into deep trouble. He was acting independent of God. He was trying to self-navigate his own resolution regarding the desperate physical needs of his men. On that occasion he did not take the time to seek the Lord for guidance on the matter. We should realize prayer is being dependent upon God by trusting Him to do what we cannot do without Him! This is why I believe faith is the entrance or starting point to an effective life of prayer.

A Time to Learn and Listen!

The second important dynamic to an effective prayer life is knowing God wants to speak to you more than you want to hear Him. God is love, and Love wants to be known. God desires to share Himself with us through prayer. Jesus said, "My sheep hear My voice, and I know them, and they follow Me" (John 10:27). Prayer is a conversation, and to have a conversation, one has to listen and one has to speak. Let's face it. The reason prayer can be mundane or boring is because we are doing all the talking! Sometimes we just need to toss aside our list, enter His throne room "looking" for Him and listening to Him. I'm not saying don't ask! But rather, reexamine how you are asking! What is my mind-set or focus? Am I determined to hear God speak to me, coming to Him with an expectation to hear Him? Do I even really believe He wants to speak to me or to give me the direction or guidance I need for my life?

Subsequently, we must confront the defining question: How can I do God's will and purpose for my life if I don't know what it is? And how will I find out if the God who loves me does not tell me? We need to start from the fundamental premise that no one wants us to do God's will more than God; therefore, God wants us to be informed so we will know what He wants us to do for Him.

Let's consider this, how would David do God's will for his life if he did not take the time to seek Him and, most importantly, hear Him? God predicted such a man before David was even born: "And I will raise up for myself a faithful priest, who shall do according to what is in my heart and in my mind. And I will build him a sure house, and he shall go in and out before my anointed forever" (1 Sam. 2:35). David would learn the importance of prayer, that is, if he would fulfill God's will and purpose for his life.

We must understand this truth about God's heart regarding each of our lives. There is nothing more important than fulfilling His purpose and the very reason for which He created each of us. And we can't do His will if we don't know it! So more than anything, we must believe He wants to reveal to us His will more than we want to know it!

Learning to hear God's voice is supplemental to the faith dynamic we just discussed, as both dynamics are complementary to each other. I cannot hear Him without abiding intimately with Him. This includes studying His Word and discovering His heart and His character so I avoid a distorted view of Him. And most importantly, I must be resolute in being determined to hear Him and to hear Him only!

Too often, we are looking for "that word" from our brother or church leader rather than spending time with the One who wants to speak to us more than anything. Yes, God does speak to us in other ways, through our leadership, other believers, and, of course, through His written word, which is active and alive. But more importantly, He desires for you to personally hear Him because He wants you to know the experiential reality of Him. There is no substitute for experiencing the reality of hearing His personal, intimate still, small voice (1 Kings 19:12).

Let me for a brief moment offer distinctive insights in this regard. I'm aware many people have difficulty hearing that "still, small voice" of God. Like anything else, it is a process of discovery in learning how to become familiar with the Lord's voice in prayer. His voice is *prevailing*, meaning dominant, because it is inescapable. His word captivates your attention. It stands by itself. His thought, idea, or impression will not leave you.

A second distinction is His "word" is original in scope. Original in the sense He provides a spiritual insight into His character, for example. God always has a purpose in speaking, the same as He does through His written word, which is to reveal Himself and His truth. Subsequently, this "original" distinction has a weight of authority, as Jesus promised, "When the Spirit of truth comes, he will guide you into all the truth, for he will not speak on his own authority, but whatever he hears he will speak" (John 16:13). At the same time, the weight of His voice will not run over you, for He is gentle. He desires we learn from Him.

Another quality is He can say so little and say so much. His word is specific and usually carries multifaceted applications similar to His written word. But at the same time, we must always remember He will never contradict His written word. These are some specific distinctions to help guide us in cultivating conversational prayer with the Lord.

Please hear my heart, my friend. God does not want you to borrow someone else's revelation or experience from another believer and make it your own. He does want you to learn a truth about Him through someone else's testimony, but He doesn't want you to substitute someone else's spiritual encounter for your own. God wants you to encounter Him and give to you your own experience with Him. God wants you to live the life He created you to live. Your purpose for Him is distinct, different, and exclusively designed by Him just for you! After all, God is the only One who really knows you! And He knows you better than you know yourself!

Worth the Wait

This brings us to our third important aspect of prayer, which is learning to "wait on God." As we discovered, David was impetuous in his reaction. He didn't take time to seek God, which is another way of saying he didn't take time "to wait on God." We do the same, especially in American culture where we have come to expect instant gratification and immediate results. Waiting is not an American virtue!

But David did learn later the importance of this aspect in prayer as he declared, "Make me to know your ways, O Lord; teach me your paths. Lead me in your truth and teach me, for you are the God of my salvation; for you I wait all the day long" (Ps. 24:4–5). Waiting is never easy. David learned this the hard way in the Judean wilderness for ten years of his life, because God was teaching Him what it meant to have a heart after God's own heart! It would be vitally important to seek God first and foremost in order to manage the affairs of a nation, especially a people that are God's people.

Prayer, a Language of Partnership with God!

Prayer is the pathway to realize what God wants done on earth as it is in heaven. What does this mean? David learned doing God's will was most important in his life. He discovered this through prayer. This defining purpose of prayer is qualified by Pastor Jack Hayford: "Prayer is essentially a partnership of the redeemed child of God working hand in hand with God toward the realization of His redemptive purposes on earth."[6] This is really an amazing truth when one thinks about it! That God, the Eternal One, the Ancient of Days, the Creator of the entire cosmos, would limit Himself by desiring and designing each of us to "partner" with Him to accomplish His redemptive purposes on earth.

This principle of prayer cannot be overstated—it is that important. We must understand God has determined to limit Himself, because it is through prayer God desires to prepare us to do His work. God informs us that we were created to do His work: "For we are His workmanship, created in Christ Jesus for good works, which God prepared beforehand, that we should walk in them" (Eph. 2:10). No one wants us to do His work more than God, so we simply need to trust He desires to reveal His will for our lives.

This is what Jesus meant by His instruction: "Apart from Me you can do nothing." It is only through abiding in Him we can be fruitful or productive. It is through our dependence on God through prayer that God can then depend on us to do His will and work. When we realize our weight of responsibility in prayer, then we will begin to discover the blessing God has entrusted to us in the words of Paul: "For we are God's fellow workers" (1 Cor. 3:9). Prayer is God's method in allowing us to participate and to advance His purposes on earth. It should be the greatest priority and most important activity we do in our daily lives!

We must understand if we are going to fulfill our calling, we must be willing to allow God to prepare us for our designed assignment because it involves paying a price. Waiting on God involves learning His ways and will instead of working it out our own way. It also involves allowing God to teach and equip us for the work He has called us to do. This deficiency is particularly accentuated in the potentially catastrophic Nabal event. David immediately went into action without waiting on God for his answer to the situation.

We need to get this truth in our minds and hearts: waiting on God will *always* produce transformation in our lives. If we are truly learning, really learning, His ways for our lives, the effects will be transformative, especially regarding those wrong paths we have chosen for ourselves.

Gordon Fee offers this insight: "Prayer...does not make demands upon God (though our prayers often do), but humbly waits and listens to God—and trusts God."[7] Unfortunately, some believers do not want to wait or be willing to pay the price of a season of preparation. We tend to want immediate answers. But it is essential, if one desires to cultivate a heart after God's heart, one must learn to wait humbly and patiently. It will be worth it all. Just ask David!

A Time to Meet!

The fourth dynamic may very well be the most important to learn and to actualize in our lives. To know how to pray effectively is primarily the responsibility of the Holy Spirit. However, the Holy Spirit does not work alone. He needs and desires our participation. Our first responsibility is to ensure we make ourselves available on a regular basis by surrendering the time to converse with our Lord. Regular means every day! We shouldn't miss a day, or at least we wouldn't want to miss a day, because of the obvious importance, as well as the enjoyment!

Jesus emphasized an important method that would provide us with optimum effectiveness and results. He instructed, "But when you pray, go into your room and shut the door and pray to your Father *who is in secret*. And your Father who sees in secret will reward you" (Matt. 6:6). This principle forms my definition of prayer: Prayer is making oneself fully available to God!

Think about it. The greatest challenge today is turning off all the activity. Jesus emphasized, if one wants to be effective in prayer, you must "shut the world out" with the effect of also "shutting down" oneself. Stop doing by shutting out the world, and shutting yourself in with the Father! Can you imagine doing that today with the prevalence of social media? I guess it just comes down to what is most important in one's life. Talking on Facebook or with the Father who loves you more than anything in life?

But really, the greater question is, why did Jesus emphasize such a method? Why did Jesus say it is important to "shut out (the world) and shut in (self)" when it comes to prayer? There are two reasons, and the first is because you and I are seeking the Father "who is in secret!" Now the usage of the word *secret* means to be "hidden or unseen." God is hidden from our visible eyes because He is Spirit. To find or look for someone who is hidden takes a concentrated focus and effort, that is, if you are serious in wanting to discover the hidden "object." To find requires some passion in seeking. This requires enclosure—shutting out and shutting in!

Jesus emphasizes the importance of seeking the Father "who is in secret" by instructing, "But seek first the kingdom of God and His righteousness, and all these things will be added to you" (Matt. 6:33). Such an effort, mind-set, and personal availability is enhanced without distractions or disruptions. Furthermore, it accentuates the priority prayer should be in our lives.

Most importantly, Jesus foundationally provided what is commonly known as the Lord's Prayer (Matt. 6:9) as a model to teach us how to pray. For me, the most important word in the entire blueprint is *Our*! To be able to call God, Father, well, it doesn't get any better than that! It enhances the richness and value of spending time with "Our Father" in secret, don't you think?

The Reward of Prayer!

The second factor is found in Psalm 25:14: "The secret of the Lord is with those who fear Him, and He will show them His covenant" (NKJV). Again, the word *secret* is used and other translations refer to this as *friendship*. So it reads, "The friendship of the Lord is with those who fear Him." The overall meaning is a certain level of relationship, a friendship in which one can confide. Also, the word *fear* in this context means "to revere, to respect." To revere a friend is someone in whom you value and place a confidence. A friend is someone you come to know, as well as someone you enjoy! This is why prayer should be an exciting and enjoyable endeavor.

This dynamic is further amplified by Jesus's words in the vineyard on His way to Gethsemane: "No longer do I call you servants, for the servant does not know what his master is doing; but I have called you friends, for all that I have heard from My Father I have made known to you" (John 15:15). Jesus is emphasizing that those who are His friends—those who are making themselves available to Him by enclosing oneself with the Father—He will reveal to them what He is doing on earth as it is in heaven!

This truth is best modeled in the ministry of Jesus because it was His very pulse to only do the Father's will, as He described, "The Son can do nothing of His own accord, but only what He sees the Father doing. For whatever the Father does, that the Son does likewise. For the Father loves the Son and shows Him all that He himself is doing" (John 5:19–20).

Jesus was teaching His disciples what was the very heart of His effective ministry. It was prayer. Nothing was more important to Jesus than fellowship with His Father, for it was only through prayer Jesus would learn what the Father wanted Him to say and do.

Jesus has promised we can have the same type of relationship with God. Father-God will reveal to you that person who needs a prayer or an encouraging word so they will be strengthened in their faith. Perhaps the Lord will direct you to visit an individual in desperate circumstances, giving you the wisdom to say and do just the right thing that will help them in their time of need.

Trust me when I say that when you experience His Presence and hear that still, small voice with acuity, you will be able to say with complete integrity, there is nothing more exciting, enriching, and enjoyable than prayer. When the Father shows up by His Spirit, speaking and revealing in a conversation with you, His friend, it is incomparable to any other activity on earth! Simply put, it is His *reward* to you and you will never be disappointed in time spent with Him!

For this reality to occur we must fully depend upon the Holy Spirit. Scripture tells us we do not know how to pray, and so we must rely on the Spirit of God to facilitate our prayers, if we are going to be effective prayers (Rom. 8:26–27). Gordon Fee amplifies the scriptural truth: "Prayer, therefore, is not simply our cry of desperation or our grocery list of requests that we bring before our heavenly Abba; prayer is an activity inspired by God Himself, through His Holy Spirit. It is God siding with His people and, by His own empowering presence, the Spirit of God Himself, bringing forth prayer that is keeping with His will and His ways."[8] This is the reward Jesus promised for those who would shut out the world and shut themselves in secret with the One who is secret (hidden)! (Matt. 6:6).

Prayer Is Transformative!

All we must do is respond to the impulse of the Spirit as He prompts us to pray at any time or any place. Personally, I have seen some of the most dramatic answers to prayer when I'm fully dependent upon the Holy Spirit to lead my time of prayer. I have discovered the most enriching and exciting moments of prayer is when God shows up by His Presence and I acutely hear and experience Him. It is transformative and causes one to want to spend more time with Him. In such moments, He is like an appetizer! You just want more of Him!

This I believe is the ultimate purpose for God in providing this gift of grace to us. Prayer directs our lives, but it also changes us. Listen to Richard Foster, a noted author who has written several classics on the subject of prayer, and his claim regarding God's purpose for prayer: "To pray, is to change. This is a great grace. How good of God to provide a path whereby our lives can be taken over by love and joy and peace and patience and kindness and goodness and faithfulness and gentleness and self-control. The movement inward comes first because without interior transformation the movement up into God's glory would overwhelm us and the movement out into ministry would destroy us."[9]

If you noticed, Foster listed the attributes of God that are more commonly described as the "fruit of the Spirit" (Gal. 5:22–23). In essence, Richard Foster is saying prayer is one of God's methods for changing our hearts by allowing the Holy Spirit to cultivate His attributes in us. Indeed, this was what God was doing in David's life, particularly in the appointed season of preparation during his wilderness wanderings for survival.

Through the Nabal incident, God provided David another test. God desired to teach David how to be merciful to the merciless. To be forgiving to the unforgivable. To be humble to the haughty! To return kindness to the unkind! And most importantly, to become more God-dependent by fully trusting and surrendering to God's will since Father-God knows best! But it is important to remember it almost didn't happen because David did not pray. That is the lesson we should learn from this incident.

As we close this important chapter, let's hear the timeless words of our Savior Jesus Christ, which echo a thousand years later from the time of David, Father-God's ultimate purpose of prayer, transformation:

> *If you love those who love you, what benefit is that to you? For even sinners love those who love them. And if you do good to those who do good to you, what benefit is that to you? For even sinners do the same. And if you lend to those from whom you expect to receive, what credit is that to you? Even sinners lend to sinners, to get back the same amount. But love your enemies, and do good, and lend, expecting nothing in return, and your reward will be great, and you will be sons of the Most High, for He is kind to the ungrateful and the evil. Be merciful, even as your Father is merciful. (Luke 6:32–36)*

This is the kind of heart God was cultivating in David. And it is the same kind of heart God desires for you and me.

As we have discovered thus far, David was learning what God's heart was like. And it was through prayer, David's dependency upon God, he would learn God's character and how God desired him to serve. David was teachable, even during the most painful of circumstances. As a fugitive in a desolate wilderness, God was teaching David the preeminent priority of doing God's will, no matter the cost. For God had an ultimate destination for David, and it was encased in learning to have a heart after God's own heart and all it would embody.

We are given some indication what that goal is in the words of Jesus just cited in chapter 6 of Luke's gospel. But know this, child of God, it is the same destination for you and me. Let it suffice for now that it would be premature to reveal God's goal at this moment of our journey with David, for we have more to discover and learn regarding the meaning, purpose and value of having a heart after God's own heart. Let us, therefore, continue our pursuit, as we realize the "undergraduate" time of study is over for David as the shepherd, soldier, and servant. For David, who has learned his lessons well, now graduates to his next position and purpose in life for which he was destined!

CHAPTER 5

....

The Shepherd Boy Becomes King... and a Pivotal Moment!

*Create in me a pure heart, O God, and renew a
steadfast spirit within me. Do not cast me from Your
Presence or take Your Holy Spirit from me
—Psalm 51:10–1(NIV)*

O n the battlefield of Mt. Gilboa, Saul's forty-year reign
ended tragically in defeat, and by his own self-inflicted
death. Three of Saul's sons, including David's best friend,
Jonathan, also died in the fierce battle. When David received this
tragic news, David immediately tore his clothes, wept, and fasted.
David mourned publicly and privately. He publicly lamented their
deaths, as recorded in the first chapter of 2 Samuel: "Your glory, O
Israel, is slain on your high places! How the mighty have fallen."

This Hebrew poem poignantly expresses David's grief for the
loss of Saul and Jonathan. It also indicated something more. David
still maintained a wholesome respect for Saul's position as the
anointed king of Israel. Even despite the murderous attempts on his

life and being dislodged from his home for a good part of ten years, David still demonstrates genuine brokenness for the demise of the first king of Israel.

This is the initial inkling of who David has become, changed by his wilderness experience, reflecting not only a lack of bitterness or resentment toward an enemy, but respect for Saul's accomplishments, as he wrote these words: "Saul and Jonathan, beloved and lovely! In life and in death they were not divided; they were swifter than eagles; they were stronger than lions" (2 Sam. 1:23). It is through this lamentation we get another view into David's heart, as we see humility, mercy, kindness, a servant's heart, and, more importantly, unconditional loyalty and love. Yes, David learned to love his enemy Saul.

The former shepherd boy is now ready. God directs him to go to Hebron, the main city of southern Israel, where the men of Judah, the largest tribe of Israel, anoint him king at thirty years of age over the house of Judah in the year 1011 BC.[1]

However, Abner, Saul's army commander, installs Ish-bosheth, Saul's lone surviving son, over the northern part of Israel, which include the other eleven tribes. War ensued between the house of David and the house of Saul for several years. Ish-bosheth's reign lasted only two years as he was eventually assassinated by two captains from his own army.

The elders of Israel then came to Hebron and anointed David as their king. David reigned at Hebron over Judah for seven years and six months (2 Sam. 5:5). In 1004 BC, David finally captured Jerusalem from the Jebusites, which was a monumental feat because since the time of Joshua, control for the city went back and forth.[2] David's entire reign over Israel was forty years, including thirty-three years from Jerusalem.

The Philistines were eventually subdued by David. But the Ammonites became the major focal point during much of David's reign. The Ammonite wars began with Israel about 993 BC.[3] David had reigned for eighteen years at this point in time and is about forty-eight years of age. It is then another life-changing incident occurs in David's life. Scripture provides the context: "In the spring of the year, the time when kings go out to battle, David sent Joab, and his servants with him, and all Israel. And they ravaged the Ammonites and besieged Rabbah (the capital city). But David remained at Jerusalem" (2 Sam. 11:1).

David's Worse Nightmare!

As we realize, this account begins with the inference, David was not where he was supposed to be. Typically, during ancient times of warfare, kings led their armies into battle. However, on this occasion David decided to stay home. So one day, from the balcony of his palace, he happens to observe a beautiful woman bathing. The woman's name is Bathsheba, and she is married to Uriah. David already has three wives: Ahinoam, Abigail, and Michal. Apparently, this is not enough, as David invites Bathsheba to his bedroom.

Unexpectedly, Bathsheba becomes pregnant. To cover it up, David sends for Bathsheba's husband, Uriah, from the battlefield with the hope he would return to his home and sleep with his wife. However, Uriah does not comply with David's unspoken scheme as he wanted to honor the military code of abstinence when the army was engaged in battle. Finally, David ordered his army commander Joab to send Uriah to the frontline to ensure his fate. David's plot was successful as Uriah was felled by enemy archers. David then took Bathsheba for his wife, and she bore him a son.

The cover-up lasted almost a year when the Lord sent His prophet Nathan to speak to David. Now we must not forget a king had the power to put to death the prophet, especially if the king did not like what he heard. This occurred throughout the history of Israel's monarchy under other kings! Nevertheless, Nathan boldly confronts David regarding the adulterous affair and the murder of Uriah:

> *Thus says the Lord, the God of Israel, 'I anointed you king over Israel, and I delivered you out of the hand of Saul. And I gave you your master's house and your master's wives into your arms and gave you the house of Israel and Judah. And if this were too little, I would add to you as much more. Why have you* despised *the word of the Lord, to do what is evil in His sight? You have struck down Uriah the Hittite with the sword and have taken his wife to be your wife and have killed him with the sword of the Ammonites. Now therefore the sword shall never depart from your house, because you have despised* Me, *and have taken the wife of Uriah the Hittite to be your wife. (2 Sam. 12:7–10)*

Perhaps the thought has already occurred in your mind (as it did for me), and you have found yourself asking, "How could God characterize David, as a man after His own heart, when he had committed such grievous sins?" After all, David has committed adultery, then resorted to murder in his attempt to cover up the affair. Furthermore, as if that were not enough, he took Bathsheba for his wife, adding her to his collection (wives), while producing him a son, and seemingly carrying on with the life of managing the nation without missing a beat!

Does this sound like a man who reflects the heart of God? One could readily conclude there apparently is a "big disconnect" with such a description of David, or at the very least, an issue regarding the veracity of scriptural understanding of God's characterization. Of course, the latter is a more diplomatic way to avoid possible incredulity of God's inscription of David's heart!

Again, we must be mindful that David is in pursuit of God's heart. This is the essence or meaning of God's inscription regarding David's life. God was saying, "I have found a man who desires to know My heart. David desires to know Me!"

David's actions were heinous by standards of any culture. Further yet, in today's world of psychology, he probably would be diagnosed as a sociopath. So it is obvious that David's actions did not align with God's characterization of him. Subsequently, we need to dig deeper to find out what God knew about David that we did not—because God always tells the truth, since He is truth. God's inscription of David has to be accurate. This is crucial and, therefore, a pivotal moment regarding David's journey, largely because of David's personal contradictions—his hypocrisy.

Let's explore the confrontational scene in our attempt to discover the authenticity of God's statement as David initially reacts to the prophet's indictment and the naked reality of his dire circumstances. First, David is aware that capital punishment is the penalty for adultery under the Old Testament Law, which perhaps led to the cover-up. Also, it must be underscored that David knows the prophet Nathan is God's mouthpiece as he offers his initial response to the prophet. Now let's consider the scene:

> *Thus says the Lord, "Behold, I will raise up evil against you out of your own house. And I will take your wives before your eyes and give them to your neighbor, and he shall lie with your wives in the sight of this sun. For you did it secretly, but I will do this thing before all Israel and before the sun.' David said to Nathan, 'I have sinned against the Lord." And Nathan said to David, "The Lord*

also has put away your sin; you shall not die. Nevertheless, because by this deed you have utterly scorned the Lord, the child who is born to you shall die." Then Nathan went to his house. (2 Sam. 12:11–15)

David's first response to the charges made against him is very clear and clean in his personal acknowledgment of what he has done. He states concisely, without condition, and absent of any excuse, reason, or explanation, "I have sinned against the Lord!" David takes complete ownership of the wrong he has committed. It is so important, it is worth repeating. David takes complete and unconditional ownership by saying, "I am the man! I did it...I did it all! I have sinned against the Lord!"

But why is this so important for us to recognize? There are several factors, but before we discuss them, it must be emphasized David accepts full responsibility for his actions *before* Nathan announced to David, "You shall not die!"

Therefore, we might conclude, "What a relief for David since he learned he was going to survive!" But not so fast. Though he may have felt some reassurance, there is plenty of insight provided through God's word that David did not experience immediate relief in learning he would live and not die for his adulterous affair. In fact, through his own words, recorded after the confrontation with Nathan, the weight of these sins was excruciatingly heavy and self-induced with guilt, deep-tormented sorrow, and desperate remorse. Let's listen to those opening words of deep brokenness:

David's Desperate Heartache!

> *Have mercy on me, O God, according to your unfailing love; according to your great compassion blot out my transgressions. Wash away all my iniquity and cleanse me from my sin. For I know my transgressions, and my sin is always before me. Against you, you only, have I sinned and done what is evil in your sight, so that you are proved right when you speak and justified when you judge. (Ps. 51:1–4)*

This prayer of David is one of the most personal and powerful moments of brokenness in all the Bible. It is Psalm 51, known as the penitent psalm or the psalm of "repentance." Most Bible scholars believe it was written by David during the days that ensued after his meeting with Nathan. It is very personal and unpretentious. There is no time for pretense when one is desperate. And, since this time in David's life was radically life-changing, it is important to portray a more brutal and honest depiction of this dramatic scene and aftermath.

Perhaps David, to avoid disruptions or distractions from his royal court and family, would have immediately left the palace to seek solitude in some isolated place where he could be alone with the Lord. The visual we should view is not a serene picture of a man kneeling at a rock calmly and quietly praying to God with an upward gaze toward the heavens. Instead, we should see a broken, guilt-ridden, devastated man with his royal robes torn and dirty as he lays prostrate with his face in the dirt, pounding his fists into the ground as he desperately seeks forgiveness and mercy from the God he loves. It is a time of great despair and desperation!

The haunting of David's soul is much worse than the insidious murder, adultery, and cover-up. As heinous as those sins are, the horrific torment deep within him can be found in the reverberating echo of God's indictment against him: *"You have despised My word... therefore, you have despised Me!"*

Such words coming from the God, whom David had come to know intimately, as well as the many blessings he had received from Him, is excruciatingly unbearable. Consequently, he is explicitly direct and specific in his appeal, for David's words are personally addressed to God and no one else. However, they are not words spoken without assistance, of which I will explain in a moment.

Before we look at the content of David's prayer, let's consider two primary reasons this penitent prayer is recorded for our benefit. The first is that God provides for you and me today a blueprint or a map for the priceless gift known as repentance. It is a gift. Therefore, we should not approach this vital dynamic to the Christian life with some type of formulaic mind-set. That will not work with the Lord, for no one knows our heart and motives better than God. However, there are principles we can learn from regarding this life-changing process, as David learned, when convicted by God's Word and led by the Holy Spirit in his prayer.

Since we live in a culture where a "victim mentality" pervades western society in which there are always excuses or justifiable explanations for one's wrongdoing, it's important to understand the dynamics of repentance. These principles are so foundationally significant, they will determine whether reconciliation will occur in one's relationship to God, as well as with others.

Secondly, and most importantly, insights of this prayer help answer the question as to why God would give David such an inscription regarding his character. They provide a deeper glimpse and understanding into this very broken man, who definitely was not perfect, but maintained his passionate pursuit of God's own heart!

Repentance: Entrance to a Restored Relationship with God!

The priceless value of repentance cannot be overstated. It's the only entrance to a restored relationship with God. Martin Luther contended that repentance should be constant in the life of a Christian, therefore viewed as a lifestyle. Certainly, it is the cornerstone to growing and reaching the ultimate destination God has established for every one of His children. That's how important this dynamic is to the Christian life.

But there is much misunderstanding within the Church and outside of it regarding the meaning of this biblical truth. It is grossly misperceived, due in much to Hollywood's portrayal of the urban street-corner preacher, typically a characterization of an angry, self-righteous evangelist spewing ominous, ultimate warnings, "Repent or perish!" Of course, Hollywood did not need to originate the "script" as they were given such a message from some pulpits, past and present. This has only contributed to an ugly and negative perception of this all-important dynamic, which was the centerpiece of Jesus's gospel message: "Repent, for the kingdom of heaven is at hand" (Matt. 4:17).

The word *repentance* is derived from the Greek word *metanoia*. It means to have a "change of mind." Pastor Jack Hayford qualifies this dynamic as "a radical upheaval of the human will."[4] Indeed, it is a radical change to one's paradigm of living. Repentance is about transformation, a change in lifestyle.

To develop it further, I would offer this definitive meaning: a radical reorientation of the individual person, which comprises the heart, soul, mind, and body of the human being. In contemporary language, this radical reorientation subsequently produces a paradigm shift in the life of the believer. This is what happens when the Holy Spirit convinces a person for the need to change. Repentance is the genesis for a reawakening of the interior being of the individual when wrongful acts have been committed against God and others. We should understand, repentance creates in the life of the child of God a constant, good, positive, and transformative power that engenders an intimate and deeper connectivity to God! We shall see this as we closely view David's prayer of repentance.

There are several important steps in the journey of repentance. The first is taken by David when he reacts initially to the divine indictment from Nathan by declaring, "I have sinned against the Lord!" This is the most important necessary step. One must *acknowledge* what one has done by accepting full responsibility without blaming anyone or anything pertinent to one's circumstances in life. There is no momentary hand-wringing uncertainty, memory lapses, posturing, or excuses. David's acknowledgment is clean and concise. His acceptance for what he has done is immediate, without pretense.

This first step of being accountable is a huge challenge to most people in general. We can understand this by taking a brief look at Adam and Eve, where it all started. After they sinned, the first occurrence was God initiating a conversation by asking Adam a question: "Where are you?" (Gen. 3:9). Though they were hiding among the trees in the garden, of course, God knew exactly where they were located. But did they?

That was the point of the question. God in effect was asking, "Where have you gone, Adam? Where are you located in relationship to Me?" As we know, sin causes alienation from God—a displacement. And God's Presence had departed from them. They knew something was radically different because of it. That is what Adam meant when he said, "I was afraid, because I was 'naked,' and I hid myself" (Gen. 3:10). They were not simply naked, literally. Yes, they discovered their physical nakedness. But there was a greater problem. Their acute naked condition was the departure of God's Presence they had never experienced. Declaring one's independence from God produces such a result. Then, when Adam finally answered the Lord's inquiry of eating the forbidden fruit, he blamed his wife. Adam did not want to take ownership for his actions.

In effect, the "blame game" continues today. It is why true reconciliation is preempted in the Church-at-large, and unforgiveness in relationships is like a pervasive cancer. People have a difficult time with this first step regarding repentance because they cannot humble themselves and take full responsibility for their actions. Typically, people want to blame their parents, their family heritage, their environment, spouse, or other relationships for their problems, circumstances, or issues.

God has given me the privilege of ministering in our local homeless shelter, and I love each person with whom I interact. But in ministering to people struggling with various addictions, I've discovered their narratives persist in blaming their families, friends, or the other person for their condition. The tendency is not to take responsibility for choices made. Many cannot break free from the horrific bondage in their lives, either due to the lack of humility or not recognizing their desperate need for *someone* greater than themselves. They struggle with taking complete ownership for their broken condition! Inevitably, they stay stuck, not able to move forward in their journey with Christ because of the inner struggle to surrender and their lack of knowing *how* to surrender. The real tragedy is the powerful transformation Christ promises evades them!

However, this is not the case with David. David is immediate in wanting to be clean and clear about his conduct. This is the second dynamic of repentance and such action by David is described as a "confession." The Greek word for confess is *homologeo*, which means "to say the same thing." It also has a judicial application in which it carries the meaning of "a binding and public declaration that settles a relationship." David is saying, "Whatever, Lord, You say about my sins is true and accurate and I agree with everything you say about me...I am a sinner...I am an offense to You!" Through these two initial steps, David is *agreeing* with God by his acceptance of God's verdict regarding his immoral actions.

This is the impactful meaning of his profound declaration: *"Against you, you only, have I sinned and done what is evil in your sight, so that you are proved right when you speak, and justified when you judge."* It is not that David is in denial or ignoring the reality he violated Bathsheba, her husband, and the nation (the king was viewed as a Shepherd of Israel—a representative of God to the people). Instead, David's focus is on the character of God and who God is in relationship to him. David *affirms* God is truly the only One who knows the ontology of sin and is the only One who has the capacity to measure the depth of its destructiveness to an individual human soul. He alone is able to judge it rightly due to the righteousness of His own heart. This is the third important principle in the map of repentance. God is the only Person who can effectively adjudicate the nature and power of sin.

We must listen very carefully because many well-intended believers miss this significant dynamic regarding the process of repentance. A believer's ability to grow in their life with God can be stunted as a result. The most important effect of David's acknowledgment (confession) is his humble movement toward God by bringing his heart into alignment with God's own heart. He does this by consenting to and affirming God's judgment of his personal, human condition in relationship to the character of God's rightness!

The Heart of David's Brokenness!

After his initial confession of wrongdoing, David then takes the next and fourth incremental step in the progression of "turning toward God (repentance)." David makes an *appeal*. But it is not an ordinary appeal. David knows he has committed egregious acts, worthy of capital punishment. But the most grievous violation David has come to realize is he "*despised*" God by his actions.

The Hebrew word for *despise* means "to hold in contempt or to have disdain." To hold in contempt or to be contemptible toward someone is to *not* value, or in other words have little regard for that person. It is much the same as saying to that person, "I don't care what you have to say, I'm going to do, what I want, when I want, however I want!" The key component in the statement is "I don't care!" And when we say "I don't care," we are in effect saying, "You don't matter!"

It is this context, for David, he makes the most heart-crushing discovery of his actions. David has come to realize that his actions demonstrated a reckless disregard for God's goodwill. With the backdrop of Israel's history, David is very much aware of Mt. Sinai and God's purpose in giving His Ten Commandments to his nation. It was to reveal who He was, His will, His heart, His desire and destiny for how Israel was to live for Him, and with Him, in relationship as His chosen people.

David discovers he committed contemptible acts toward the God he professed to love. And nothing could have caused more anguish of soul than to realize how he had hurt and offended the God he had come to know personally. Such heartache was even more compounded and magnified for him because David knew all that God had done for him. God had anointed him with His Holy Spirit, and so he was quite familiar with the awesome Presence of God. God's Presence went with him wherever he went. God had protected him from the murderous assaults of Saul. God had made him king over all Israel and victorious against all his enemies. David didn't lose a battle, and David knew the very reason he didn't suffer defeat. So David had known the goodness and favor of God in which he had been greatly blessed by God, and he loved God for such undeserved blessings.

Is it any wonder David finds himself broken, devastated, and desperate? Now he believes everything is in jeopardy. He has been told by Nathan "that he is not going to die" for his sins, but that doesn't matter to him. In fact, he probably would find death a more merciful remedy than the broken heart he has to endure.

But what is in jeopardy for David? Is it the pronounced sentence of death for David's son from Bathsheba? No, though it grieves him to suffer such a loss. Is it the ominous consequence that the "sword will not depart from his household (family)," which indicates family conflicts and premature deaths (the first four sons of David died prematurely, three by the sword)? No. Regardless how painful such repercussions would be, that is not it for David!

David knew what had happened to his predecessor, Saul. God's anointing had departed from Saul. God's presence had left him because Saul was too independent and bent on self-navigation. An important lesson we could all learn from Saul's demise—God will not go where He is not wanted! David's greatest fear was what happened to Saul would now happen to him. Nothing would break David's heart more if such would occur.

Humility Breeds Reconciliation; Reconciliation Bleeds Humility!

But David was different. The biggest distinction is David *wanted* God in his life. Not only that, David knew he *needed* God in his life. Author, John Ortberg, refers to such a moment as "a God-given ache for goodness."[5] The brokenness David experienced was the "ache" for the goodness of God to be restored in his life. And he knew such goodness was God's actual Presence.

David knew his effectiveness as a king and as a warrior was completely determined by being fully dependent upon God. This is the qualitative essence of a man who is truly humble. Humility breeds reconciliation, and reconciliation bleeds humility. And at this point, nothing, nothing else, mattered more to David than reconciliation with God and his relationship being restored to the Lord! David would have preferred death rather than the departure of God's Presence in his life!

Now listen to his desperate plea: *"Create in me a pure heart, O God, and renew a steadfast spirit within me. Do not cast me from your presence or take your Holy Spirit from me" (Ps. 51:10–11, NIV).* Can you hear the despair in his cry to God? Let me paraphrase: "Please, Lord, don't leave me. I know I'm not worthy of you, but I know I can't do 'life' without you. Don't depart from me, Lord. I need you, and I will not be effective without you. Besides, I would not want it any other way, because I know your way is best!"

Clearly, David is showing deep remorse that he grieved the Lord by committing such contemptible acts and disregard for God's commandments. David had learned God's commandments were from God's heart. David's actions were a personal rejection of God. David is desperately pleading God would "not cast him from His presence or take His Holy Spirit from him." David knew God's Holy Spirit was inseparable from experiencing the reality of God daily in his life.

At this point, all the success David had achieved didn't matter to him. All the wealth he had acquired because of his status he could care less. You see, God has a way to getting us reoriented toward what is really important in life. David's heart during the year of cover-up had become desolate, deserted, and lonely.

The place David found himself wasn't simply because he had been "busted." David was desperately broken and engulfed with inconsolable grief—the kind of grief one experiences when they have lost someone of great value and meaning in their life.

David's greatest fear was estrangement from God and the loss of personal relationship he had enjoyed with the Lord. David had gotten a glimpse of what it was like to experience such alienation as he suffered the past year under the weight of shame, guilt, and conviction, of which he cries out for God's mercy quite early in his prayer: *"For I know my transgressions, and my sin is always before me... Cleanse me with hyssop, and I will be clean; wash me, and I will be whiter than snow. Let me hear joy and gladness; let the bones you have crushed rejoice. Hide your face from my sins and blot out all my iniquity"* (Ps. 51:3, 7–9).

David's appeal is embedded in deep anguish of soul and remorse. David is not groveling. He simply is a broken man. Too often this is a missing component when it comes to the repentant dynamic in the Church today. The Christian philosopher Dallas Willard offers important insights regarding the significant and deep emotion of remorse:

> To prosecutors and judges in our court system, as well as to people in ordinary situations of life, it still matters greatly whether wrongdoers show signs of remorse or seem to be truly sorry for what they have done. Why is that? It is because genuine remorse tells us something very deep about the individual. The person who can harm others and feel no remorse is, indeed, a different kind of person from the one who is sorry. There is little hope for genuine change in one who is without remorse, without the anguish of regret...Much of what is called Christian profession today involves no remorse or sorrow at all over who one is or even for what one has done. There is little awareness of being lost or of

a radical evil in our hearts, bodies, and souls—
which we must get away from and from which
only God can deliver us.[6]

The emphasis is not that remorse or tears of regret are by itself enough. Nor is one ignorant of the fact that regret can certainly be contrived or manipulated through tears. That is not a new thing. However, Dr. Willard contends, a person who is broken may be a good indication one is genuine in wanting to change based on their choices made. In other words, remorse is a good starting point toward transformation in the person who has a sincere and broken heart because of what they have done.

This is evident as David prays a significant insight regarding God's heart: *"You do not delight in sacrifice, or I would bring it; you do not take pleasure in burnt offerings. The sacrifices of God are a broken spirit; a broken and contrite heart, O God, you will not despise" (Ps. 51:16–17).*

Now it was alluded to earlier, David did not pray without assistance. How did David discover that God did not delight in sacrifice or take pleasure in burnt offerings? After all, the Old Testament sacrifices were instituted under God's direction. Was David disregarding God's ordained commandments regarding sacrifices by this new declaration? No, he was not. David had simply received a revelation of God's heart about what was most important to Him. God was teaching David an important lesson he would not forget.

God's first priority in having a relationship with man begins with the heart. Remember, when Samuel was going through the selection process and following God's instruction in the anointing of the next king of Israel, God reminded Samuel of this important truth: *"For the Lord sees not as man sees: man looks on the outward appearance, but the Lord looks on the heart" (1 Sam. 16:7).* It is the heart of the individual that God sees as His "altar" of true sacrifice.

So David is learning what is important to the God he loves during this most critical crisis in his life. David is discovering the centerpiece to repentance. It has everything to do with brokenness and a contrite heart. David realizes these "sacrifices" are encased in humility. One of the reasons humility is so important to God is, one will never start their journey with Him unless they recognize their need for Him. The following scripture explains why humility is very important to God as described by the prophet Isaiah:

> *Heaven is my throne, and the earth is my footstool;*
> *what is the house that you would build for me,*
> *and what is the place of my rest? All these things*
> *my hand has made, and so all these things came to*
> *be, declares the Lord. But this is the one to whom I*
> *will look: he who is humble and contrite in spirit*
> *and trembles at my word. (Isa. 66:1–2)*

This passage of Scripture is a forecast of the New Testament Covenant in which God is looking for a place to dwell (rest), and it is the heart that responds to God's invitation with an attitude of humility. Again, humility is the personal acknowledgment, one needs and desires God, because one has learned they are incomplete or inadequate without Him. Humility is man's invitation to want and realize his need for God. God is constantly looking for such a person who simply wants Him and wants Him desperately and decisively!

This is the heart of David. It is the characterization of David's heart toward God with regard to his personal sins. He is broken, contrite, and filled with anguish and deep regret. I believe you can say his remorse or anguish of regret is a byproduct of his passion to have his relationship restored to God as David makes his humble request: *"Restore to me the joy of your salvation and grant me a willing spirit, to sustain me" (Ps. 51:12).*

Nothing is more important than for his relationship to be restored with God. Nothing is more important to David than to be reconciled to God. This priority surpasses any other concern and care for his life. Humility produces such a passion and hunger. He wants to be in right relationship with God no matter the personal cost and consequences that God has already pronounced. For David, the personal cost of his sins is incomparable to the potential loss of his relationship with God. Nothing compares to this highest priority of David!

Indeed, not only is this the essence of repentance, but it is an accurate alignment with one who is portrayed as "a man after God's own heart!" David is learning to want the same thing God wants for his life. God wants David to know Him. But let us remember, such a lesson learned by David was not learned alone. The Holy Spirit taught him this invaluable truth.

David's Greatest Hope!

When David begins his prayer of repentance in pursuit of reconciliation and restoration to God, he appeals to the greatest attribute of God's nature he has come to know in his life. He appeals to what he has discovered of God's heart as a shepherd boy in the hills of Bethlehem, as a fugitive in the Judean wilderness, and as king of the most powerful nation in the entire region during his first twenty years of rule. David appeals to the only thing he knows—He appeals to God's grace!

Consider the opening words of David's prayer: "*Have mercy on me, O God, according to your unfailing love; according to your great compassion blot out my transgressions. Wash away all my iniquity and cleanse me from my sin*" *(Ps. 51:1–2)*. David's direct appeal is for God's mercy, and God's mercy is enfolded in His "unfailing love." He knows God's mercy is fashioned from His grace, which flows from His unfailing love. David knows this from his personal interactions with God as he records these attributes in one of his prayers of worship: *"The Lord is merciful and gracious, slow to anger and abounding in steadfast love...He does not deal with us according to our sins, nor repay us according to our iniquities" (Ps. 103:8, 10)*. David is providing a description of God's grace in which God does *not give* him what he deserves for his sins!

But it is also most important to realize David is not presumptuous or sloppy regarding God's grace. He knows it is his only hope. He knows God's grace because he has been the beneficiary of it throughout his life. David knows God chose him when he was a young, irrelevant, insignificant shepherd boy. David experienced God's grace when God chose him over his seven other brothers. David knew God's grace when he was anointed by the Holy Spirit while Saul remained king of Israel. And David had seen God's grace work in his life as a fugitive in the wilderness while experiencing the provision and protection of God until the appointed time he would assume the throne of Israel according to God's time schedule.

However, David does not presume God's grace at this particularly painful intersection of his journey with God. This is why he is found imploring God, *"Do not cast me from your Presence or take your Holy Spirit from me."* David, appealing to God's grace is his only hope, for nothing is more important that his relationship restored to God. Nothing else will satisfy him. Nothing!

The Awesome Grace of God!

God's grace by many believers is viewed as a mystery. In one respect, it will always have some depth of mystery, primarily due to the incomprehensible nature of God. But we can gain some sense of meaning regarding this attribute of God. The technical definition of grace or the common definition every Bible college student learns when referring to the grace of God is known as unmerited favor. Indeed, grace is God's underserved favor toward every sinner.

But I also like an expanded version that deepens, for me, the meaning of grace as offered by Dallas Willard: "Grace is God acting in our lives to accomplish what we cannot accomplish on our own."[7] So true, because of our humanity—our limited, finite humanness— we need God to do in our lives what we cannot do for ourselves. In essence, we not only need God's grace when we sin, but also we need God's grace constantly working in our lives because of our human limitations. We will always need God's grace!

With God just showing up in our lives it is important to understand this vital foundation—it is because of His grace! Everything we receive from God is due to His grace. Consider Abraham. What did he do to earn God's visitation? Did he acquiesce to a qualified status that warranted God showing up in his life? No, because at the time, he didn't even have any idea who God was because he lived in a pagan society (Sumerian), which worshiped the moon god Nanna.[8] Then one day, God shows up in his life, changes his environment, moving him to a new residence, all the while revealing to Abraham His heart and purpose for his life. All God wanted to do for Abraham was to bless him by offering several promises: "I will make you a great nation…I will bless you and make your name great…I will make you a blessing…and through you all the nations of the world will be blessed" (Gen. 12:2–4). What did Abraham do to earn such gifts from God? Nothing. Nada. Absolutely nothing!

So there was nothing Abraham could do to earn God's blessings in his life through his own individual self-effort. However, there was one condition required of Abraham. Abraham must trust God to do what only God could do for him! Abraham would have to trust God to do that which was inconceivable or impossible according to all human limitations. Abraham would need to fully rely on God's grace for God's will and purpose to be realized in his life! And indeed, Abraham did just that. Abraham chose to believe in God's promise, a male heir, and to receive what God wanted to do in his life! That is God's grace!

It was also the same conditional requirement for others: Jacob, Joseph, Moses, Joshua, and David. We must never forget, all of these individuals in the Bible were sinners and their missteps are well documented in their stories. During various occasions in their lives, they "missed the mark," one of the biblical definitions of sin. There is not one personal story that does not include a time each person missed it. The only reason they were able to do great exploits for God's purpose in their lives was based on two primary principles: God showed up, and they trusted in God to do what only He could do for them! All of them stumbled and failed God at some point during their journey with Him, simply because they were sinners, just like you and me. Then they would allow God to pick them up and move forward by allowing Him to bring them to their God-ordained destiny.

The invitation is the same today for everyone, as it was for all the men and women in the Bible: to trust in God's grace! This explains the statement by Jesus, "Truly, I say to you, whoever does not receive the kingdom of God like a child shall not enter it" (Luke 18:17). Jesus underscored the importance of being childlike in order to receive God's promises. To be childlike means to be humble and vulnerable. When one is humble and vulnerable, one is very reliant and trusting upon those to whom the child is entrusted. And, of course, a child doesn't have all the answers. A child simply trusts and relies on those for their care. Likewise, God desires we trust in His grace to do what only He can do for us!

To further qualify the meaning of grace, it is important to recognize the Greek word for gift is the word *charis*. Gift or charis is synonymous with "grace or favor." All of God's blessings should be viewed as gifts flowing from His grace. They are undeserved and even unexpected, as it was in Abraham's life. And the greatest gift God gives to the world is His Son, Jesus Christ. All we must do is to fully trust Jesus to do in us what only He can do because of that which we cannot do for ourselves. That my friend is God's grace in action!

A Summation of David's Prayer!

Now, it's important for us to review this important dynamic in the Christian life. David's prayer of heartbreak comprises five major dynamics of repentance:

- David *acknowledges* his sins by fully taking ownership without excuse, explanation, or evasion;
- David confesses his sins by *agreeing* with God, everything God says about his conduct;
- David *affirms* God's character, as God is the only one who truly understands the ontology or character of sin, and therefore is always right in His judgment of it;
- David *appeals* to the only hope he has, which is God's mercy fashioned by His grace and flowing from His unfathomable steadfast love;
- And the fifth is the one dynamic we have not discussed yet, but it is most important to the process: David *accepts* God's mercy and forgiveness through the grace expressed to him by the God who loves David very much!

We do not want to glide too quickly over this fifth dynamic. It is commonly a big issue for many believers as many people have a tension in this regard: accepting God's grace. One factor in this tension is the human proclivity toward religiosity. We have this tendency to think there is something we must do to improve on what only God can do. So we decide there must be some penance or work we must do to get back on the right track from which we have been derailed. We feel we have to earn God's approval, so we readily have difficulty in simply accepting His gracious forgiveness and mercy into our lives.

The second factor has everything to do with the first. It is the insidious malignancy of the human condition known as pride. It is usually pride that keeps us from receiving God's grace. Why? For obvious reasons pride insists on self-navigation. Pride demands making its own decisions and setting its own course. Pride is a blinding power by which we can be deceived into thinking we "know a better way." This explains the declaration by the apostle Paul in Ephesians 2:8, "*For by grace you have been saved by faith, and not of yourselves, it is the gift of God, lest anyone should boast.*"

But if one genuinely applies the first four principles, the fifth one regarding the acceptance of God's grace will fall into place because they are a perfect antidote to pride. Those four principles can't help but cultivate a brokenness that causes one to cry out to God, "*You do not delight in sacrifice or I would bring it. You do not take pleasure in burnt offerings. The sacrifices of God are a broken spirit. A broken and contrite heart, O God, you will not despise!*"

Humility Fed David's Hunger for God

As David approached the midpoint of his reign, he did a life-changing pivot in his journey with God, evidenced by what God was willing to do later for David in the last years of his life. This will be our discussion for the next several chapters. But have we now answered the defining question regarding the inscription God had given to David?

Deeply encased in the essence of David's prayer is one of the attributes God values most in the human heart. It is humility. Humility is the very antithesis of pride. Humility acknowledges one's personal inadequacy, nothingness, and incompleteness without God. Please note, there is a more extensive delineation regarding the qualitative traits of humility in chapter 12 because this godly attribute was foundational to David becoming a man after God's own heart. But in the meantime, listen to the sobering call by the South African missionary-evangelist Andrew Murray regarding this all-important virtue:

> The call to humility has been too little regarded in the Church because its true nature and importance has been too little apprehended. It is not something which we bring to God, or which He bestows; it is simply the sense of entire nothingness which comes when we see how truly God is *all*, and in which we make way for God to *be all*. When the creature realizes that this is the true nobility, and consent to be—with his will, his mind, and his affections—the form, the vessel in which the life and glory of God are to work and manifest themselves, he sees that humility is simply acknowledging the truth of his position as creature, and yielding to God His place.[8]

In the most awful of circumstances, David comes to this personal realization of God's character and His heart. David has learned, he is utterly nothing without God in his life. Through his greatest adversity yet, David discovers his utter and complete need to be abandoned to God by being fully dependent upon God to do, what he could never do for himself. This is the mark of humility. And the effect of such is teachability.

David learned he was not willing to live without God, so he was willing to pay whatever cost to have the intimacy of his relationship with God restored. And, though David was the most powerful and effective monarch in the region at the time, nothing could compare to his relationship with God as he penned such thoughts late one evening as a refugee in the wilderness: "*O God, you are my God; earnestly I seek you; my soul thirsts for you; my flesh faints for you, as in a dry and weary land where there is no water. So I have seen you in the sanctuary, beholding your power and glory. Because your steadfast love is better than life, my lips will praise you*" *(Ps. 63: 1–3).*

Yes, David was an adulterer and a murderer, but also a man who desired to turn it around and do a complete pivot back onto the right pathway, no matter the cost. David would have preferred death rather than live another moment without God's Presence in his life. David was committed to learning from his tragic transgressions. Learning is growing, and growing is changing, all of which engenders a radical reorientation of the human heart. Such is the Godly gift of repentance being worked out in one's life through the grace of God.

Through this horrific "dark night" of David's soul, he learned some important truths regarding God's heart and one of particular importance: the value of God's word. This principle is given more attention in the next chapter. He also learned what God values most. It produced in David a heart that was reoriented to the priorities of God's heart—that which was important to God. This is the kind of heart God said He had searched for, and found, in a shepherd boy who would someday be a king of Israel!

CHAPTER 6

The Deficiency for David's Derailment!

Why have you despised the word of the Lord, to do what is evil in His sight? Now therefore the sword shall never depart from your house, because you have despised Me...
—2 Samuel 12:9–10

As God confronted David through Nathan, His prophet, the Lord informed him regarding the *cause* for his transgressions. We must visit this scene again so we can dig deeper in understanding the cause for this temporary derailment of David. Let's listen to the account:

> *Thus says the Lord, the God of Israel, "I anointed you king over Israel, and I delivered you out of the hand of Saul. And I gave you your master's house and your master's wives into your arms and gave you the house of Israel and Judah. And if this were too little, I would add to you as much more. Why have you despised the word of the Lord, to do what is evil in His sight? Now therefore the sword shall*

never depart from your house, because you have despised Me." (2 Sam. 12:7–10)

The Lord loved David, so God wanted to fully arrest David by not only attending to the deep ramifications of his sins and the effects on his household, but more importantly, how God wanted David to learn from his horrific actions by discovering the cause for doing what he did. So God cuts directly to the issue: *"You have despised My word... You have despised Me!"*

God Kept His Promise!

As we look at this text, it is interesting to observe the sequence of God's address to David. The Lord begins with a chronology of David's life as it concerns God's personal involvement in his life. God begins with that sacred moment when He sent Samuel to anoint David as the next king of Israel while David was yet a young shepherd boy, resulting in God's Spirit *"rushing"* upon David. Then the Lord reminds David, He protected him during all those years he spent as a fugitive fleeing from the conspiracy of Saul and the attempts on his life. God reminds David, during his darkest hours, God preserved his life.

Furthermore, David is reminded of how he is blessed with the women he had been given in marriage (polygamy was allowed during ancient times). Finally, the Lord concludes the chronology with how God made David king over a united Israel!

God's ultimate indictment is wrapped around David's life chronology, as the Lord declared, "You have despised the word of the Lord!" (2 Sam. 12:9). It is significant to underscore that it isn't until God has reminded David of all that He has done for him, the Lord provides the cause for David's spiritual impairment.

This begs the question, why did the Lord address David in this manner? Didn't David already know or understand that he had been the beneficiary of the Lord's great blessings in his life? Yes, David knew this reality, which explains his authorship of 75 of the 150 psalms of praise and worship. Without question, David knew all these blessings found their origin in God, based on such prayers of thanksgiving and worship expressed to Him.

However, God had a message for David that was bigger and greater than his own personal circumstances. God wanted David to understand there was a direct correlation with the blessings God had given David and the value of His Word. God desired that David would learn they were more than mere blessings. They were *promises* made and *promises* kept by God!

First and foremost, God wanted David to realize there was not a promise made to him God had not kept! God wanted David to understand all the blessings he had received from the Lord were based on His grace. There was nothing David had done to earn and acquire God's blessings or the destiny God had chosen for his life. God chose to bless David because of Who He is and His good will. God was teaching David that His promises were inseparable from His invaluable Word that embodies His character!

God Is a Promise Keeper!

God wanted David to remember, there was not one, *not one*, promise He had made to David that He had not fulfilled—not one! And again, it was most important for David to understand the blessings he received from God were based on God's promises initiated by God alone. Even when it seemed the odds were unrealistic for David to ever realize his destiny as the next king of Israel, God wanted David to remember it was because of the Lord working on his behalf and

His faithfulness that made the impossible become possible! However, it was also a teaching moment for David—a brief history lesson. For with the backdrop of David's story was the larger narrative of his own people, Israel.

David was familiar with how things got started with the "Father of Israel's faith"—Abraham. It was shared in the previous chapter how God one day merely showed up and introduced Himself to Abraham, making him a wonderful promise by which God would bless him with many descendants, and through them, form a nation in which God would bless the world. This promise later became known as the Abrahamic Covenant. The word *promise* is synonymous with *covenant*!

David now understood this promise initiated by God was not something Abraham conceived. Abraham did not become inspired with the concept or idea. In fact, in order for Abraham to receive this promise of God it would require him to move his entire family about one thousand miles to an unfamiliar and unknown land (Gen. 12:1).

This was all God's idea done by God's initiative. It was God's unconditional promise. The only responsibility Abraham had regarding this offer from God was simply a response to trust God to do what Abraham could not do. Both Abraham and his wife, Sarah, did just that, since they were beyond the biological capacity to have a child. And so a nation was born from their "miracle child," Isaac. The nation would later become known as Israel.

David recalled all of this happened in Abraham's life because of God's grace. David was beginning to understand there was a similar parallel between what God worked out in Abraham's life and his own personal journey. God had simply showed up and introduced Himself to Abraham, totally unexpected, and gave him a glimpse of Who He is and what He is like. God desired to bless Abraham's life with a wonderful promise that could not be earned or acquired through self-effort. God's promise to Abraham is simply, God's gift.

As David continued the review of his heritage, he remembered it would be many years later, God again showed up in another man's life—Moses. God told Moses to go tell the Israelites, *"I have observed you and what has been done to you in Egypt, and I promise that I will bring you up out of the affliction of Egypt to the land of the Canaanites…a land flowing with milk and honey" (Exod. 3:16–17).* We know the "affliction" was slavery, for God desired to use Moses as His instrument to rescue Israel from the horrific bondage they had been subjected over four hundred years.

Only with God's help, Moses succeeded in his assignment. As instructed by God, Moses brought over two million Israelites to Mt. Sinai, where God would introduce Himself to all the people with an awesome display of His power and Presence. It was occasioned with God's audible voice for the first and only time in human history as He spoke to a collective group of people.

Subsequently, through this personal introduction, God gave His commandments to teach the people how to live with Him and others, as well as giving to them their purpose and destiny, based again on a promise: *"Tell the people of Israel: You yourselves have seen what I did to the Egyptians, and how I bore you on eagles' wings and brought you to Myself. Now therefore, if you will indeed obey my voice and keep my covenant, you shall be my treasured possession among all peoples, for all the earth is mine; and you shall be to me a kingdom of priests and a holy nation" (Exod. 19:3–6).* This became known as the Mosaic Covenant or the Covenant of the Law.

David was discovering the true meaning, as well as the value, for his personal blessings received from God and how they had a direct correlation to Israel's historical narrative—sown in the promises God had initiated. It was not based on merit, qualifications, or worthiness of any individual person. It was merely about a God who decided to start with one man. Then a particular people, who God desired to bless and form into a nation He could call His own. And then a nation through whom God desired to bless the entire world and to reveal Himself!

God was teaching David that his blessings were similar to Israel's blessings. They were embedded in the promises of God—conceived, constituted, and consummated in the goodness of God. They were promises formed and fashioned by God's grace. Promises made by God, and promises kept by God!

It's Personal to God!

After David's brief history lesson, God then pronounces the indictment that crushes David's heart inconsolably: "*Why have you despised My word? Now therefore the sword shall not depart from your house, because you have despised Me*" (2 Sam. 12:9–10).

The second lesson David is to learn, sin is personal with God. God's statement effectively says as much. Sin is very personal with God because it is antithetical to His character, and God wants David to understand this important truth. For what David did by taking another man's wife, then conspiring and murdering her husband was without question evil. But beyond these obvious sinful deeds, God wanted David to learn his sin was much deeper than such acts. David's conduct was a personal affront to God. This explains why God told David, to paraphrase, "You despised My Word; therefore, you despised Me!" God took David's sin personally!

We learned in the previous chapter the meaning of the word *despise*. It means to hold in contempt or to have little regard for someone. Can you imagine David's thoughts when he heard such an indictment against him? So let's translate God's indictment accordingly: "David, you have devalued Me and everything I am to you. You have acted with disdain toward Me. By your actions, you have shown very little value or regard for Me!"

110

Nothing could cut David so deeply and crush his heart more than to hear such words from the God he had grown to know and love. But God did not only want David to know how he had offended Him, God was also teaching David an important truth regarding sin.

Before we now fast-forward a thousand years, we must understand an important characteristic of God's nature. The eternal God, who is timeless—no beginning and no end—is omniscient, meaning all-knowing. Consider this as applied to *chronos* time—the Greek word from which is derived *chronology*. It refers to time measured in its development marked by milestones and events. Obviously, God knows the chronology of time in our world (for He created it—day and night) involving the past, present, as well as the future—all of which He can view at the same time.

When God confronts David with the cause for his sin, "despising His Word," I believe God has in view another time in the future. A thousand years after David's reign, His greatest Promise arrives on the scene. A gospel writer describes the arrival of His Promise: "*In the beginning was the Word, and the Word was with God, and the Word was God. He was in the beginning with God...And the Word became flesh and dwelt among us, and we have seen His glory, glory as of the only Son from the Father, full of grace and truth*" (John 1:1–2, 14).

Regarding this context of scripture, the author is deliberate in using the Greek word *logos* to characterize the long-anticipated Messiah of Israel as the Word of God. The usage of *logos* in this passage carries the meaning of "person or personality." Therefore, this gospel account conveys the eternal, "one-of-a-kind," only begotten Son of God having now entered the world, being born in human form and the very self-expression of God. In other words, Jesus was sent into the world to communicate the very character and life of God and was self-described as the Bread of Life, promising those people who would come to trust in Him—"They would never hunger!" (John 6:36). Such people would always be satisfied.

111

This is the meaning of Jesus as the Living Word of God. Jesus, the Christ—the Anointed One—is the self-expression of God in the flesh because He is God and was always with God! In fact, this is further amplified in the book of Revelation regarding the Second Coming: *"And the name by which He is called is The Word of God"* *(Rev. 19:13).*

This explains why God's Word is so personal! This passage illustrates God's Word is inseparable from His character or Person. When God speaks, His Word is a reflection of His character. Scripture informs us, Jesus mirrored God's heart—His character and will. For Jesus taught His disciples this truth: "Whoever has seen Me, has seen the Father" (John 14:10). And He also said, "And He (the Father) who sent Me is with Me. He has not left Me alone, for I always do the things that are pleasing to Him" (John 8:29). The Father is inseparable from His Son, and the Son is inseparable from the Father, for they are One!

Furthermore, let's not overlook the last verse that describes "the Son as full of grace and truth." Grace, because Jesus is God's Promise and gift to humankind. Truth, because Jesus is the Living Word. This enhances our understanding of Jesus's reassuring response to His disciples on the night before He was to be crucified and their fearful apprehension of not knowing where He was going: "I am the way, and the truth, and the life. No one comes to the Father except through Me" (John 14:6).

This should crystallize our understanding of the importance of God's Word. To ignore, neglect, or distort is to devalue the veracity and vital worth of God's Word. This should explain why God took David's sin so personally: "You despised Me!" And the same applies to us, doesn't it?

Despised the Riches of God's Goodness!

This brings us to the third most important lesson God wanted David to learn and serves as a corollary to the second principle. In order to fully comprehend the impact of this third dynamic, we must consider the premise of two New Testament passages written to a church in Rome by the apostle Paul, one of which states, *"Or do you despise the riches of His goodness, forbearance, and longsuffering, not knowing that the goodness of God leads you to repentance?" (Rom. 2:4, NKJ)*.

The context for this scripture is the rhetorical argument Paul is making to the fellowship of believers in Rome at the time, in which it is his contention, that the "richness of God's goodness"—the Cross of Christ—is that which leads men to repentance! The character attributes of God, such as His mercy, kindness, and goodness are enveloped and expressed in the grace of God—the genesis for radical reorientation toward God—repentance.

Again, we see the usage of the word *despise* in which Paul is applying it specifically to the grace of God, exhorting believers *not* to devalue or disregard the "goodness" of God's character. We must be mindful of this truth. For Paul, the Cross of Christ was the greatest expression of God's grace to anyone who would receive such a "gift" from God: *"For it is the power of God to salvation for everyone who believes" (Rom. 1:16)*.

Ultimately, Paul passionately contends, the richness of God's goodness has the power to transform the human heart! Therefore, Paul's prominent message is *not* to devalue God's gifts or blessings, for it is those very expressions of God's grace that begin to lead men to the Lord, generating the desire to know Him and to grow in their life for Him.

It was the same message from God to David. This explains why God started with a biographical sketch of what God had done for

David. God chose him to be king when he was but a shepherd boy. God protected and preserved David's life from the hatred of Saul. God gave David the family he desired. All these blessings, which found their origin in the gracious initiative of God, represent the richness of God's goodness. This is what David had despised when he despised God by his conduct. David had been reckless by his actions toward the goodness God had shown him, and subsequently, the sad effect was David demonstrating little regard for God's grace that had been working in his life.

But it all still begs the greater question in each of our minds: Why, David, did you act in this manner? You and I may qualify the question further: "Why did you commit such acts, when you had so much and knew God had blessed you with the life He had given you? Did you feel entitled, David, because of your position and had consequently become seduced by power? Did you have a distorted sense of yourself that somehow you had a license to do what you did because you were God's favorite? Or perhaps you presumed on God's grace by thinking, *One time won't hurt*, for God will understand and forgive, right? Or did you become blinded with pride and deceived into thinking it was your efforts that made you successful? Well, what was it exactly, David?

God Wasn't Good Enough!

Perhaps, some or all those issues factored in David's failure. However, I also believe we are given the sobering answer to this defining question in the text. After God delineates all He has done for David—as if all those blessings were not enough—God then emphasizes an important point in verse 8: *"And if this were too little, I would add to you as much more" (2 Sam. 12:8)*. This statement more than implies that God was saying to David, "And if all my blessings were not enough, I would have given you more!"

Heartbreakingly was this stark reality God conveyed to David: *"I was not enough for you!"* Is it any wonder David was crushed to the core when he heard those words from the Lord: *"You have despised Me!"* This was the ultimate message God was willing to teach David. In my view, it was an "unintended consequence" of David's transgressions. It did not excuse it; however, God instead, in His patience and love for David, wanted him to learn this eternal lesson. To know God in all who He is—His goodness, kindness, mercy, and His unfailing and perfect love—God is incomparable and therefore *good enough*!

This truth is too important to glide over it with an attitude this only applies to the context of David's life. For Scripture reminds us, *"For whatever was written in former days was written for our instruction that through endurance and through the encouragement of the Scriptures we might have hope (Rom. 15:4)."* God wants us to learn from David's life.

A moment I will never forget occurred several years ago. Simultaneously, several prominent Christian leaders were experiencing scandals or controversies in their personal lives, and the incidents received broad and extensive media coverage. It had the effect of "one shoe dropping," then another, and another. Several national ministries were being investigated for extravagant lifestyles and possible financial improprieties by congress. Then there was another who decided "There is no hell!"

All this came to my attention during a span of two weeks. One day, while running some errands, I had been thinking about these shortcomings and the adverse impact on the Body of Christ. As I returned home and drove into the garage, I felt an impulse from the Holy Spirit and became overcome with deep sorrow and grief. As I became broken and while praying, I heard myself say to the Lord, "Jesus, what's wrong with You, that somehow we find, You are just not enough!" Please understand, it was not a condemning or self-righteous posture toward any of these ministers but a grief-bearing stance that humbled me with such truth for days: "Jesus, what is it about You that seems to say, 'You're not good enough!'"

Scandals among Christian leadership have left their tracks throughout Church history. This is not news (despite the media's ventures)! But perhaps a new view for the Church is this gut-wrenching, heart-crushing reality in which we have said unintentionally—not necessarily through adultery or committing murder—but in other ways, "Knowing God is not good enough, rich enough, or complete enough, I need someone or something else to add to the mix!" This too can devalue the importance of God's word in our lives.

This was the cause of David's derailment in which for a moment he took his eyes off the "prize" of knowing God and cultivating an intimate relationship with the Lord. Today, it is the major contributing factor for many believers being disconnected in their relationship to God. Since this is a more comprehensive issue, we will attend to this in more detail in offering a complete remedy in the last chapter of this book. However, we can consider part of the answer that will begin to facilitate a healing process to one who is disconnected in their relationship to the Lord.

George Barna, the contemporary research monitor for faith and spirituality in our culture, conducted a survey in 2001 regarding the belief of absolute moral truth in American culture. George Barna found "only 33 percent of Americans accept the idea of absolute moral truth. His poll indicated that born-again Christians do better, but still only 49 percent of them accept that moral truth is absolute."

That is an ominous and startling fact, keeping in mind the survey is from 2001. Only "49 percent of born-again Christians" believe in absolute moral truth. Where is the other 51 percent? And what does that say regarding the value of God's Word in the Church at large today? Clearly, the "49 percent" has suffered some erosion as indicated by the Church seemingly convulsing in confusion and finding itself marginalized with the ability to address current cultural issues because of a compromised stance regarding the value of God's Word.

If ever there has been a time when the Church needs to rely on her compass, it is today. Every believer must decide regarding the eternal question posed by the enemy of our souls since the Garden of Eden, "Has God said?" Thus, when it comes to God's Word, this is the premise from which to navigate the moral quagmire of life: *"All Scripture is breathed out by God and profitable for teaching, for reproof, for correction, and for training in righteousness, that the man of God may be complete, equipped for every good work" (2 Tim. 3:16–17).* In essence, this Scripture is stating, though men wrote it, God authored His Word by the Holy Spirit! God's word is as relevant today, as it was for David, but do we believe that?

Each of us must make the determination of how we view and value God's Word. There is every indication David learned what God was teaching him because that was the passion of his heart, evidenced by his prayer at one point during his journey: *"Make me to know your ways, O Lord; teach me your paths. Lead me in your truth and teach me, for you are the God of my salvation; for you I wait all the day long" (Ps. 25:4–5).*

Indeed, David learned the importance of God's Word, and he determined God's Word was truth! And, yes, painfully he learned, for God had warned him regarding the future consequence for his sin: "The sword will not depart from your house." The first four children (not including Bathsheba's first born) of David's family died premature deaths, three of them violently by the sword (2 Sam. 3:2–5). And, as costly a lesson this was for David to experience—as the record indicates that he loved his family much—the greater pain he endured was discovering the truth about himself, of which he had despised God by somehow believing in a rare, weak moment the lie that "God was not good enough to trust!"

Incidentally, I don't think it is mere coincidence God used the "sword" as the means of disciplining and teaching David the value of His Word and the adverse repercussions, if one chooses to ignore or compromise God's Word for whatever the reason. In the New Testament, God's Word is metaphorically referred as a "sword" for an effective "spiritual weapon" in the engagement of spiritual warfare for the believer! (Eph. 6).

The outcome of Saul and David was very different. This can be largely attributed to David's response to God's correction. David had the humility, therefore, the desire to be a student of the Lord and to learn from Him, as well as from his mistakes. This is a quality in having a heart after God's heart. David remained eager to learn. A humble spirit causes one to believe there is always something valuable to learn from the Lord.

More than anything, David wanted to know the Lord and to grow and honor Him with his life. David never wavered from such a posture before the Lord. No matter how painful the lesson, he did not give up. He soon realized there was nothing comparable to God as he declared as much, in one of his psalms: *"Because your love is better than life, my lips will glorify you. I will praise you as long as I live, and in your name I will lift up my hands. My soul will be satisfied as with the richest of foods"* (Ps. 63:3–5, NIV).

It is clear, David eventually learned that God was definitely more than enough, for David had become "satisfied" with God as he experienced Him daily and grew in his personal walk with the Lord. David had unintentionally discovered the darkened depths of what it meant to "despise the Lord"—a black abyss of spiritual deadness in his soul he would never want again to visit in his life! For through such an ordeal of personal failure, David learned a preeminent eternal truth: God is inseparable from His Word and should be trusted accordingly!

Therefore, let us not forget this important truth about David's life. There is probably no one man in all the Old Testament who learned more about the attributes of God's character than David, largely due to his thirst to know God. This is evident based particularly on what God does during the last ten years of David's reign and is shared in our next chapter in which David again rediscovers in a most new and powerful way the richness of God's goodness and how truly God's love is incomparable to anything in this life!

CHAPTER 7

David: "I Want to Build God a House!"

So I have looked upon You in the sanctuary, beholding
Your power and glory. Because Your steadfast love is better
than life, my lips will praise You. So I will bless You as
long as I live; in Your name I will lift up my hands.
—Psalm 63:2–4

From my point of view, we now enter one of the most personal and profound scenes in the Bible. But before we begin, we must consider this reminder that was shared in the introduction of this book. The historical background to a scriptural passage is a key factor involving a solid and consistent interpretation of Scripture (exegesis). In other words, the historical context for an event that occurred at a particular time, enlightens, as well as enhances, the meaningful interpretation of a biblical account. It certainly does that as we visit this momentous event in the life of David.

The Event Chronology!

Now it is important to set-up the context for this exchange between God and David. For this event carries the impetus of this book and constitutes the ultimate objective of God's own heart regarding His Church. It is that important, due to its rich historical significance, and is found in the second book of Samuel, chapter 7. Since the incident is recorded early in this book, it would suggest this encounter with God occurred early in David's rule. However, several historical facts and scriptural accounts corroborate this event occurring late in David's reign.

The first fact directly involves King Hiram and the ancient city of Tyre. Records of antiquity indicate he did not come to power until 980 BC.[1] Scripture indicates King Hiram gave David the rich resources, particularly the cedar from north of Israel, in nearby Lebanon to help build and complete David's palace: "Hiram sent messengers, cedar trees, carpenters, and masons to help build David's palace" (2 Sam. 5:11). David would not have had access to the cedar until king Hiram began to rule and the alliance with David was forged. This alliance occurs sometime during the last ten years of David's reign, since history records his death in 971 BC.[2]

Secondly, the building projects David undertook and described in Scripture (1 Chron. 15) would not have happened during the early years of his reign because he was fully engaged in the wars with the "surrounding nations," such as the Philistines and the Ammonites. These conflicts would have inevitably occupied most of David's time, energy, resources, and required his complete attention and focus.

A third reason is David's respite from war. The battlefield consumed most of David's rule. This would be an ideal time for capital improvements. It would have been an excellent opportunity for a king to conduct renovations, especially completing the building project of his own living quarters, as described in the opening sentence in chapter 7: "Now when the king lived in his house and the Lord had given him rest from all his surrounding enemies" (2 Sam. 7:1).

The fourth factor deals with the Ark of the Covenant. The Ark seemingly was not moved to Jerusalem until late in David's reign.[3] Scripture reveals such: "David built houses for himself in the city of David. And he prepared a place for the ark of God and pitched a tent for it" (1 Chron. 15:1)."

Finally, this event ensued well after the "Bathsheba incident," which involved at least a distance of ten years. This profound exchange between God and David not only confirmed God had indeed forgiven David, but it is a powerful revelation regarding the depth of God's grace toward David.

It is from such a chronological and historical context God desires to speak to you and me today. In fact, David himself actually makes such a declaration in his response to the Lord's overture toward him in this scene: "You have spoken also of your servant's house for a great while to come, and this is instruction for mankind, O Lord God!" (2 Sam. 7:19) Therefore, through this event and its timing, God desires for us to see the depth of His love and mercy that flows from such grace!

The Ark and the Tent!

We must now consider some background regarding the Ark of the Covenant and the "Tent" referred to in this scene. The Ark of the Covenant had very special meaning and significance for Israel. The Ark signified the Covenant (Mosaic) God had made with the people of Israel and represented "the place" where the Lord would manifest His Presence, as described in the book of Exodus, in which God gave directions to Moses regarding the construction and purpose of the

Ark of the Covenant: *"And you shall put the mercy seat on the top of the ark, and in the ark you shall put the testimony (two stone tablets of Ten Commandments) that I shall give you. There I will meet with you, and from above the mercy seat...I will speak with you about all that I will give you in commandment for the people of Israel"* (*Exod. 25:21–22*).

The "mercy seat" was the structure on the top part of the ark and was a small, more limited "picture" of God's throne in heaven. So the Ark of the Covenant symbolized God's enthronement in heaven and was determined by God to be the place He would manifest His Presence to meet and converse with Moses.

Much of God's purpose in the construction of the Ark was to offer a window into His nature and character. For example, the mercy seat demonstrated that He preferred mercy as a God of love. The Ark of the Covenant signified God's Presence was with the nation but also was a shadow or preview of "better things to come" with regard to the New Covenant (Heb. 9:11). It was also a limited snapshot of the metanarrative regarding the eternal plan of redemption that God had prepared "before the foundation of the world" (Eph. 1:4–5).

The tent to which David referred is a central part of the intimate conversation between God and David. It was set-up adjacent to his palace and was known as the Tent of Meeting or the Tabernacle. However, it was not a mere tent. Based on God's instructions to Moses, it was a rather comprehensive structure with the following dimensions: 45 feet long, 15 feet wide, and 15 feet in height (Exod. 26). It was a wooden skeletal structure covered by four layers of cloth and skin and overlaid with gold with no solid roof or front wall. The Tabernacle interior comprised "two rooms" separated by a very large veil. The "innermost place" known as the Most Holy Place was 15 feet in length and was the location of the Ark of the Covenant. Once a year, only the High Priest could enter the Most Holy Place on the Day of Atonement. The outer room was known as the "Holy Place" and was 30 feet in length. This Tent was no small structure.

David Makes a Request!

It very well could have been springtime, which would be a good time for renovations and building projects. It is also a rare time of peace for David as the opening verse of chapter 7 indicates. David's palace has been recently completed. David has settled in and is enjoying the comforts of his new living quarters, when he looked out his window and says to the prophet, Nathan, *"See now, I dwell in a house of cedar, but the ark of God dwells in a tent. And Nathan said to the king, 'Go do all that is in your heart, for the Lord is with you.'"*

Nathan immediately knew what David meant. David was expressing his desire to build God a house, and David was seeking the approval of God's prophet in order to expedite the venture. Such spontaneous approval by Nathan would have been understandable since the prophet knew how successful David had been throughout his rule.

David had subdued all the nations of Philistia, Moab, Zobah, Damascus, Ammon, Amalek and Edom, which surrounded the small nation of Israel.[4] But Nathan also knew the sole reason David had been so effective. Nathan had known, throughout the thirty years of his reign, David honored the Lord, and as a result the prophet knew God had blessed David's military leadership. David had not known defeat on the battlefield, for the Lord was with him. Therefore, David's desire to honor the Lord by building a Temple, a building worthy of the Lord, would be a natural fit for David to do, according to Nathan's thinking.

However, the only problem with Nathan's response was that it was presumptuous. Nathan hadn't checked in with the Lord on the matter, and in that regard, neither had David. But David probably felt relieved and reassured that he had the prophet of God's blessing on his new building project for the Lord. For this had not been a fleeting thought or a moment of inspiration for David, but rather something he had been deliberating and contemplating for some time now. And now David had the prophet's blessing as Nathan bid the king a good night: "Go, do all that is in your heart, for the Lord is with you!" (v. 3).

A Temple Is Top Priority!

At the time, David was the most powerful ruler in the entire region. He naturally would want the privilege or honor of building "a house" that was worthy of the Lord. For David, not only desired Jerusalem to be the central governing power of the nation, but also the spiritual center for the life of Israel. This is indicated by the extreme measures David undertook in bringing the Ark of the Covenant to Jerusalem.

Now we need to understand in our thinking, building a temple for the Lord was not a secondary thought but rather a "big idea"—a top priority for David. By the way, prophets just didn't "hang out" arbitrarily in the royal court. Unless they had a specific message from God to deliver to the king, it was by invitation-only one could enter the presence of the king. This is another indication David had been considering this building project for some time and, in effect, solicited Nathan to the palace to discuss the matter with him.

But let's consider what extraordinary measures he took in his first, yet failed, attempt to merely bring the Ark to Jerusalem, because in this venture we can learn how important to David the prospect of building a temple for the Lord was for him:

> *David consulted with the commanders of thousands and of hundreds, with every leader. And David said to all the assembly of Israel, "If it seems good to you and from the Lord our God, let us*

send abroad to our brothers who remain in all the lands of Israel, as well as to the priests and Levites in the cities that have pasturelands, that they may be gathered to us. Then let us bring again the ark of God to us, for we did not seek it in the days of Saul." All the assembly agreed to do so, for the thing was right in the eyes of all the people. (1 Chron. 13:1–4)

Obviously, David went to great lengths in bringing the Ark to Jerusalem by appealing to the nation for its approved transfer. This was a big deal for Israel because during Saul's reign, as this scriptural passage underlines, the priority of God's Presence and subsequent worship was not attended to by the nation due to the leadership. This of course amplifies the distinction between Saul and David's leadership. The appropriate worship and such attendance to the Lord was not a priority for Saul.

However, the worship of the Lord was preeminent in David's life, which made "building a house" for the Lord a top priority for David. This is reflected in David's meticulous efforts to confer with the priests and Levites relative to the spiritual implications of the Ark's removal to Jerusalem, as well as wanting their consent. Many of them lived in various cities throughout Israel. Furthermore, David also not only consulted with the leadership of his army regarding their affirmation of the Ark's transfer, but when it came time to move the Ark, he gathered thirty thousand soldiers to escort it on the journey to Jerusalem (2 Sam. 6:1:1).

All of this would have required a substantial investment of time, organization, and skillful planning on David's part. With so much responsibility, perhaps it is reasonable to understand, though difficult to believe, how neglecting the sacred protocol in moving the Ark on the shoulders of the Levite priesthood could have possibly occurred. Nevertheless, it did, resulting in a delay of three months in bringing the Ark to Jerusalem (2 Sam. 6:11).

Also, one must consider the substantial area required to provide for the Tabernacle, which David had to prepare in advance. The courtyard that was the enclosed area for the Tabernacle was to be 75 feet in width by 150 feet in length (Exod. 27:18). This is at least half the size of a football field. So with all the renovations taking place and the need to cordon off an area large enough to accommodate the Ark of the Covenant, David wanted the preparations to be just right in receiving the Ark into the new capital city of Israel. But this was only a temporary arrangement in David's thoughts and plans.

David's Interest for God's Well-Being!

When David invites Nathan to his palace and presents his idea of building a house for the Lord, David is expressing his interest regarding the "well-being" of God! David is not merely interested in God's living conditions. He is interested in God's reputation. David primarily desires to provide God a place that will give Him the honor he believes God deserves! In essence, it is the deepest expression of David's motivation toward the Lord. David wants the Lord to receive all the glory for that which God has accomplished for him throughout his life as well as for the nation of Israel!

To be interested in the well-being of God is to be concerned for what benefits God, such as His reputation and personal knowledge of Him. This had become the heart of David. At this time, David is at least sixty years of age. David had grown in his knowledge and love for God, in which he had moved from self-interests, to the interests of God. This is a vital attribute in cultivating a heart for God, according to Dr. Dallas Willard:

To love God with all your heart is to have your will set on what is best for Him above every-thing else. Love is the disposition to bring good to the object that is loved, and God has so dis-posed Himself toward His creation—and His human creation, in particular—that we are able to participate in His life by setting our will toward what is good for Him.[5]

This is what it means to be interested in the well-being of God. David is concerned with what is good for God! More than anything in his life, David desires for God to be glorified. David wants God not only to be glorified throughout Israel, but beyond the borders of Israel and throughout the world. David wants God's name to be magnified above and beyond any other so-called "deity" on the face of the earth. David especially wants the surrounding nations who have fought Israel over the past thirty years of David's reign, to know the reality of the One and only true God, and the One who has made Israel so powerful and successful. This is the very heartbeat of David, to glorify God, and is the very essence of David's heart, which is to set his will toward what benefits God!

David's greatest desire in building God "a house" is for God to receive the credit for all that the Lord has accomplished for David and Israel. He wants the people not to forget and to remember the Lord in their practical activities by creating a central place of worship in which they will be reminded of the importance of worshiping and expressing their gratitude to the Lord for all that He has done for the nation in their daily lives. And now, by what means does David pro-pose such a goal should be accomplished? By building God a house, a house that is worthy of the Lord! But it cannot be just any kind of house. It must be an extraordinary House, a House of worship!

David, the Worshiper!

David knew something about worship, and such a reality was formed by his relationship with the Spirit of God. More than likely, he learned to play his lyre and sing his songs to the Lord as a young teenager during the many secluded hours while shepherding for his father in the fields of Bethlehem. Many of the psalms (poems, songs) he wrote originated from the depths of his heart as David learned to express his love, adoration, and thanksgiving to the Lord. Yes, there were those moments too of despair, sorrow, remorse, and desperation when David would experience trials that would cause him to cry out to the Lord. But regardless of his circumstances, one thing is certain about David—he desired to acknowledge the preeminent importance, purpose, and priceless role the Lord had in his life. Consider David's words as he speaks of how intimate the Lord knew him:

> *O Lord, you have searched me and known me! You know when I sit down and when I rise up; you discern my thoughts from afar. You search out my path and my lying down and are acquainted with all my ways...Where shall I go from your Spirit? Or where shall I flee from your presence? ...For you, formed my inward parts; you knitted me together in my mother's womb. I praise you, for I am fearfully and wonderfully made. Wonderful are your works; my soul knows it very well. My frame was not hidden from you, when I was being made in secret, intricately woven in the depths of the earth. Your eyes saw my unformed substance; in your book were written, every one of them, the days that were formed for me, when as yet there was none of them. (Ps. 139:1–3, 7, 13–16)*

Do you see the personal, interactive intimacy between David and the Lord he worshiped? The worship of God is about intimacy. Throughout this psalm, David speaks in the first person regarding his relationship to the Lord, and the Lord in relationship to him: "You have searched me and known me!" Indeed, what David is describing regarding his relationship to the Lord is very personal, for he acknowledges God "formed him in the womb" and the Lord also "saw him," before David was even formed (born) as well as the number of "days" he would live in this world!

Without question, these are intricate details regarding the source, conception, and formation of David's life, and, most importantly, how David captured the Lord's attentiveness even before he existed! Before David was, God had already thought about him! How amazing is that? How personal, how intimate are God's thoughts of David? All of which brings us to an important question: how did David know such details? The simple answer is the Lord revealed it to David through His Holy Spirit!

We must remember when Samuel anointed David with oil, the Holy Spirit "rushed" upon him. David knew what it personally meant to experience God's Presence daily in his life. God never abandoned David, for God's Presence was always with him. This explains how God's Presence was inescapable for David as he described such a reality in this psalm: "Where shall I go from your Spirit? Or where shall I flee from your Presence?" (139:7–8).

David's thoughts seem to be continually upon God. When David awakens from a night of rest, right away he realizes God's Presence is still with him. How many of us can relate to that? If we're honest, most of us are merely trying to "get our bearings" or attempting to navigate our first cup of coffee in the morning! Not David! David's thoughts immediately are focused on the Lord as he began a new day. David's first morning moments are filled with thoughts of the Lord and worship! This truth is reflected in his word, "How precious to me are your thoughts, O God! How vast is the sum of them! If I would count them, they are more than the sand. I awake, and I am still with you" (Ps. 139:17–18). Wow! What a window into the life of the king of Israel. This is the heart of a worshiper of God!

One could probably say that worship defined David's life. We must not forget, David was a very important and busy man. He was a king and his schedule was much occupied with managing the affairs of the most powerful nation in the region. David's military and domestic responsibilities for Israel were very demanding. David had reached an unparalleled pinnacle of success, and with it some measure of self-importance, so it could be understandable for David to become preoccupied with his affairs or even presumptuous by taking the Lord's blessings for granted. Saul did. Other kings in Israel's history did. But not David.

We come to discover one of the most prominent and pronounced qualities of David's character that compelled God's inscription of David. Above everything in life—David's position as king, his military genius, or his administrative acumen—nothing was comparable to his insurmountable love, expressed in worship, to the Lord. David loved to worship the Lord! It was almost like he could not worship the Lord enough! Look at such words David wrote in another psalm: *So I have looked upon you in the sanctuary, beholding your power and glory. Because Your steadfast love is better than life, my lips will praise you. So I will bless you as long as I live; in your name I will lift up my hands"* (Ps. 63:2–4).

David had discovered, through personal experience, encountering God's love was better than anything this life could offer. For him, there was no more important priority than his worship of God. A. W. Tozer articulates a poignant description regarding this pervasive passion of David: "David's life was a torrent of spiritual desire, and his psalms ring with the cry of the seeker and glad shout of the finder."[6]

This explains how worship defined David's life and was the primary motivation in him wanting to "build God a house." David was a true worshiper of God. But such a description of David does not merely mean worship was his top priority. We know it was a priority from the seventy-five psalms he recorded. But greater yet is the dynamic truth: David knew *how* to worship!

Before we go further, we need to consider an appropriate understanding and definition of the term *worship*. Across the spectrum of the Church-at-large, we would find many diverse descriptions of what comprises worship. Some would say worship is a form of praying. Or worship involves certain music instruments, as well as lifting our voices to God. Some would offer worship is an outward physical expression of clapping or raised hands. Or dancing before the Lord with celebratory jubilation as David did when he successfully brought the Ark to its new home in Jerusalem (2 Sam. 6:14). Others would say worship is the reading and studying of God's word or writing about God. All of these expressions, indeed, describe to some extent the dynamic of worship; but they do not define it!

Worship Defined

If we are going to understand what it means to have a heart after God, we must understand the definitive meaning and purpose of worship. The actual word *worship* comes from an "old English" word *weorthscipe*.[7] It had the connotation to "ascribe worth." A fundamental understanding for worship would mean to ascribe or to assert a worth or value of the object or the Person being worshiped. Therefore, I submit to you my personal definition of worship: *worship is an intimate language of love!*

Now think about it in these terms as we live out this meaning, though mindlessly at times, in the practical realities of daily life. In pop culture, people will have expressions of adoring a celebrity or fashion style or a remarkable achievement or talent. Whoever that person may be (hoping it's not true), it goes without saying that "celebrity" has captured the heart of the person. The individual is celebrated as distinct or valued above the norm in today's culture! But let's consider what true worship is and its applied meaning to the Only One who is worthy of worship! And there is no better place to start than with Jesus in His exchange with the Samaritan woman at the water well. The Samaritans were of Jewish heritage who believed they garnered the "right way to worship" because they worshiped in the "right place."[8] Jesus then corrects her thinking by emphasizing what worship is really all about by giving her a definition: *"But the hour is coming, and is now here, when the true worshipers will worship the Father in spirit and truth, for the Father is seeking such people to worship Him. God is Spirit, and those who worship Him must worship in spirit and truth"* (John 4:23–24).

Jesus gave us definitive criteria that describes the essence of worship. Jesus addresses four major aspects regarding the dynamics of worship in His conversation with the Samaritan woman by defining true worship, how it should be expressed, as well as the purpose. Jesus establishes two foundational principles that define true worship: *true worship is expressed in "spirit and truth."* Another way of saying the same thing is *true worship is expressed in authenticity and accuracy!*

The Authentic Heart!

When we consider authenticity, this quality applies to the human spirit or heart. Scripture informs us, it is the heart of man that captures God's interest the most, as God emphasized this reality to Samuel during the selection process for David: *"For the Lord sees*

133

not as man sees: man looks on the outward appearance, but the Lord looks on the heart" (1 Sam. 16:7).

Unfortunately, so much of our worship can be wooden and rigid because our heart is absent. Jesus addressed this spiritual malady when speaking to the religious leaders of His day, as He quoted the prophet Isaiah, *"This people honors me with their lips, but their heart is far from Me; in vain do they worship Me, teaching as doctrines the commandments of men" (Matt. 15:8–9).* We tend to be perfunctory or performance-oriented in our worship, largely because the focal point is ourselves and what is happening around us, and therefore having our hearts disconnected from Whom we worship! Authentic worship treasures and values God for who He is which is based on His character!

But why is the heart so important to God when it comes to worship? God's Word states, "Keep your heart with all vigilance, for from it flow the springs of life" (Prov. 4:23). Dallas Willard qualifies this truth: "The human heart, the will, or spirit is the executive center of a human life. The heart is where decisions and choices are made for the whole person. That is its function."[9]

This is one reason worship has everything to do with authenticity, involving the heart, because it has everything to do with our will! There may be times when we do not feel like offering our worship because of our life circumstances, but we must determine we *will* become what He desires us to be, true worshipers of Father-God because He alone is worth it!

Jesus also underscored the importance of the heart of man throughout His Sermon on the Mount and in particular: "For where your treasure is, there your heart will be also" (Matt. 6:21). Jesus was presenting that the type of worship that Father-God desires is honest, real, and genuine worship that comes from the heart. What is it we treasure (or worship) most in life? We must never forget this important truth: *the activities and priorities of our lives correspond with what is most important to us!*

Accurate Worship!

But it is important to understand worship is not expressed in a vacuum. Worship—that is, true worship—cannot be abstract; otherwise it will not have meaning but rather a superstitious, mystical, fog-like response. Therefore, true worship is based on knowledge. Jesus underscores this truth to the Samaritan woman, which can be easily overlooked: "You worship what you do not know; we worship what we know for salvation is from the Jews" (v. 22).

Jesus was qualifying one cannot truly worship someone they do not know. Jesus was enunciating the Father desires people to "know" Whom they worship and why they worship Him. When people have encountered the experiential reality of God in a direct and personal way, it naturally leads to worship. Worship of God is to be concrete and substantial. We cannot truly worship someone we don't actually know or someone whom we have not experienced. And you cannot acquire a true knowledge of a person without taking time to spend with them, gaining insights into their character and discovering who and what they are like. This is what David learned. When you begin to know someone, you then start to realize their true nature. We should then understand authenticity is inseparable from accuracy, since authenticity treasures God's character and His character is truth!

This explains the meaning of Jesus's statement, "The Father is seeking such people to worship Him." God's greatest desire is for people to know Him. God is love, and love desires to be known. This truth is particularly captured in the opening words of Jesus's longest recorded prayer: *"And this is eternal life, that they may know you the only true God, and Jesus Christ who you have sent" (John 17:3)*. Jesus was articulating to the Samaritan woman the other foundational principle of worship, which is truth, and how it must be constructed on a personal, intimate knowledge of God!

We Are Wired for Worship!

With regard to the type of people God desires for worship, Jesus's statement could be misconstrued that God somehow "needs" our worship. He does not. But we do. God is Spirit, and He is self-sufficient. He is perfectly complete within Himself. The apostle Paul, while preaching, reminded his audience of this dynamic reality regarding God's nature: "Nor is He served by human hands, as though He needed anything, since He himself gives to all mankind life and breath and everything" (Acts 17:25).

Therefore, we need to understand the Lord is quite secure with Himself, for He knows when given the opportunity to introduce Himself, He is quite impressive to any human being—just ask Moses (Exod. 33:18–23). He does not need anyone to tell Him how impressive He really is, as if He is an egocentric being! He is not. For if that was His nature, there would never have been a Cross. However, through authentic and accurate worship, it is we who are reminded of Who He is and what He is like based on substantive and concrete attributes of His character!

So now we must ask, why is God seeking a particular type of people to worship Him? Simply because we do need to worship! This is the third dynamic in Jesus's defining purpose of worship. *We are built for worship.* We should understand, since we are made in His image, we are spiritual beings living in physical bodies and *we are wired for God.* This is why worship is a matter of the heart. God is Spirit, and God is love. The only way we can connect with God is through our spirit, as God's Word tells us: "God is love, and whoever abides in love abides in God, and God abides in Him" (1 John 4:16).

Yes, worship is about God, Who He is and what He is like; but worship is also God providing a pathway to know Him more intimately. Jesus was revealing to the woman that true worship will encounter Father-God and bring transformative benefits. Pastor Jack Hayford further delineates this powerful descriptive purpose of worship:

> With this statement—God is Love—God's Word has suddenly turned the tables on us. It is as though He is balancing the tables on us. It is as though He is balancing something for us, as though He is saying: "You may come to worship Me. I welcome your appropriately bringing glory to Me because it is right. But it is also good for your own sake that you worship Me, not because I need your worship, but because through it, you will be progressively liberated from yourself (which is life's worst bondage). By worshiping Me, you are also being brought to a place of intimate relationship—one of knowing, understanding and walking with Me."[10]

God is love, and He created us to be loved by Him and to know His love and to love Him. God wants to be wanted. He will not go where He is not wanted. So God waits to be wanted. He waits for His invitation from us, which is our worship! Worship is our personal acknowledgment: "We want You, we need You, we welcome You!"

God desires us to want Him, for He knows when we experience His Presence, it will be life-changing for us. It was for David as he declared, "Oh, taste and see that the Lord is good! Blessed is the man who takes refuge in Him!" (Ps. 34:8). To *taste* the Lord means to experience Him. God wants the same for you and me. He wants us to see (discover), like David, the Lord is good! Listen to the words that parallel David's experience and also from one who was known to practice worship in his daily life, A. W. Tozer:

> For it is not mere words that nourish the soul, but God Himself, and unless and until the hearers find God in personal experience they are not the better for having heard the truth. The Bible is not an end in itself, but a means to bring men to an intimate and satisfying knowledge of God, that they may enter into Him, that they may delight in His Presence, may taste and know the inner sweetness of the very God Himself in the core and center of their hearts.[11]

The Holy Spirit Helps Us

This, of course, brings us to the fourth most important dynamic that actualizes true worship with authenticity and accuracy. We need God's Spirit in us, He who is the bond of love between our Father and us. *It is essential that we have this "bond of love" connecting us to the Father and leading us to worship Him in "spirit and truth."* The simple reality is we cannot experience true worship without the Holy Spirit leading and enabling us in our worship of Father-God. We cannot truly worship alone. I don't mean we cannot be by ourselves when we worship. That would be a contradiction of God's word. We need the Holy Spirit to do what He enjoys doing—glorifying Jesus! This is what Jesus taught in preparing His disciples for His departure from them, just before He went to the Cross the next day: "*When the Spirit of truth comes, He will guide you into all the truth...He will glorify Me, for He will take what is Mine and declare it to you" (John 16:13–14).*

The Holy Spirit delights in pointing people to Jesus because He knows Jesus is the genesis for all worship. Worship starts with the Son of God, which begins for you and me at the Cross. The reason for this is God has appointed Jesus to be the Mediator of the New Covenant because He reconciles us to the Father (Heb. 9:15). This is God's ultimate and greatest gift to us, for it is through Jesus, the shedding of His precious blood, we are reconciled into right relationship with God (2 Cor. 5:17–21), provided we choose to accept His gift!

We should always remember all worship must be centered in Jesus Christ, for when our full attention is on Jesus, we also see God (John 14:9). Therefore, we must depend upon the Holy Spirit to give us order to our worship, an authentic and accurate order of expressed love. The only way we can worship Father-God accurately is based on His character and authentically with our hearts is with and through the assistance of the Holy Spirit.

But we need to humble ourselves by acknowledging we need the Holy Spirit to help us do what only He can do for and with us. We are not passive in this expression of love but willing participants as we ask Him to help us assert the right, worthwhile value of God in our lives. This is what the Holy Spirit is committed to do and loves to do—to help us glorify Jesus by leading and teaching us how to treasure Father-God based on the right value He is certainly worth: incomparable pricelessness!

A Personal Moment!

As a pastor/teacher, I've never wanted to be one who taught about something I didn't know personally. The apostle Paul made such a commitment, and one I desire to emulate: "For I will not venture to speak of anything except what Christ has accomplished through me" (Rom. 15:18).

As I share with you a personal page from my own narrative, I begin with a very important passage of Scripture. One day when Jesus was worshiping in the Temple in Jerusalem, He stood and cried out, *"If anyone thirsts, let him come to Me and drink. Whoever believes in Me, as the Scripture has said, 'Out of his heart will flow rivers of living water'" (John 7:37–38).*

Always a poignant scene for me, as Jesus broke rabbinical protocol by His unique posture of standing in the Temple, instead of remaining seated, underscoring the message and the passion He expressed because He did not want people to miss His vital and pivotal announcement. Knowing Jesus was speaking about the Holy Spirit, I would simply pray, "One touch, one taste, one glimpse, oh, Lord!" For years I sought this promise of Jesus, the promise of His Holy Spirit.

Then one day, unexpectedly, and in a seminary classroom no less, it happened. It was during simple prayer as we began our day of study. Of course, it was a very clinical environment due to the academic setting. There was no external, emotive impulse that provoked or contributed to the moment. There was no music, preaching, or an invitation extended. It was just a moment of simple prayer. Students, most of them pastors, were leading out in their individual public prayers.

As the prayers ensued, suddenly and without anticipation, I began to sense God's familiar Presence. But this soon became different. Much different. His Presence intensified and manifested like nothing I had known before. From the top of my head to the soles of my feet, I felt encased in His Presence. Initially, I was overcome with fear because I was in awe. I knew it was Him. No one had to tell me. Fear would, of course, be a natural response since the supernatural—

God's Spirit—was intersecting my humanness. I was overwhelmed by His Presence because my entire body was immersed in Him. The Holy Spirit permeated all my being.

Though physically my eyes were closed the entire time, everything I could see was a "brilliant white." In my sobering awe of Him, I naturally raised my hands in worship with tears running down my face. This seemingly lasted at least seven to ten minutes. But my hands did not move. They remained lifted upward in worship. I never considered this posture until after the moment ended. But I know if His Presence had remained in such form, my hands would have stayed upwardly outstretched and without fatigue. It was a natural posture and inclination in that moment. Oh, what a moment! "Astonished reverence" as someone once described worship. Yet words defy human description. Even now, in my attempt to explain this encounter, I am overcome with emotion, as words seemingly fail to express the pronounced effect of His Presence. What remains is a vivid moment forever etched in my memory regarding the unfathomable depth of God's awe and goodness!

On occasion, when led to share this experience, there are two prominent distinctions I offer. The first is regarding the manifestation of His Holy Spirit. His Presence was a power that enveloped my entire being. His Spirit permeated my body, bathed in His Presence, outwardly and inwardly. Though I was conscious of my surroundings and had control of all my faculties, His power was beyond my control, overwhelming all my physical senses, emotions, as well as my thoughts—totally engulfed.

The second distinction is instructive personally. This encounter occurred based solely upon His grace! Probably due to my religious background, God wanted me to know I could not earn this gift. This was His gift, and a gift cannot be earned, it can only be received. But then I'm reminded, to receive, one must ask. God's word tells us as much: *"Ask, and it will be given to you; seek and you will find; knock, and it will be opened to you. For everyone who asks receives...How much more will your Father who is in heaven give good things to those who ask Him!" (Matt. 7:7–8, 11).*

Yes, for some time I had asked. Now I don't know why it happened—the when, where, and way of it. It doesn't matter. What is important is it did happen, just the way Jesus promised. It was, and is, all about His grace that flows from His unending stream of love. Indeed, true to His word, "Rivers of Living Water flowed out of my heart!"

This is what I meant earlier when I stated we cannot truly worship alone. As it is the same with our prayer lives, we need the Holy Spirit to lead and enable us in our worship of Jesus, and our Father, to get it right. The Holy Spirit enjoys leading us more deeply in our worship of Jesus, making our assertion of His worth and value much more authentically real and accurate.

However, this is not intended to imply one must have the same type of encounter I experienced. Not in the least. Or that somehow a singular experience indicates one has arrived and that is all you need. My contention is we should all experience His Holy Spirit in a very real and tangible way. For when one does, you don't need anyone to tell you because you know the distinction and it is transformative. Besides, this is God's intended purpose for our lives: to personally experience the reality of Him, just as David did, and therefore, this should give us perspective regarding the actions of Jesus declaring such a promise in the Temple!

Dr. Stephen Seamands provides additional clarity to this dynamic truth:

> What does it mean to be filled with the Holy Spirit? Although it is a spatial metaphor, being filled with the Spirit is not really about space, like filling up a cup with water. We will be mis-

led if we conceive of it that way. Essentially this metaphor describes a personal relationship with the Holy Spirit characterized by surrender and abandonment to the Spirit. For though the Holy Spirit is present in all believers, in some He is not preeminent; though He is resident in all, in some He is not president. That is why Paul exhorts believers who already have a relationship with the Holy Spirit (Eph. 1:13) to "be filled with the Holy Spirit" (Eph. 5:18).[12]

What Dr. Seamands explains here describes best my experience with the Holy Spirit of God. It also reminds me of another promise Jesus gave: "And he who loves Me will be loved by My Father, and I will love him and manifest Myself to him" (John 14:21). Oh, what grace, my friend, for this is Jesus's promise for everyone, that is, if you love and want to know Him!

Let's remember the Father knows what He brings to the table, so to speak. He knows that if we want Him like He wants us, we will not be disappointed with Him. In fact, we will enjoy Him like nothing else in life. Why? We were created to be loved by Him, to know His love, and to love Him. We are incomplete without Him. We were wired for God. So we cannot truly worship Him alone. This was the very pulse of Jesus's teaching to the Samaritan woman.

The Sweet Psalmist!

And this was the pulse of David's life as he learned to worship God in all aspects of his life. This was his entire motivation in desiring to build God a house that would be the worship center for the spiritual life of Israel. He wanted a "house" that would rightly "honor" God throughout the region so the nation would acknowledge their value of the Lord and always remain thankful for the many blessings He had given to them. This passion of worship in David's life marked him, so much so, when he died, he was lamented by the entire nation as "the sweet psalmist of Israel," a worshiper of God!

Now then what was God's response to David in his request to build the Lord a house? Would God allow the worshiper of Israel his passionate request? Let's find out.

CHAPTER 8

The Lord: "No, David, I Will Build You a House!"

But the Lord said to David my father, "Whereas it was in your heart to build a house for My name, you did well that it was in your heart!"
—1 Kings 8:18

Nathan returned home, and David retired for the evening. David probably did not get much sleep that night, perhaps too euphoric as he replayed the conversation with Nathan and particularly the prophet's parting blessing: "Go, do all that is in your heart, for the Lord is with you!"

Just as important it was to gain consensus of the nation's leadership to move the Ark to Jerusalem, it was even more important to have the prophet's blessing to build a Temple for God. The prophet's blessing was the same as receiving God's approval on a course of action. Needless to say, David was elated, for this idea of building a house for the Lord had resonated in his soul for years during his reign, and finally, it was now on the threshold of becoming a reality. For this idea was "big" as far as Israel's history was concerned. And David knew it was a pivotal moment to construct the plans for building it!

However, all of David's plans were about to change because the Lord showed up in a vision that same night and spoke to Nathan (v. 17):

> *Go and tell my servant David, Would you build Me a house to dwell in? I have not lived in a house since the day I brought up the people of Israel from Egypt to this day, but I have been moving about in a tent for My dwelling. In all places where I have moved with all the people of Israel, did I speak a word with any of the judges of Israel, whom I commanded to shepherd My people Israel, saying, Why have you not built Me a house of cedar? (2 Sam. 7:5–7)*

An Original Idea!

This is an interesting way in which the Lord began His response to David's request. The Lord starts with a brief history lesson of Israel and then presents a rhetorical question of how this idea originated because the Lord wants to be clear it did not come from Him! This is a significant factor, so we don't want to miss it. The Lord even goes to the extent of saying, He had not even inferred the idea, let alone expressed such an interest or made the request to anyone throughout Israel's history. We easily could presume the Lord was rather "irritated" with the suggestion because it appears the Lord is being sarcastic in the tenor of His words. But that is not the case.

There are two things the Lord is emphasizing. The first is no one throughout Israel's history had thought of this idea until now. The second point is that this is entirely David's idea, and David's alone. It did not come from God because He had not even spoken about the matter to anyone previously. The Lord qualifies this reality with a rhetorical question, "Why have you not built Me a house of cedar?" The Lord wants it to be absolutely clear this has not been a point of conversation in times past with anyone in Israel. It was not a concern or interest of the Lord's, for He was quite content with a tent!

Therefore, it is like the Lord intentionally wants everyone to know this idea of building a house for the Lord is totally David. It is just like David. It is David's original idea. Further yet, the Lord is not displeased with the notion. In fact, the Lord is affected by David's desire to bless Him with such a venture. We must remember David's primary motive is to glorify the Lord by building a marvelous "house" that would give God the honor He deserved for all He had done for Israel. Also, David wanted Israel's enemies and all the surrounding nations to know the One true God Whom Israel served. Now wouldn't God agree with David's desire that others would come to know Him through the building of this Temple?

It is this writer's view, the Lord was "affected" because David was thinking of Him in this regard! Mind you, no one else had until now, but David did! I'm sure there may be those who may disagree with such an assertion. However, this belief is based on two things. When David's son, Solomon, prays for the dedication of the Temple, which is recorded in 1 Kings 8:18, he declares these words to Israel: *"But the Lord said to David my father, 'Whereas it was in your heart to build a house for My name, you did well that it was in your heart.'"* Yes, it was a great idea that David had thought of it, because it was God's will that a Temple would be built for Him. It was the right idea, just the wrong man to do it!

The second aspect is based on the Lord's remaining response to David. In my view, it's the Lord's way of saying, "Thank you, David, for thinking of Me. Thank you, David, for wanting to give Me such an honor throughout all of Israel, as well as the entire world. Thank you, David, for desiring to glorify Me!" But I'm getting ahead of myself, so let's read more of the Lord's answer to David:

> *I took you from the pasture, from following the sheep, that you should be prince over My people Israel. And I have been with you wherever you went and have cut off all your enemies from before you. And I will make for you a great name, like the name of the great ones of the earth. And I will appoint a place for My people Israel and will plant them, so that they may dwell in their own place and be disturbed no more. And violent men shall afflict them no more, as formerly, from the time that I appointed judges over My people Israel. And I will give you rest from all your enemies.' Moreover, the Lord declares to you that the Lord will make you a house. (2 Sam. 7:8–11)*

The Unexpected Promise of Promises!

We have come this far in our journey with David for just this moment. David is in the twilight of his years, and yet he is going to receive a new insight and revelation of the heart of God. This scene reveals the depth of God's love and His grace for David as the Lord reminds David of His steadfast and unwavering commitment to him throughout his life. This principle is unveiled in the intimate words of God: "And I have been *with you* wherever you went..." The Lord wants David to remember, He has never abandoned him, no matter his given circumstances in his journey with the Lord. Whether he was a young shepherd boy killing a lion or a bear, a teenager facing a formidable giant warrior, or a fugitive fleeing for his life in a desolate, unending desert—the Lord never left his side. The Lord was always there for him, even though there may have been times David felt abandoned and alone. We should find comfort in this important reality and remember this truth in our journey with God.

The Lord does this primarily to remind David there has not been a promise God has made to him He has not kept. For the Lord has consistently shown David through the years, He is not like man, in which He withdraws His commitment or breaks His promises. And, of course, David discovered this from personal experience that caused him to create and write songs of gratitude and worship, exalting God for His steadfast love, as he wrote on one occasion: "Your steadfast love, O Lord, extends to the heavens, Your faithfulness to the clouds" (Ps. 36:5). So the Lord was preparing David for His answer because God's response would be in future tense. It would be in the form of a promise, a promise that would be fulfilled long after David had died. For the Lord is going to *give* David an unfathomable blessing. It will be a "Promise of all promises!" But it is not the answer David expected!

The Lord provides David, initially, the answer to his idea of building Him a house by stating what He will do for David in verse 9: *"And I will make for you a great name, like the name of the great ones of the earth."* We would understand this to mean in our contemporary language, "God is going to make you famous!"

But David would view this in terms of what was important to monarchies during ancient times—a legacy. Every king wanted to be remembered, which accounts for some of the great monuments built in ancient times by the Pharaohs of Egypt or the Caesars of Rome. Everyone wants their life to have meaning after they're gone. One wants to know their life made a difference in this world. Everyone wants to leave an inheritance, if not for anyone else, at least for their own family.

Therefore, this is a blessing of epic proportions God is giving to David. This part alone would have been enough for him. David viewed such a gift from God—a great name, among the greatest—as one who is named among the "fathers" of Israel. To be named among the progenitors of Israel, like Abraham, Isaac, Jacob, Joseph, and Moses, was indeed an overwhelming and great honor!

After this pronouncement, the Lord begins to tell David the other three blessings, beginning with verse 11: *"Moreover, the Lord declares to you that the Lord will make you a house."* This is not the answer David was expecting to hear. In fact, it is quite a reversal because in the following verses of this passage, the Lord lets David know it will be his "son" who will build Him a house: *"I will raise up your offspring after you, who shall come from your body, and I will establish his kingdom. He shall build a house for My name, and I will establish the throne of his kingdom forever. I will be to him a father, and he shall be to Me a son"* (2 Sam. 7:12–14).

For David, these blessings from God are a stunning turn of events. But it doesn't end there because there is a fourth blessing regarding this "promise of promises" from God to David: *"And your house and your kingdom shall be made sure forever before Me. Your throne shall be established forever"* (2 Sam. 7:16). Again, it cannot be overstated this is a most unexpected answer for David. David is stunned. It is overwhelming, to say the least. Now let's summarize what the Lord has promised David:

- "I will make you a great name, like the name of the great ones of the earth."
- "I will build you a house!"
- "Your son will build Me a house, and I will be like a father to him."
- "And your house and your kingdom shall be made sure forever before Me. Your throne shall be established forever!"

As we can see, God has promised David four powerful, profound blessings for his life and legacy. But, before we can go any further, we must have clarity regarding the type of "house" God plans to build for David. The Greek word for house is *oikos*, which has a broad meaning and application.[1] It can literally refer to a physical dwelling, such as one's home or in the context of that which David desired to build for the Lord, a temple. But especially during ancient times, it referred to one's household, family, and heritage. One's family would be known as the house of Abraham, the house of Saul, or the house of David. The use of the term was commonplace, particularly among royalty.

It could also be applied to nations. When Israel became a divided nation, frequently in the Old Testament, the prophets would refer to the northern kingdom as the House of Israel and the southern kingdom as the House of Jacob.

David understands the type of house God has promised to build him. It refers to his heritage—his descendants. Not only that, God has promised David's house and his kingdom will always remain and endure without end. For David, these promises are not just beyond his expectations, they are beyond anything he could have possibly conceived, considered, or even asked for himself!

All of which brings us to a very important truth. These promises were given to David based on God's initiative. Again, they originated with God. They were God's promises based on God's purpose for David's life. This is the core principle of God's grace. God showing up in one's life and doing for you and me what we cannot possibly do for ourselves is the work of grace.

David knew these promises of God could not be earned, and they were certainly not deserved. They could not be acquired through some human effort, religious posture, nor were they predicated upon preferential treatment. They came from God, and no one else, for these promises were formed by His will, given to David because of His grace.

God's Metanarrative

Now this is very important. There is a story larger than the story of David. This is known as the metanarrative of God. The Greek prefix *meta* means "beyond." A metanarrative refers to the "grand or larger story." These promises are so significant for David, they have everything to do with God's greater and grand purpose for all of humankind. Consequently, David's view of the full ramifications of these promises of God is limited. A New Testament scripture says as much: "For we know in part and we prophecy in part, but when the perfect comes, the partial will pass away" (1 Cor. 13:9–10). David had no way of knowing the larger story of God's purpose and plan regarding the promises He made to David. David only knows "part" of the bigger picture. He does not know God's grand story!

However, we can detect that David does sense his story is part of God's larger narrative, though he does not know the specific details. Seemingly he thinks there is more to these blessings from God during his initial response to what God has promised him by his summation: *"And yet this was a small thing in your eyes, O Lord God. You have spoken also of your servant's house for a great while to come, and this is instruction for mankind, O Lord God!" (2 Sam. 7:19).* David recognizes these promises of God are a revelation of a greater plan and purpose that will benefit all of mankind. Yes, David had a sense of a greater purpose in God promising him a "house and throne" destined for eternity. David understood *forever* is a very long time, and he knew God wouldn't make such a promise, if there would not be a greater purpose to this promise after his death.

For instance, David did not know over a one thousand years later, on the dusty streets of Jericho, a blind man by the name of Bartimaeus would desperately cry out to the miracle worker passing by, followed by throngs of people all hoping for His healing touch: "Jesus, Son of David, have mercy on me! Son of David, have mercy on me!" (Mark 10:47–48).

Notice that Bartimaeus did not call out, "Jesus, son of Moses" or "Jesus, son of Abraham" but instead "son of David!" For this was the fulfillment of God's promise to make David's name a "great name on the earth" because God had predetermined the Messiah would be the "righteous Branch" from the House of David!

You may be asking, why would people during the time of Jesus be referring to Him as the son of David? It has everything to do with the Old Testament prophecies of the Messiah! The promises God made David became the "promise" of promises or that which became known as the Covenant of David (Davidic Covenant).

Though the word *covenant* is not used in the text, the use of the word in ancient times was understood to mean *promise*. Consequently, Israel was traditionally taught later by Jewish religious leaders, including the prophets, the Messiah would originate from the bloodline of David, as promised by God: *"I will raise up your offspring after you…and will establish His kingdom forever."*

The following are just a few of the prophecies that underscore the Jewish tradition regarding the Anointed One (the Christ), corresponding to the Davidic Covenant and the expectation, "the Christ" will come from the house of David:

- *There shall come forth a shoot from the stump of Jesse, and a branch from his roots shall bear fruit. And the Spirit of the Lord shall rest upon Him, the Spirit of wisdom and understanding, the Spirit of counsel and might, the Spirit of knowl-*

edge and the fear of the Lord. And His delight shall be in the fear of the Lord. (Isa. 11:1–3)

- *Behold, the days are coming, declares the Lord, when I will raise up for David a righteous Branch, and He shall reign as king and deal wisely, and shall execute justice and righteousness in the land. (Jer. 23:5)*

- *For to us a child is born, to us a son is given; and the government shall be upon His shoulder, and His name shall be called Wonderful Counselor, Mighty God, Everlasting Father, Prince of Peace. Of the increase of His government and of peace there will be no end, on the throne of David and over His kingdom to establish it and to uphold it with justice and with righteousness from this time forth and forever more. (Isa. 9:6–8)*

These Old Testament prophecies of "the Christ" inform us regarding Israel's identification of the Messiah with the royal line of David. Since the nation had been prepared by its religious leaders to expect the Messiah to come from the "House of David," consider this text in the gospel of John as the people respond to Jesus's teaching in the Temple: *"When they heard these words, some of the people said, 'This really is the Prophet.' Others said, 'This is the Christ.' But some said, 'Is the Christ to come from Galilee? Has not the Scripture said that the Christ comes from the offspring of David, and comes from Bethlehem, the village where David was?' So there was a division among the people over Him"* (John 7:40–43).

This substantiates how the Davidic Covenant was viewed by the people of Israel. It was the defining qualifier in determining the pedigree of the "Promised" Messiah for Israel! It also contributed to the confusion among the Jewish leaders and the people. Jesus was known to have been raised by Mary and Joseph in Nazareth, located in the Galilean region. This would effectively disqualify Jesus as the expectant Messiah in many of their minds. Either people didn't know Jesus was born in Bethlehem or some chose to ignore that fact, preferring to discredit Jesus since His ministry was a threat to the religious establishment of Israel.

David did not know that the Messiah for Israel and for the rest of the world would originate from his line of descendants. Nevertheless, David did trust God to do what God said He would do. He had come to know the Lord in a very personal way in this regard. David's ability to trust and depend upon the Lord had become for him a relational faith. He did not merely know "about Him," but rather, He had come to know the experiential reality of His heart, God's word for his life, His will, and His ways. David had learned to trust and depend upon God's word and His promises because God had only given him reasons to trust Him with his life! He had learned throughout his life the Lord was faithful and true to His word!

What to Do When God Says No!

But now a bigger question remains for David, or should we say a test. How would David respond to the Lord's answer? In another scriptural passage, we are informed as to why God did *not* want David to build Him a house. David had explained the answer before he died to his son Solomon: "My son, I had it in my heart to build a house in the name of the Lord my God. But the word of the Lord came to me, saying, 'You have shed much blood and have waged great wars. You shall not build a house to My name, because you have shed so much blood before Me on the earth'" (1 Chron. 22:7–8).

In the same passage, the Lord then qualifies further this answer by stating to David, God desired the builder of His house, if it is to be a house of worship, to be "a man of peace" and not war. Let's remember, the Hebrew word for peace is *shalom*; and though it comprises the meaning, "a state of tranquility," it does refer to an "absence of conflict." God desired His house to be built by a man of peace, not a man of war—a man, whom God had given "rest from his enemies."[2]

We must not forget how much David really, really wanted to build a house for God! It meant everything to him. He loved God very much, and he wanted to build a house that would give God the glory he knew the Lord so richly deserved. It would not be unreasonable to conclude this was a burning desire in the heart of David, to build a house that would honor the Lord in all Israel as well as for all the world to see!

What would David do? What would you do? What would I do? I'm sure we could all identify with David. From time to time in our journey with the Lord, we all have had that similar experience in which we wanted or badly desired something, a certain vocation, a specific relationship, or a definite dream to be fulfilled but then God said no!

How did you feel, and what did you do? Did you become angry and resentful toward God because of your disappointment? Did you become disillusioned with Him over the matter? Did you become dysfunctional for a season because you had become embittered by your circumstances? Did you withdraw from church for a while? Or did you in fact persist and continue doing everything you knew to do to ensure the reality of your heart's desire? As we know this is only self-navigation or manipulation in order to achieve one's own way. Or perhaps, after much internal wrestling and vacillation, did you finally accept and surrender to God's will for your life? Yes, I know. It's not easy when our want is greater and more important than His will! But a constant lesson in our journey of the Christian life is learning God's will is always—yes, *always*—better for us than what we think we need or should have for ourselves!

We would do well to respond to the Lord the way David did. David worshiped! David went into the Tent to be alone with the

Lord. This is probably the first thing we should do when the Lord tells us no! We should enclose ourselves alone with the Lord and pour out our heart to Him, and to the Lord only, for a moment. Now let's read the account of what David did in his response to the Lord:

> *Then King David went in and sat before the Lord and said, "Who am I, O lord God, and what is my house, that you have brought me thus far? And yet this was a small thing in your eyes, O Lord God. You have spoken also of your servant's house for a great while to come, and this is instruction for mankind, O Lord God! And what more can David say to you? For you know your servant, O Lord God! Because of your promise, and according to your own heart, you have brought about all this greatness, to make your servant know it. Therefore you are great, O Lord God. For there is none like you, and there is no God besides you, according to all that we have heard with our ears." (2 Sam. 7:18–22)*

The text says he went into the Tent and *sat* before the Lord. The word *sat* or to *sit* before the Lord indicates a posture of worship. The Hebrew word *yashab* means "to inhabit, dwell in, or to settle for a period of time."[3] David desired to *settle in* or *to abide* in God's presence. Also, to connect this word with the phrase, "Before the Lord," infers a face-to-face meeting or encounter with a person.[4] David wanted an encounter with the Lord, to abide in His Presence.

It is important to recognize David's response is not a hurried or fleeting reaction. He is deliberate and thoughtful. He is contemplative. He is definitely not in a hurry or rushed. David desires to abide in God's Presence. He is going to take his time because nothing is more important than this moment. David's response to what the Lord has promised him, well, it is a special moment. Because David doesn't have many years left, most likely there will not be another moment quite like it. So he wants this moment to count. He takes a pause from his affairs of state, the disruptions and distractions of royalty. He shuts out the world as he attends to the Lord with complete focus. He offers expressions of gratitude and love, perhaps never before expressed from his lips. It is probably unlike any other previous moment of worship in his life, of which there had been many he found enriching! He is most likely careful with each word he offers. The king of Israel just sits before the Lord. Contemplative. Quiet. Perhaps, motionless. For he is the one who recorded: "Be still before the Lord and wait patiently for Him" (Ps. 37:7).

Then finally, he utters his first words: *"Who am I…and what is my house, that you have brought me this far?"* Those certainly are not words of disappointment or disillusionment but rather words of amazement, astonishment! It appears David is stunned beyond belief. It is as if he is beside himself, with such bewilderment and overwhelming disbelief! And why shouldn't David feel that way? After all, this whole thing began with David wanting to honor the Lord by building Him a house! But instead, God has done a reversal on him!

David had every reason to be amazed at this counterproposal. It was logical as well as characteristic of David to begin his prayer and worship with expressed words of humility: "Who am I?" And what a great place to start but with the personal acknowledgment he is not worthy of such an extraordinary blessing from the Lord! This most powerful promise of God is beyond anything David could possibly conceive or imagine. Indeed, he is astounded!

David is so humbled by God's promises to him. He naturally begins with the words that reflect such humility and gratitude: "Who am I, O Lord God, and my house that you have brought me this far?" David's response is personal—very personal with this intimate expression of worship. Such expressions of gratitude are coming from a much older David, who remains in awe of such benevolence from the God he loves much. We can interpret David to be saying, "Why do you do this for me? Why do you honor me in such a way?" After all, he just wanted to build God a house but now this? Indeed, "astonished reverence" is David's posture!

Such words of humility by David are further amplified by his next self-acknowledgment: "You have brought me this far…and yet, this was a small thing, in your eyes, O Lord God!" David is contemplating what God told him previously about their journey together: "I took you from the pasture, from following sheep, that you should be prince over My people Israel. *And I have been with you wherever you went*" (vv. 8–9).

David is expressing heartfelt worship to the Lord, so let me qualify further my interpretation of his response: "Indeed Lord, it is true, You have brought me this far. You have been with me every step of the way. If it wasn't for you, I wouldn't be where I am today. It is because of Your care for me…Your steadfast love, that I have made it this far. All that has been accomplished for Israel is because of You! And, most importantly, Lord, I know, through my entire journey, You have never left me alone! Who am I?"

Do you think the Lord answered that question or that David may have discovered the answer, even though it was rhetorical? Though David does not explicitly indicate it in this passage, perhaps he did find the answer to the question that gnawed within his inner depth of soul: "Who am I?" The answer is implied as he pours out his heart in the ensuing statement: *"And what more can David say to You? For You know Your servant, O Lord God! Because of Your promise, and according to your heart, you have brought about all this greatness, to make Your servant know it."*

It is interesting that David begins this statement in third person. A name meant everything in ancient times because it did more than identify the person. It typically identified a distinguishable characteristic of the person. A name offered an identifiable trait regarding the personality or disposition of that person. This is one reason why God changed Jacob's name to Israel. The name, Jacob meant "supplanted" and had the inference of being a manipulator. *Israel* means "one who has struggled with God."[5] So a person's name in ancient times was very personal because you could become familiar with a person without ever meeting them by just knowing their name.

David begins in third person because it is connected to the application of a personal and intimate word *know* in his following sentence. The Hebrew word is *yada*. David is saying, "You know me very well. You know how I am wired for you. You know the good, the bad, and the ugly. And You know my heart toward You. What more can I tell You? Words fail me. I am overwhelmed with gratitude, but my words seem incomplete." Another time, in another place, he said as much to the Lord, "Even before a word is on my tongue, behold, O Lord, you know it altogether" (Ps. 139:4).

In the next sentence the same word, *yada*, is used. So without changing the meaning, let's rephrase David's statement to glean the intended insight: "You have made this promise to me, and have accomplished all these great things in my life, according to Your own heart, to make your servant *know* it." What is it David is to *know*? To *know* what God is able to do, if he would just fully and completely trust Him? To know the greatness of God and His power in slaying a giant warrior or great armies that outnumber Israel? Of course, those are true qualities of God that are part of David's journey to learn, but there is something more.

David's Greatest Desire!

David recognizes the reason God has done all that He has done for him is because of God's own heart. David acknowledges that all God has done for him is for this very reason: So David will come to know Him. To know His heart! To learn His nature! To discover His ways! To realize His will! To know His love through life's experience! To know Him!

Yes, all the great achievements God accomplished through David was to lead him to the ultimate destiny. For the ultimate purpose of God was to teach David, Who He is and what He is like! All of which embodies David's heart cry for the Lord as he reflects these dynamic truths in one of his psalms: *"Make me to know Your ways, O Lord; teach me Your paths. Lead me in Your truth and teach me, for You are the God of my salvation; for You I wait all the day long"* *(Ps. 25:4–5)*. Isn't this to be our passion regarding the journey of the Christian life?

It is my conviction David discovered the answer to his question "Who am I?" I believe the Holy Spirit gave him the voice in his heart to realize the most personal and priceless discovery in his relationship with God: "You told me who I am! I am Yours…and You are Mine!"

Tell me, my friend, does it get any better than that? No, I don't believe it does! For David actualized this great eternal truth for his life and serves as "instruction" for you and me and all of mankind. The greatest purpose should therefore be our greatest desire, which is to know God. Not to know about Him extrinsically or through a mere distant, head knowledge, but to know Him intrinsically, personally, intimately, and experientially. This is what David came to know and what he came to know of God's will and purpose for his life.

God knew David even before he was born in Bethlehem. God knew him before he killed his first bear, lion, or giant. God knew David before he wrote his first song about Him or before he became a prince of Israel and the shepherd of God's people. But David didn't know God until the day Samuel made a house call to David's family. He didn't know God's heart until God showed up in his life again and again. And when God did, David craved more of Him, as he recorded in one of his songs: "O God, You are My God, earnestly I seek You; my soul thirsts for You, my body longs for You in a dry and weary land where there is no water" (Ps. 63:1, NIV). Such is God's grace for David!

Then David began to know God's heart and started cultivating a heart after God's own heart. He got a taste, but David had to know and have more of Him. This was his persistent quest. He couldn't get enough of Him! He had experienced Him as he profoundly wrote, "Oh, taste and see that the Lord is good!" (Ps. 34:8).

And there was something more that drove David. It would be gross negligence if it was not emphasized. It is the motif of David's heart. It is the apex or exclamation mark, if you will, of having a heart after God. It is found in the last two concluding verses of his response to the Lord, as he says, *"Now therefore may it please You to bless the house of your servant, so that it may continue forever before You. For You, O Lord God, have spoken, and with Your blessing shall the house of Your servant be blessed forever"* (2 Sam. 7:29).

Most importantly, David is offering, "Lord, let all that You have promised, be done according to Your own heart." All of which is encased in his words, "May it please You!" If the promise to David and its fulfillment will please the Lord, David is all for it! For David has discovered, when you get to know someone intimately and grow to love that person, you want to do everything you possibly can do to *please* that person. Why? Because that person has become your world!

The Lord had become David's life in every aspect of his entire being. No one had become more important to him than the Lord. And so David wanted to do that which would please Him. Isn't this the driving motivation to do God's will? It was for David. This is the same principle mentioned earlier in which one desires to do what is *good* for God! This is why David wanted to honor the Lord by building Him a house! But God had other plans for David, and because of Who God is, God honored David. You know, it's just like God!

As we now know, David didn't know the complete and specific details of God's promises. But he did know what an unimaginable, incomparable honor God had given to him! For God's grand narrative, which instructs us today, would inevitably unveil the purpose of His promises to David in the gift of God's own Son, Jesus, who would later one day declare in the last chapter of the final book of the Bible, *"I, Jesus...I am the root and the descendant of David, the bright morning star!" (Rev. 22:16).*

Yes, a Promise of promises well kept by a God who loved David extravagantly. It's just like Him!

CHAPTER 9

The House God Promised David for Eternity!

In love, He predestined us for adoption as sons through Jesus Christ, according to the purpose of His will, to the praise of His glorious grace with which He has blessed us in the Beloved.
—Ephesians 1:5–6

Although David was not allowed to build the Temple, the Lord did permit him to acquire all the materials necessary for its construction (1 Chron. 22:14–16). David did this in the remaining years of his reign after making his son, Solomon, coregent at about twenty years of age.[1] Together they developed the building plans as well as the organization of the Levites and priests who would serve in the newly built Temple.

We must now turn our attention to the "House" God promised to build for David. We discussed in the previous chapter the Greek word for house, *oikos*, had broad meaning in antiquity. The term could apply to a dwelling place, such as one's home or a Temple of worship, which Solomon would then build. But God also told David, He would "make him a house" (2 Sam. 7:12). This engenders a defining question: What type of house did God plan to build for David?

David understood it in the context of his family heritage—his family household or his descendants. But as mentioned previously, David only knew in part, not having a more complete view of the larger divine metanarrative. He did not know the specific goal and details God had in mind when He made the pronouncement to David: *"And your house and your kingdom shall be made sure forever before Me. Your throne shall be made sure forever before Me" (2 Sam. 7:16)*. David was right in thinking the *house* God planned to build him would be comprised of people and it would consist of a family. More importantly, based on God's promise, David also knew what would make this house extraordinarily unique is that it would be an eternal family. Consequently, it would be a very special family—a distinct family or house for Whom God would be the builder! (Heb. 11:10).

Like any house that is going to be long-lasting—an eternal one, in this case—it must have a solid, reliable foundation. It must be a foundation that is "sure," which means it must be trustworthy and unshakeable. This foundation must be dependable so that no one will ever be disappointed. Over two hundred years after the death of David, one of the most prolific prophets of God, Isaiah, predicted on Whom this "Foundation" would be built by God: *"Behold, I am the One who has laid a foundation in Zion, a stone, a tested stone, a precious cornerstone, of a sure foundation: Whoever believes will not be in haste" (Isa. 28:16)*.

As emphasized, God had an eternal plan that was the central underpinning to His metanarrative or grand story. God's promise to David was a part of that grand story. Progressively and incrementally, chapter by chapter, as time marched on God provided clues or indicators, known as prophecies regarding the revelation of this "Foundation, a stone, a tested stone, a precious cornerstone" of which God would use to build the eternal house of David. This Isaiah prophecy was one among hundreds of such prophecies in the Old Testament, predicting the arrival of the Messiah.

The central Character of God's dramatic story would not be unveiled too early or too late, but just at the right time, when God knew the world was ready. As we know God is very patient and would not unfold the main Character of His-Story until the time was just right.

This reminds me of an incisive statement by the South African missionary-evangelist Andrew Murray when comparing the complementary distinctions of the Old and New Testaments of the Bible: "The New was enfolded in the Old; the Old unfolded in the New. It is possible to read the Old in the spirit of the New; it is possible to read the New as well as the Old in the spirit of the Old."[2] This is a great suggestion on how to read God's Word through the guidance of the Holy Spirit and glean some of the rich eternal truths which are hidden within it. The Old Testament prophecies unfold the New Covenant, and the New Testament unveils more fully the metanarrative of God as it states, *"But when the fullness of time had come, God sent forth His Son, born of woman" (Gal. 4:4).*

God sending Jesus Christ, His only begotten Son, born of a woman, is the beginning of God fulfilling His eternal promise to David. Listen again how another New Testament writer uses the same metaphoric language of house building and is a corollary to the Isaiah prophecy: *"As you come to Him, a living stone rejected by men but in the sight of God chosen and precious, you yourselves like living stones are being built up as a spiritual house, to be a holy priesthood, to offer sacrifices acceptable to God through Jesus Christ" (1 Pet. 2:4–5).*

This Scripture not only amplifies the Isaiah prophecy, but also is consonant with God's promise to David, as the author refers to Jesus as the "Living Stone, chosen by God and precious" and upon

Whom, you and I are "Living stones being built up as a spiritual house."

David was right! The house God promised to build would consist of a family founded by God, built on His foundation, the "precious cornerstone," His Son, Jesus Christ.

The House with an Eternal View!

Now it is important to underscore that the Davidic Covenant was always in the eternal view of God since it was central to His purpose in all of creation. That truth is further substantiated by the various New Testament scriptures that correspond with the figurative language of God's eternal plan by comparing this new family to a "spiritual house or as the temple of God":

- *Or do you not know that your body is a temple of the Holy Spirit within you, whom you have from God? (1 Cor. 6:19)*
- *Do you not know that you are God's temple and that God's Spirit dwells in you? (1 Cor. 3:16)*
- *For we are God's fellow workers. You are God's field, God's building. (1 Cor. 3:9)*
- *So then you are no longer strangers and aliens, but you are fellow citizens with the saints and members of the household of God, built on the foundation of the apostles and prophets, Christ Jesus Himself being the cornerstone, in whom the whole structure being joined together grows into a holy temple in the Lord. (Eph. 2:19–21)*
- *Now Moses was faithful in all God's house as a servant, to testify to the things that were to be spoken later, but Christ is faithful over God's house as a son. And we are His house if*

indeed we hold fast our confidence and our boasting in our hope. (Heb. 3:5–6)

Whether it is the Old or the New Testament, the figurative language describing the house God would build is constantly the same. This is a very significant dynamic. It is important to know and understand the promise to David has everything to do with the gospel message for today.

Therefore, we can equate the gospel message with God's promise to David. As we know, the translation for gospel means "Good News!" For it would be through the proclamation of the gospel message, God would fulfill His promise to build the House of David. As God promised, this house would be a family that would endure and "Be sure before Me forever!" We will revisit this truth in more detail in a moment.

So the metaphoric language has everything to do with the eternal plan of God that is all about God's original purpose in creating mankind. Therefore, the language is very much the same regardless of the historical context because God's purpose and goal for mankind's creation is in His constant view. Again, this is the grand narrative of God but revealed only in parts as it is unveiled.

Very much like a compelling and dramatic script written for a play or movie, it is vitally important the language is similar throughout the narrative. In this way, the theme will remain constant, consistent, and capture the reader's attention as the drama unfolds, gradually revealing hidden truths along the way that construct the ultimate plot, or biblically speaking, God's preeminent purpose for creating humankind. Again, this explains David's statement, "This is instruction for mankind," because he sensed God had a greater purpose that transcended the immediate promise God made to him.

The ultimate outcome of the Lord's metanarrative magnifies the veracity of God's Word transcending centuries, various cultures, and diverse personalities pointing to God's nature and causing one to discover and acknowledge, "Only God could conceive such a marvelous and perfect plan throughout human history!"

Based on New Testament language regarding the type of house God would build, there are two primary components that are presented to us. The first is that the "house" is a family, and this family is further qualified as members of the household of God. Secondly and most importantly, the New Testament writers refer to this family as a "dwelling place" for God. This is validated by the apostle Paul when he says, "Don't you know you are God's temple, and the Spirit of God dwells in you?" (1 Cor. 3:16).

This promise of God to David is a family God has desired and destined for Himself to dwell in before He even created the world! This is the essence of God's metanarrative that is detailed in the final two chapters. This eternal plan of God before time began, Paul refers to as a mystery revealed: "And to bring to light for everyone what is the plan of the mystery hidden for ages in God who created all things" (Eph. 3:9). The mystery of God's plan and purpose in creating mankind was gradually being unfolded to ultimately include all people.

We have come to a very important intersection in our journey with David. The entire exchange between David and the Lord began with one primary word expressed in David's opening sentence—*dwell*. David said, "See now, I *dwell* in a house of cedar, but the ark of God dwells in a tent." David was very interested in where God would dwell! David was concerned that a proper house be constructed for God to be glorified and to dwell.

But I don't think it was David's intention to be prophetic in his expressed concern for the "well-being of God." Nor was it David's intention to make an implicit reference that directly had everything to do with the ultimate purpose for which God had created mankind since David only knew in part. Nevertheless, his statement did just that. It was a prophetic statement, though an unintended consequence. We must remember God is telling His-Story throughout His written word. This is the reason we have spent time on the history and purpose of the Ark and the Tabernacle in chapter 7. For the Ark, the Tent or Tabernacle, and the Temple are all foreshadows of God's marvelous promise to David and the ultimate fulfillment of such a promise. They are emblematic of a dwelling place for God. But it is no ordinary house. It is such an extraordinary dwelling place, only God could conceive such a plan. A dwelling place where God would manifest His glory!

These "articles" have a direct correlation to God's promise for David and the type of house God plans on building. We should view them as predictive of "something better to come" (Heb. 8:6). They are part of the progressive and incremental unveiling of God's metanarrative. And they all have one commonality—the manifest Presence of God's glory!

God's Building Plan

Thus far, what do we know regarding the type of house God will build for David? We know God is planning to build an eternal family. We also know God desires to dwell in this family, for this is His eternal building plan! But such a house must be prepared for such a wonderful Resident, does it not? It must be a house worthy of the Lord to dwell in! This then begs the next important question. How will God build such a house?

As we know, David's son, Solomon, was chosen by God to construct the Temple in Jerusalem. However, God had predetermined to build this "eternal house" through His Son, Jesus Christ. This was God's blueprint. This eternal plan was *conceived* by Father-God before the world was even created, as it states in Paul's letter to the believers in Ephesus: *"Even as He (God) chose us in Him (Jesus) before the foundation of the world, that we should be holy and blameless before Him.* In love *He (God) predestined us for adoption as sons through Jesus Christ, according to the purpose of His will" (Eph. 1:4–5).*

This wonderful passage underscores Father-God had conceived the plan in His love for us, and it was His desire to have "many sons," who would be adopted through His Son, Jesus Christ. Paul then expands further on this eternal plan of God by delineating how all of this was made possible, as well as how it was God's intentional purpose in making full disclosure according to His own time schedule: *"In Him (Christ) we have redemption through His blood, the forgiveness of our trespasses, according to the riches of His grace…making known to us the mystery of His will, according to His purpose, which He set forth in Christ as a plan for the fullness of time, to unite all things in Him (Christ), things in heaven and things on earth" (Eph. 1:7, 9–10).*

Fundamentally, this passage is speaking of God's plan for salvation, but also refers to the metanarrative of God. And something much more. Too often the gospel message has emphasized what we are being "saved from," which is certainly important, but we must also realize and convey what we are "saved for!" This applies to the subject of repentance, which we discussed earlier in the book. Repentance is not just about subtraction, but it is complemented with addition. You cannot have one without the other because if we neglect one part, we present a "half-truth." It's not just about, "No, that is wrong, but yes, this is right for you!" The gospel message should convey not only what we are saved from, but for that which is God's purpose, plan, and destiny for our very existence!

Framed for Fellowship!

This part of God's eternal plan reminds me of a true story involving a young teenage boy who at the age of sixteen attempted to make the varsity high school basketball team. It was probably a common story then, as it is today for many teenagers, who simply want to be good at something by pursuing an athletic endeavor that will validate the reason to be accepted and valued!

This young man practiced diligently and with passion in pursuit of his dream. There were many late-school nights working on shooting skills in the dark and in the cold. Finally, the three-day tryouts had arrived, and it was now time to prove the hard work would pay dividends. But it was not meant to be. Though the young man felt he had outplayed most of the other guys, he did not qualify for the team. Have you ever felt disqualified? Have you ever felt like somehow, you didn't quite measure up or you just didn't quite fit?

That's how the young man felt on the long three-mile walk home—disappointed, dejected, and discarded. And alone. You see, his parents divorced when he was eight. He was very close to his dad, but Dad was not around. His mom remarried a man who was a musician and played the nightclub scene. They lived self-absorbed lives, so much so, the young man didn't tell them of his ambitious dream. He was totally alone in his quest and then in his despair.

By all accounts it was a long, lonely walk home, as tears streamed uncontrollably down the young man's face. The heartache was deep because the teenager thought he played well enough and was good enough for the team. But the tears of dejection would not stop. And now only two blocks from home, the young man desperately cried out, looking upward at the wintry star-filled sky, "Oh, God, I believe in you. Something deep inside tells me You are Who You are! I just don't fit. This life is never going to work for me without

You. Somehow I know I will never be worth anything to my family or fellow man without You...I need a dad! Will you be my Father?"

Yes, that was the prayer. A simple but desperate prayer. Yet it was quite a prayer for a young teenager to offer. I can remember it as if it were yesterday. You must understand I had been raised in a mainline denomination where there was not much emphasis or teaching on the Bible. Now I know, though not then, I had assistance in offering such a prayer based on the answer received. It was totally unexpected but remarkable. For the very first time in my life, I heard these words, "Yes, John. I will be your Father, and you will be My son!"

Do you know what that meant to me at that desperate moment of brokenness? Even though I was young, I did understand the magnitude of the moment. God, the Creator of the entire universe, told me He would be a Father to me. The fact God spoke to me, and that I heard that still, small voice was tremendous in and of itself.

But more than that, for the "fatherless" to be told by God, I could have such a relationship with Him, well, the tears suddenly stopped. The inconsolable found not only consolation but a deep abiding peace and joy that told me I was going to be just fine. I was no longer alone.

It would be several years later I would be presented with the gospel message and would later discover a scriptural passage that validated this first encounter with the Lord:

> *For we are the temple of the living God; as God said, "I will make My dwelling among them and walk among them, and I will be their God, and they shall be My people. Therefore go out from their midst, and be separate from them, says the Lord, and touch no unclean thing; then I will welcome you, and I will be a father to you, and you shall be*

sons and daughters to Me," says the Lord Almighty.
(2 Cor. 6:16–18)

Can you imagine the excitement and reassurance when I read such an affirmation of my experience with the Lord? I hardly knew anything of God's Word, let alone this profound promise of God. To finally discover I was destined for such a personal, intimate relationship with God was overwhelming and incomparable to anything in this life! For me then it was more meaningful to read David's words as he described his relationship to the Lord: "Because Your steadfast love is better than life, my lips will praise you" (Ps. 63:3).

It didn't matter anymore if I didn't fit everyone else's expectations. Because I now knew I fit with Father-God. This was the very pulse of my discovery as I grew in my relationship with the Lord, that just as we are wired for worship, we are framed for fellowship with Father-God! *You and me were framed by God for Him to dwell with and in us!*

We are the *framework* for God to dwell in and to manifest His Presence. This was God's eternal plan and the house God promised David He would build and would endure forever. It was to be the house Father-God would dwell eternally!

As Jesus prepared His disciples for His departure—He was going to the Cross the next day—He said to them, "I will not leave you as orphans; I will come to you...If anyone loves Me, he will keep My word, and My Father will love him, *and we will come to him and make our home with him*" (John 14:18, 23). There is that constant and consistent metaphorical language throughout His-Story. It doesn't matter who is speaking regarding the eternal plan, whether it is the Father to David, Jesus to His disciples, or the apostle Paul to believers, the language is the same, because God's purpose for mankind is a unified narrative with one ultimate goal.

THE HOUSE GOD PROMISED DAVID FOR ETERNITY!

And what is that goal of God regarding our purpose? Father-God desired, and thereby, planned to have a family—many sons (non-gender)—who would mirror the image of His only begotten Son, Jesus Christ, with the purpose of ruling with Jesus throughout eternity.

God Reveals an Identity for Israel

This was and always has been God's eternal plan. He began to unveil His plan through the introduction of Himself to the nation Israel. Let me set up the scene. God had just rescued two and half million Israelites from slavery in Egypt, through His agent, Moses.[3] They have just arrived at Mt. Sinai, which took about sixty days of travel.[4] God prepares the people for His special visitation to give them the Law or more commonly known as the Ten Commandments. But before the dramatic scene in which God speaks audibly for only the one-time to a collective group of people in human history, the Lord relays a message to them through Moses. Listen to the Lord's introductory words to the people:

> You yourselves have seen what I did to the Egyptians, and how I bore you on eagles' wings and brought you to Myself. Now therefore, if you will indeed obey My voice and keep My covenant, you shall be My treasured possession among all peoples, for all the earth is Mine; and you shall be to Me a kingdom of priests and a holy nation. These are the words that you shall speak to the people of Israel. (Exod. 19:4–6)

175

The Lord tells the people His plans and purpose for them. All they have known for four hundred years (Gen. 15:13) is slavery, and they have never been a nation. For the first time in their lives, God wants to give them their identity! Their identity has everything to do with their God-ordained destiny of which God wants to define who they will become!

Their purpose is conceived in God's desire for them to be His "treasured possession, a kingdom of priests, and a holy nation." This is constituted on Israel's responsiveness to the Lord's proposal. Would they want a relationship (covenantal) with God or would they not? Their answer to that ultimate question would be determined by one dynamic reality—would the people do what God wanted them to do? Would they love Him in the same way He loved them as His "treasured possession?" Tragically, we know their decision and outcome—they rejected the Lord (Num. 14:22–23).

Personal Identity Provides Purpose!

Just like ancient Israel, no one can know their purpose in life, independent of their God-given identity. Tragically speaking, millions of people do not know or understand their destiny God designed for them. Even within the Church-at-large, there are many believers who profess Christ who do not know their God-given purpose and identity. Sadly, the adverse effect of not knowing one's destiny in life is the inability to learn one's identity for they are complementary and inseparable.

Peter Scazzero, in his book *Emotionally Healthy Spirituality*, emphasizes the importance for believers to develop spiritual maturity and how to do just that in their journey of the Christian life. Since he is a pastor of an urban church, he, of course, writes from his personal background experience and makes this astonishing but profound claim: "The vast majority of us go to our graves without knowing who we are. We unconsciously live someone else's expectations for us. This does violence to ourselves, our relationship with God, and ultimately to others."[5]

Scazzero's statement underscores a common, deep spiritual malady that affects the entire human personality. Keep in mind he used the word *violence* regarding the impact of not knowing one's identity. This contributes toward many of the perplexing issues that immerse contemporary society—from absentee fathers, fragmented families, a broken educational system, to an insidious drug culture, much of which can be attributed to a personal pursuit of happiness that people continually find elusive.

This self-navigation in which we pursue our dreams, not knowing why and for Whom we were created, currently generates a culture convulsing in moral chaos. All of which reverberates throughout all segments of society, "Doing violence to ourselves, our relationship with God and others," because one simply does not know their purpose in life, thereby not realizing their true identity.

This reality is further substantiated by Dr. Larry Crabb, well-known from the profession of Christian counseling, who contends the primary personal need of every human being is personal worth. He then qualifies the "two inputs" he believes that people attempt to fulfill, but through self-navigation results in creating and contributing to most problems incurred in life, of which he offers:

> The most basic need is a sense of personal worth, an acceptance of oneself as a whole, real person. The two required inputs are significance (purpose, importance, adequacy for a job, meaningfulness, impact) and security (love—unconditional and consistently expressed; permanent acceptance). I believe that before the

Fall Adam and Eve were both significant and secure. From the moment of their creation their needs were fully met in a relationship with God unmarred by sin. Significance and security were attributes or qualities already resident within their personalities, so they never gave them a second thought.[6]

Dr. Crabb contends our inherent need is to be loved and accepted unconditionally in our relationship with God. He also offers, before the Fall, the attributes of *significance* and *security* actualized our personal worth because they gave us meaningful purpose (significance) and unconditional acceptance (security) by God.

If this is true, that we were created with these innate attributes of significance and security in our relationship with God and they were then shattered due to a self-centered pursuit of independence from God (the Fall), the violence done to ourselves, others, and God Himself is incalculable! Of course, we can merely rewind the video of human history and gain some insight into the immeasurable depths of such violence, all of which ensue, poverty, pestilence, greed, wars, Holocaust, genocides, Hitler, Stalin, and the likes!

Dr. Willard further qualifies the original innate attribute of significance in the human being: "The drive to significance is a simple extension of the creative impulse of God that gave us being. It is not filtered through self-consciousness any more than is our lunge to catch a package falling from someone's hand. It is outwardly directed to the good to be done. We were built to count, as water is made to run downhill. We are placed in a specific context to count in ways no one else does. That is our destiny."[7]

All of this provokes the ultimate question: If God created us with these attributes, then wouldn't it be reasonable to believe they could not be restored to each of us, independent of God?

Of course not.

On that cold, November evening, the invaluable principle the Lord began to teach me was my personal value could not be measured by what I did or how I performed in a particular athletic endeavor. Qualifying for the varsity high school basketball team did not validate the reason for me to be loved and accepted. Yes, it will inevitably impress some for the moment, but it will only be short-lived until you make an error or stumble or fail. After all, one cannot base their security or significance on how well they perform!

What happens to the reality when you do qualify to make the team? The season is over and the cheering stops, what then? What happens if you have that beautiful singing talent, but it wears out in time and the ticket sales diminish? How then do you measure your worth? What do you do when unwanted wrinkles appear, along with some graying hair, or your spouse discovers greener pastures, leaving you behind? Where do you go, and what do you do to recover your value? Or perhaps the family business fails, you lose everything and become bankrupt? Does the financial statement now set your worth or your meaningfulness and purpose in life?

You see, my friend, if we are motivated to meet our inherent needs for "significance and security," using such temporal methods to measure our worth, independent of God, the result will always be spiritual bankruptcy. This explains why some people tragically end their own lives when their dreams are crushed, finding no meaning and purpose at the end of the rainbow.

Our Inheritance!

Please hear the heart of this pastor. It is never too late to turn away from the self-navigation of meeting these two primary needs inherent in each of us. Remember, I was a young, lonely, awkward teenager, feeling like my life didn't count for much. I knew I didn't fit and didn't feel too worthwhile. But it didn't stop God from showing up for that young, lonely, unappealing, unacknowledged kid and whispering, "Yes, John, I will be Your Father, and you will be my son!"

You must understand what I didn't know then, but have now since learned, regarding this profound wonderful truth the apostle Paul describes as "our inheritance." Too often our understanding of inheritance has been limited to going to heaven. Don't get me wrong. Heaven is a great benefit. It is our reward. But our inheritance has everything to do with God's purpose in creating us. Our inheritance God planned before the world's creation: "He predestined us for adoption as sons through Jesus Christ" (Eph. 1:5). Paul then further qualifies this truth: "In Him, we have obtained an inheritance, having been predestined according to the purpose of Him" (Eph. 1:11). Our inheritance is to be known as His adopted sons! And most importantly, the "guarantee" or the "deposit" of our inheritance has been sealed in us by the indwelling of God's Holy Spirit, until we receive our full inheritance with Christ (Eph. 1:13–14). This, my friend, is the house God planned to build for David!

What amazing grace to think the Creator of the universe planned and destined you and me to become a part of His eternal family. To be able to call Him Father is simply beyond words. It is incomparable to anything this life could offer! Nothing can compare to hearing Him tell you through His still, small voice: "You're My son, and I'm Your Father!" It doesn't get better than that.

Now, if I may, I'm led to pray for you, my friend.

> Father-God, I know I do not ask for a light thing. For Jesus, you said, "With men it is impossible, but with God all things are possible." I ask you, Dear Father, do a new work that

only you can do in the person praying with me now. Align their priorities with the priorities of Your heart. May they come to know You experientially, personally, and intimately according to the destiny You designed for them and each of us. In the Name, that is above every Name, our Lord Jesus Christ, Amen.

Now let's find out more about God's building blueprint and how the Lord planned to build David's eternal House long before He created the world!

CHAPTER 10

The Perfect Plan: A Precious Foundation for David's House!

For in Him (Jesus) all the fullness of God was pleased to dwell, and through Him (Jesus) to reconcile to Himself (the Father) all things, whether on earth or in heaven, making peace by the blood of His Cross
—Colossians 1:19–20

The building blueprint was perfect. The chosen "Foundation" was sure and reliable! The plan was perfect because Father-God *conceived* it. Of course, there probably was a conversation between them—the Father, the Son, and Holy Spirit. It would be just like the Father to let the Son know what He was thinking, planning, and desiring to do. For the decision would be mutual. It had to be. That is just the way they are.

We don't know exactly the conversation between them, but we do know there had to be a plan in place because they knew in advance man would reject them. Man would prefer to go it alone. Therefore, we know the "Plan" was established before the world was created, as Scripture enunciates this profound purpose of man's creation by Father-God:

> *Blessed be the God and Father of our Lord Jesus Christ, who has blessed us in Christ with every spiritual blessing in the heavenly places, even as He chose us in Him (Christ) before the foundation of the world, that we should be holy and blameless before Him.* In love *He predestined us for adoption as sons through Jesus Christ, according to the purpose of His will. (Eph. 1:3–5)*

This passage emphasizes Father-God *conceived* the plan on this basis: "Even as He chose us in Him (Jesus) before the foundation of the world." It was Father-God's original idea because "He chose."

Furthermore, the Scripture then states the purpose of Father-God's plan—He desired a family, an eternal family, *conceived* in His love. Everything God does is motivated by Who He is: "God is love" (1 John 4:16).

This speaks to the purpose in creating mankind, for God destined this family to be comprised of "adopted sons (non-gender) through Jesus Christ." The purpose, the family, the plan—all of which was Father-God's idea—is summed up best: it was His will and therefore His initiative!

The central Person of God's divine story is His only begotten Son, Jesus Christ. Jesus is central to God's eternal purpose, as well as to Father-God's plan. In other words, the destiny of "many sons" for the Father can and will only be realized through His Eternal Son, Jesus. Jesus is the beginning and the completion of the Father's eternal plan. This means the fulfillment of the plan is wholly dependent upon Jesus—His devoted willingness to accept the assignment as well as to complete it. The promise to David—this eternal family of God—would rest entirely upon Jesus!

Sin Defined!

Now before we can discuss how God will build His house, we must discuss a condition, a human condition, that produced cataclysmic ramifications for all of creation. It is the human condition known as sin. It is the issue that got David into trouble.

When sin entered the world, it changed everything—radically. It had immeasurable repercussions that affected all God's creation. It did untold damage to the earth, the environment, the animal kingdom, all living species, and, of course, mankind.

A term, which is biblical and Hebrew in origin, gives clearer understanding and definitive meaning to sin, which is the word *shalom*. Theologian Cornelius Plantinga Jr. describes the destructiveness and damage of sin in the context of "shalom," which as he offers carries a broader meaning than peace and the absence of conflict:

> The webbing together of God, humans, and all creation in justice, fulfillment, and delight is what the Hebrew prophet's call *shalom*. We call it peace, but it means far more than mere peace of mind or cease-fire between enemies. In the Bible, shalom means universal flourishing, wholeness, and delight—a rich state of affairs in which natural needs are satisfied and natural gifts fruitfully employed, a state of affairs that inspires joyful wonder as its Creator and Savior opens doors and welcomes the creatures

in whom He delights. Shalom, in other words,
is the way things ought to be.[1]

Based on this description, the essence of *shalom* is a universal flourishing, a wholeness, if you will. Plantinga subsequently qualifies the horrific and devastating repercussions on God's creation as, "Sin, violating shalom—the way God had originally intended for life to exist."[2] A comparable conclusion would be that sin fractured the "wholeness" of God's creation. Sin was, and is, a violent intruder; and consequently, life as God intended was "broken" and a fragmented distortion from what He originally intended!

However, the worse catastrophic effect of shalom's violation was the alienation of man from God. The very purpose for man's existence was shattered. Sin does that—it destroys relationships. Sin did violence to *shalom*. Therefore, the magnitude of such brokenness would require an extraordinary and radical fix. Yes, it would demand divine rescue by the greatest power the world has ever known, and will ever know—the extravagant love of God!

But this only describes the effects of sin. It is important to define it. What is sin? The Bible says, sin is lawlessness (1 John 3:4). This means those who practice sin do not respect or recognize boundaries. The word *transgression* applies to this meaning of sin. Sin not only crosses boundaries, but falls short by "missing the mark." We do not "see" the boundaries clearly because sin has a blinding effect. Sin knows no restraint. When we sin, we not only violate our own boundaries but the boundaries of others, as well as God's boundaries, resultant in tremendous grief and pain for everyone. Sin does not live in isolation.

But sin is also more than an inability to see or respect boundaries. Plantinga takes us to a deeper understanding of sin: "Sin is not only the breaking of law but also the breaking of covenant with one's savior. Sin is the smearing of a relationship, the grieving of one's divine parent and benefactor, a betrayal of the partner to whom one is joined by a holy bond...All sin has first and finally a Godward force."[3] When David was convicted over his sin, he cried out, "Against You, You only, have I sinned and done what is evil in Your sight" (Ps. 51:4). This definition amplifies the personal nature and effects of sin toward God.

Plantinga is underscoring that sin, first and foremost, violates God, His being and very nature. It is not that David's sins did not affect others, they did. But David's first discovery is the realization he had "smeared" his relationship with God or "despised the Lord." David had betrayed the Lord by Whom "he was joined by a holy bond!" No wonder his heart was crushed, for sin in all that it embodies is a personal affront to God.

This is the starting point in understanding the issue of sin. However, we can never understand sin and its insidious force independent of realizing God's nature. For sin is antithetical to God's nature and His very essence. In God's world, sin is a violent intrusion of all that is God. It is an inordinate disposition, an anomaly of God's created order and His goodness. Sin desensitizes and makes abnormal, normal. Sin distorts and disfigures God's original creation. This explains God's holy hatred of sin.

The Genesis account of God's creative capacity reflects His nature: "And God saw everything that He had made, and behold, it was very good" (Gen. 1:31). The uninvited stranger, sin, is a spoiler of all that is God and all that is good. As Plantinga further qualifies, "Sin does not build shalom, it vandalizes it." Consider this, if God made our soul for him and to always need him, any means by which we determine to fulfill that deep need in each of us, without God, is sin. Therefore, sin is a thief. It steals, kills, and destroys all that is good. All that is God! Sin vandalizes God's highest creation, mankind.

As emphasized previously, sin is the issue of the human heart because the heart is the residence of the human will. Sin is a heart condition. Scripture amplifies this truth: "The heart is deceitful above all things, and desperately sick" (Jer. 17:9). Paul Billheimer explains the very essence of this heart condition with his own incisive definition: "Self-centeredness is the very essence of all sin, and misery and results in self-destruction."[4]

Sin by its very nature is inimical to God's nature. Sin takes without giving. God gives without receiving. Sin is enslaved self-centeredness and a far cry from *shalom*. It is our natural inclination and the reason God hates sin. Sin does violence to the goodness of God. This was acutely reflected when Adam and Eve, in effect, declared by their decision, "We know a better way. We want to go our own way."

God was left no choice. From their view, God was the intruder, the unwelcome guest. Thus, God would not impose and go where He was not wanted. God gave them up to do what they wanted but without giving up completely. Though He was grieved beyond what we would understand, the estrangement had to occur. There was no other alternative for the time being, so God departed from them and with Him, His glory! But love would not give up. Or would He?

A Radical Remedy Needed!

We could not discuss how God would build His house for David without first discussing the condition of the human heart. It is much like a visit to the doctor's office. Before the physician offers the prescribed remedy, there must be a determination of the cause and type of malady the person is suffering.

God was not blindsided in the Garden. He had already made the diagnosis long before man breathed his first breath. The Plan was already established by the Father, agreed to, and accepted by the Son. It was a radical remedy demanded by the desperate heart condition of humankind. And yes, it had to be a comprehensive and complex remedy. So complex and radical, the remedy would be incomprehensible to human intellect and reason. Man could not ever understand it alone. He would need assistance through the Holy Spirit!

The Plan would be perfect. It would be able to affect and reach all aspects of the human being—the mind, thoughts and emotions, the body, soul, and, most importantly, the heart. The Plan would need to be powerful enough to capture the interest of a wandering soul imprisoned in a darkened dungeon, lost in despair, disillusionment, and devaluation. Lost in a condition God never intended for any human being to know.

Uniquely, the Plan would make its appeal on a rough, crude altar made of wood. Rightly, the altar would be outstretched toward heaven, high enough for man to view and to arrest his wandering nature. This altar would be God's new Tree of Life. But instead of a garden, it would be located on a dusty, rocky hill on the outskirts of Jerusalem.

Again, no one could understand the Plan and method alone. This was especially true for those of Jewish origin who were taught by OT Scripture: "A hanged man on a tree was cursed by God" (Deut. 21:23). This method, this altar, the Cross, would not make sense to human rationale; but for God, His plan fit perfectly for its divine, designed purpose! But to behold the truth of such a Perfect Plan, one would need to have it revealed by God's Holy Spirit. For God's Word underscores the defect of human reason and intellect: "For Jews demand signs and Greeks seek wisdom…a stumbling block to Jews and folly to Gentiles" (1 Cor. 22–23).

The Father's Conceived Plan!

Now this is important as it is the very pulse of God's Plan, or if you will, the design of the divine Plan. When God makes His announcement to Samuel, telling him He has found Saul's replacement, the Lord states, "I have *sought* out a man after My own heart" (1 Sam. 13:14, PAR). Central to this declaration of the Lord is the use of the word *sought*. The Hebrew meaning for *sought* has broad applications. But in this context, it means "Seek to find, to search" or "to call on, to request, to desire, to pursue."[5] Therefore, we can conclude, the Lord pursued David. It was God's initiative, He chose David. God pursued David. This is the grace of God that is constantly active and not passive.

The design of God's eternal Plan refers to God's intentional purpose involving the method He determined to use to reach and reconcile the human condition. God's eternal Plan and its design is His *Pursuit* of you and me! Yes, God is the *Pursuer* of you and me—your heart and mine—*constructed* in the Cross of Jesus Christ! The Cross is God's pursuit of you and me!

Constructed through the Son

This should help us understand why God's Plan is a perfect fit. What do I mean by a perfect fit? The plan would need to be dualistic in purpose. Since man had become separated from God and had become more distant and ignorant of God's nature, the Lord would need a radical sign to reveal a glimpse of His heart. Through a Perfect Sacrifice, God would convey His very nature and His heart toward mankind, which is summed up in selfless and sacrificial love.

At the same time, not only is the "altar" designed to reveal God's nature, it's also the Lord's purpose to reflect man's disposition by revealing the horrific price of sin. There is probably no crueler form of capital punishment ever invented, than crucifixion. It was typical for someone to suffer for days.[5]

Both the nature of God and the nature of man are juxtaposed on the Cross. We must not forget, sin, because of its antithetical nature and inimical disposition toward God, required a radical treatment—death! But then God's nature becomes dominant since it is His Beloved who hangs on the Cross, revealing God's character through two primary active dynamics that embody His Person. The two dynamics expressed are God's *righteousness* and His heart of *reconciliation*.

Rightfully so, sin requires God's righteous judgment. And there is only one payment that will satisfy such a right and perfect judgment: God's love! Amazingly, God's love would not give up on humanity. However, the *only* available remedy for sin would demand God give up Jesus, God's Beloved! Yes, a payment had to be made, for God's *righteousness* required it. This is what Paul meant when he declared the major theme in his letter to the Romans: "For I am not ashamed of the gospel, for it is the power of God for salvation to everyone who believes, to the Jew first and also to the Greek. For in it (the gospel) the righteousness of God is revealed from faith to faith" (Rom. 1:16–17). God's righteousness is revealed in His right adjudication of sin, expressing His right payment for sin because of His love. This is good news!

The power of God's designed plan cannot be overstated. With His Beloved hanging on the Tree, God is in pursuit while providing payment for you and me the expression of God's justice!

This is how selfless love shattered selfishness; where humility met hubris, holiness absorbed brokenness, and gentleness swallowed violence. The Cross is where the greatest power ever to be displayed, and known, the perfect selfless love of God pulverizing the putrid abyss of hatred, anger, contempt, and bitterness through the pouring out of every single drop of blood from His Beloved Son. This is God beginning to build David's house.

Through the willingness of Jesus to offer Himself, God is able to rip apart the powerful bondage and chasm of hostility—the utter cold, naked, lonely, dark, perilous separation of man's bent toward self-navigation. All of it was finally crucified and buried with Jesus, as He exclaimed, "It is finished!" Debt paid in full, the right payment made. It is God's love, which ultimately conquers and destroys the power of sin! What a plan! What a Savior! What a God, and what manner of love is this?

And what a purpose captured in one of the most powerful scriptures in all of the New Testament:

> *But God shows His love for us in that while we were still sinners, Christ died for us…For if while we were enemies we were reconciled to God by the death of His Son, much more, now that we are reconciled, shall we be saved by His life. More than that, we also rejoice in God through our Lord Jesus Christ, through whom we have now received reconciliation. (Rom. 5:8, 10–11)*

Essentially this passage captures God's intentional purpose in the design of His Plan through the second primary dynamic, *reconciliation*, God's pursuit of mankind. But to understand the purpose of God's plan of salvation, we must consider the definition of reconciliation from a two-fold premise: a technical definition as well as a biblical qualification.

First, according to Webster's dictionary, *reconciliation* is to *reconcile*, which means to restore to friendship or harmony or to settle, to resolve a dispute.[6] Based on this definition, we may view this scriptural truth to say, "While we were sinners and the enemies of God, He gave us Jesus and restored us to harmony with Himself." Such hostility, our sinful disposition, is the violent assertion toward God, revealed in the statement, "I can do better without you."

Therefore, Christ's death has reconstituted *shalom* between God and man—peace has been restored. All of which is now dependent on how each individual person responds to God's personal invitation and overture through His Beloved Son, Jesus!

The second defining factor is effectively captured by the theologian Kenneth Wuest while citing Marvin Vincent, a Greek scholar, who further qualifies the divine work of reconciliation through the Cross of Jesus Christ:

> Reconciled is "katalasso (Greek)," "to change, exchange." The verb means primarily to exchange, and hence to change the relation of hostile parties into a relation of peace; to reconcile. In the Christian sense, the change in the relation of God and man effected through Christ. This involves a movement of God toward man with a view to break down man's hostility, to commend God's love and holiness to him, and to convince him of the enormity and the consequence of sin.[7]

Reconciliation is an "exchange" of a relationship, formerly hostile but now *shalom*. We should recognize Dr. Vincent underscores reconciliation as "God's movement toward man." *Reconciliation* is God making the first move—God's pursuit!

It is true, sin alienates us from God, primarily because sin is incompatible with the very nature of God. However, remember this other important dynamic truth. Sin does not stop God from moving toward us in the hopeless and broken condition we find ourselves. It is just the opposite, based on Who He is and His nature. It is His love for us that causes God to rescue us from our wayward plight and hopeless enslavement. It is the Cross that fits perfectly with His nature, in essence, His movement or pursuit of man—you and I—with the primary mission of restoring "shalom," the life God originally intended for each of us! This is what the apostle Paul meant when he challenged the church to understand, "It is the goodness of God that leads men to repentance" (Rom. 2:4). These are the effects of reconciliation.

Salvation, which should be understood more as deliverance—deliverance from the displacement of God's original purpose for our lives—to the ultimate replacement of God's eternal embrace and purpose for our lives here now on earth as it is in heaven. This was the life God originally intended for each of us: to share His life with us! Such is the essence of reconciliation: an exchange occurring that reconstitutes *shalom* from the damage of sin, a lost and broken condition!

Many who profess Christ are not aware of the powerful and priceless benefits reconciliation provides by God through the death of His Son, Jesus. Let me share four benefits God's movement toward us does provide. The first benefit God provides through reconciliation is (1) He *redeems* us through the shed Blood of Jesus Christ in which we receive the forgiveness of our sins (Eph. 1:7). To redeem means to purchase or buy back. A price had to be paid, a payment needed to be made according to the righteousness of God. Scripture says there can be no forgiveness of sins without the shedding of blood.

This was the "New enfolded in the Old" when it came to the institution of animal sacrifices, as they were a precursor of the Perfect Sacrifice as the writer of Hebrews describes, *"Not by means of the blood of goats and calves but by means of His own blood, thus securing an eternal redemption" (Heb. 9:12).* Redemption has the power to cleanse our hearts from all sins and to purify our conscience so we may freely live for God (Heb. 9:14).

A second provision is (2) He *rescues* us, from the jurisdiction or authority of the devil. In fact, God's Word says this is the very reason God sent Jesus into the world: "The reason the Son of God appeared was to destroy the works of the devil" (1 John 3:8). Because of Christ, no one has to live any longer under the subjugation of Satan.

Man had capitulated to Satan his God-given authority to govern the earth by surrendering to and believing the devil's lie. Such surrender resulted in mankind living under the authority of the devil since he is the "ruler of this world" as well as living separate from God. This estrangement or exile from the One who created us out of love for the purpose of knowing His love produced such catastrophic repercussions, it would require God Himself to rescue us from the enslaved entanglements of Satan's rule. Jesus died on the Cross to destroy the devil's jurisdiction over mankind. This truth is encapsulated in Paul's words as he describes what Jesus accomplished: *"He disarmed the rulers and authorities and put them to open shame, by triumphing over them in Him" (Col. 2:15).*

A third provision in God's pursuit of us is (3) He *restores* us to a right relationship with Him, which is the very reason we were created. Through the design of His Plan, the Cross, He extends the invitation to anyone who will accept to be His adopted son. Thus, God's revealed purpose for us: *"In love He (the Father) predestined us for adoption as sons through Jesus Christ, according to the purpose of His will" (Eph. 1:5).*

This is what I began to discover on that wintry November night—that I was destined for such a relationship. And so were you, my friend! This eternal truth is further amplified by Paul in another letter to the church in Rome: *"For all who are led by the Spirit of God are sons of God. For you did not receive the spirit of slavery to fall back into fear, but you have received the Spirit of adoption as sons, by Whom we cry, Abba! Father!" (Rom. 8:14–15).*

A fourth provision of God's movement to us and a continuous work in our lives today is (4) God *recovers* in us His image. We were all created in His image, but sin greatly damaged that image in us.

When God created the world, the Genesis account informs us He merely spoke the world into existence. But with His highest creation, man, it would be different. The Bible says, "The Lord God formed the man of dust from the ground and breathed into his nostrils the breath of life" (Gen. 2:7). Only with man, God deliberately breathed life into him. This reflects God's intimate involvement in man's creation, as well as His purpose for us to mirror His likeness.

The Lord invites us every day to allow Him to fashion and form the character of Jesus Christ in us that we may live for Father-God in the same way Jesus did. This is one of the great benefits of the Cross, in which we can become a person who looks and lives with the qualities of Jesus. This is a personal, intimate journey that leads us to our ultimate destination, which is further explained in the final two chapters.

The Ultimate Price for God!

As we have discussed the powerful benefits of God's reconciling work through His Son, Jesus, we should now be able to better understand why God designed such a Plan. It had to be a radical remedy, powerful enough to transform the human heart from its self-centered condition to a heart like Jesus! The Cross would reveal the love of God while at the same time reflect the horrible, twisted disfigurement of sin itself in the innocent body of God's only begotten Son, Jesus Christ. Such a powerful demonstration of God's love would affect the entirety of a human being—the heart, soul, mind, and body. This is the perfect fit of the divine plan.

Now it would be gross negligence not to emphasize the pervasive strand of the Cross regarding complete darkness and futility of being lost or abandoned. One cannot fully understand the design of God's eternal plan, the Cross, without assistance from the Holy Spirit. At the same time, there will always be a mystery about the Cross such as now when we consider the "ultimate moment" the Father and Son had never known.

It is that personal, most intimate, moment when hell unleashes all its fury and the sinless, innocent Lamb of God becomes the sin-bearer for humankind. As sin rips the Beloved from the embrace of His Father, we hear Jesus cry out to Him in the most excruciating, indescribable torment and anguish, surpassing all the great physical agony He endured, "My God, my God, why have you forsaken Me?" (Matt. 27:46). Should there be any wonder why darkness covered the entire scene for the final three hours the Beloved hung on the Cross? (Luke 23:44).

The heart-crushing moment was the horror Jesus wanted to avoid, if it was at all possible, as He desperately prayed in Gethsemane. No, there were no other options. There was no other way. The ultimate price of sin must be paid—abandonment and alienation, the horrific effects of sin on the human soul. This was the real agony for Jesus in the garden, causing Him to profusely sweat drops of blood. So much so, an angel had to be sent to "strengthen Him" (Luke 22:43–44).

Nevertheless, Jesus was determined to do the Father's will, no matter the price. Jesus's love for His Father caused Him to willingly surrender to the altar of sacrifice, as He recounted the final words of instruction He had received from the Father: "No one takes it (His life) from Me, but I lay it down of My own accord. I have authority to lay it down, and I have authority to take it up again. This charge I have received from My Father" (John 10:18).

What a perfect eternal Plan, because of a Perfect Sacrifice. The Father gave up His Son, in order to have many just like Him. The Son willingly gave up His Father to become the bearer of all sins. This was the exchange that had to occur to produce this new eternal family of God. Paul captures this dynamic truth: "For our sake He (the Father) made Him (Jesus) to be sin, who knew no sin, so that in Him (Jesus) we might become the righteousness of God" (2 Cor. 5:21).

This should cause us to pause and ask ourselves, "What kind of love is this?" Indeed, it is a love not of this world but an extravagant love of unfathomable depth. It is a sacrificial love that can give, and give, and give, even without receiving. Such love can only be understood through the assistance of God's Holy Spirit. Human reason cannot comprehend it. Human effort cannot apprehend it alone. This is why there are those who can't accept such a sacrifice. It does not conform to their preconceived image of God because "if God is a benevolent God, how could He allow such violence to be done to His Beloved Son?" And since it does not reconcile with the consistency of what they believe about God or their human understanding, well, they cannot accept it.

The real tragedy of such a conclusion is they do not understand the real nature of God. For when one sees Jesus, one sees God! Jesus, willingly surrendering to God's will was a joyful surrender because of His love for the Father, as the writer of Hebrews described it (Heb. 12:2). This is reconciliation: God's movement toward us and inviting us to respond in the same way Jesus did through His surrender to the Father's will. *He surrenders what He always knew, to become what He had never known. We surrender what we always knew, to become what we have never known, God's adopted sons!* What kind of love is that? Dear friend, the decision is yours as to how you will respond to the divine overture!

Truly, the epitomized power of the Cross is reconciliation. The purpose of its mission was actualized in Jesus giving Himself up to the Father in order to produce a family of "many sons" and fulfilling the eternal purpose of God. This is why Jesus is known as the Mediator of the New Covenant (Heb. 8:6), for He is the Reconciler on man's behalf. No wonder God would tell a prophet how He planned to construct the House He promised David, which would "be made sure forever before Me," *"Behold, I am the One who has laid as a foundation in Zion, a stone, a tested stone, a precious cornerstone, of a sure foundation: Whoever believes will not be in haste" (Isa. 28:16)*. Thus is the perfect Foundation for the eternal house of David!

Consummated by Holy Spirit

What a blueprint! What a building plan! And what a Foundation! Transcending thousands of years of human history and divergent cultures, God tells His-Story. Yes, His metanarrative! Father-God conceived the plan and constructed it through His Beloved Son, Jesus, the tested stone, a precious cornerstone, the sure foundation. But there is one more piece of the plan that remains to be unveiled.

Jesus knew the next day He would surrender Himself on the altar His Father had prepared for Him. So the night before, Jesus wanted to prepare His disciples for His departure by telling them, "I will not leave you as orphans!" (John 14:18). Jesus wanted to comfort and reassure them, He was not going to leave them alone. He was promising to them the rest of God's eternal plan that would be fulfilled.

They were still having a difficult time understanding. Jesus had already told them, "And I will ask the Father, and He will give you another Helper, to be with you forever, even the Spirit of Truth, Whom the world cannot receive, because it neither sees Him nor knows Him. You know Him, for He dwells with you and will be *in* you" (John 14:16–17). Since Jesus was with them, so was the Holy Spirit. However, before the Helper could dwell in them, Jesus would need to do His work of reconciliation at the Cross. After all, this was the final piece to the design of God's plan.

Still yet, it was difficult for the disciples to accept, as they remained sorrowful, so Jesus gave it one more shot by informing them, "I tell you the truth; it is to your advantage that I go away, for if I do not go away, the Helper will not come to you. But if I go, I will send Him to you" (John 16:7). Jesus again reassured them of His promise, just before He ascended to heaven: "He told them not to depart Jerusalem, but wait for the promise of the Father" (Acts 1:4).

So they waited in prayer, all 120 of them in the upper room. And then at the appointed time, not too early or too late, but just at the right time on the day of Pentecost, with the "sound like a mighty rushing wind" (Acts 2:2), the Holy Spirit arrived in glorious power and filled all of them (Acts 2:4).

The *House* God promised to build David was now beginning to be built. The Father kept His promise. Jesus kept His promise to send a Helper. His promise not to leave them alone was fulfilled. The Holy Spirit who "rushed" upon David and anointed him to be the next king of Israel was the same Holy Spirit Who rushed upon the 120 over 1000 years later. Make no mistake about it, God's Spirit made a "violent" entrance, for Scripture enunciates as much, "Like a mighty rushing wind!" There would be no doubt Who actually showed up!

Such was the beginning consummation of God's eternal plan. This event was the fulfillment of God's promise to build a house for David, which is the creation of God's new eternal family. It was also an encouraging affirmation, as the arrival of the Holy Spirit signified to the 120, Jesus had been enthroned at the right hand of the Father, just as it was predicted in the Old Testament (Ps.110:1).

This is the most beautiful, powerful, and perfect plan that could ever have been devised to recapture man's interest. And to again reconstitute an intimate relationship with his Creator for which man was originally destined. Only God could have designed such a plan. A plan Father-God *conceived, constructed* through His Son on a Cross, and *consummated* by His Holy Spirit. All three Persons of the Triune Godhead participated in this marvelous enterprise of reconciliation!

Most importantly, it was a plan designed to not only allow God to once again *dwell with* man but to *dwell in* him! Think about it, friend. God and Creator of the entire cosmos and His only begotten Son, Jesus, desired and purposed to live in you and me "before the foundation of the world."

This is the relationship we were destined to experience with the Triune Godhead from the very beginning until sin shattered shalom. Such is the community we are invited to participate and experience. This is the intimate union we are called to actualize daily in our lives with the Father, the Son, and the Holy Spirit, as Jesus promised the night before He went to the Cross: "If anyone loves Me, he will keep My word, and My Father will love him and we will come to him and make our home with him" (John 14:23). Yes, my friend, not only were we wired for worship and framed for fellowship with God, but we have been designed as a dwelling for the divine. What a plan, what a house, and, more importantly, what a Savior!

God's perfect plan for us gives us the central purpose for our worship. When one truly realizes what Father-God, through Jesus Christ, has provided us, it seems to make thank you so insufficient! In order to reconstitute man's original purpose, shalom—the way God intended life to be—we begin to discover how much God truly gave, deeply, of Himself. Yes, God made the first move. The next move is yours and mine.

So how do we express our gratitude to God? The answer is found in the exhortation of Paul's words: "That you may be filled with the knowledge of His will in all spiritual wisdom and understanding, so as *to walk in a manner worthy* of the Lord, *fully pleasing* to Him, bearing fruit in every good work and increasing in the knowledge of God" (Col. 1:9–10).

The most excellent way we can express our love to the Lord is to allow Him to continue to fashion and form us into the person He wants us to become every day of our lives. He wants us to become a "son" who is growing maturely in the character of Jesus. God knows this will be the greatest benefit to our lives, because like David, we too will develop a heart after God's own heart—the essence of which is found in living and doing what is good for God! The remaining chapters, therefore, will reveal how and what is involved in such an enterprise, as we endeavor to reach God's appointed and ultimate destination for our lives!

CHAPTER 11

The Design:
"Look and Livability"
of David's House!

For those who Honor Me, I will Honor!
—1 Samuel 2:30

We must now consider the "look" of this *House* God promised David. This includes the livability of God's House. Essentially, how should this *House* now look and live?

The *House* comprises the community of God's adopted sons and daughters. Our focus will not be the "outward appearance" but instead the interior, which applies to the priority emphasis of the human heart as God informed Samuel in His selection of David (2 Sam. 16:7). For it is the "inward décor" of the House that determines the overall livability, affecting the outward presentation of this extraordinary *House* that is God's dwelling!

Now we have come to a pivotal point in our journey with David as we consider the preeminent theme of this book. It is the foundation to cultivating a heart after God and is the major theme for both books of Samuel, stated early in the first book when the Lord speaks this eternal principle to the prophet: *"For those who honor Me, I will honor!" (2 Sam. 2:30).* This dynamic truth defines the décor of God's eternal family and is the design of what this house is to look like!

A Life to Honor God!

Therefore, it's imperative we understand the meaning of this eternal truth: "For those who honor Me, I will honor," as a practical reality in daily living. If I'm honest, years ago I was not familiar with the scriptural significance and application of such a principle. However, it came alive to me with new meaning and understanding when working in the state legislature in May of 2001. At the time, I was serving as the committee administrator for the House transportation committee and Bruce Starr, my boss and a good friend, was the chair of the committee.

Bruce wanted to do something for the state that had not been done for over ten years, which was to pass a transportation bill that would address congestion and improve roads. Due to various stakeholders (lobbyists) who represented various vested interests, it was difficult, if not impossible, to build a consensus that would ensure passage in the House and Senate as well as approval from the governor.

Nevertheless, despite all past failed attempts over the years, Bruce conceived and drafted a transportation package he was convinced most legislators, including the governor, could support. But there was one powerful lobbyist giving Bruce a hard time. He went to the airwaves disparaging Bruce's reputation. Unfortunately, this is "Politics 101"—when you disagree with an opponent, demonize them. Bruce is a solid Christian and family man, but he became very discouraged. After all, how many of us enjoy being publicly misrepresented, especially through the media?

On the drive to work one day, I was praying for Bruce and simply said to the Lord, "Lord, we need to help Bruce!" And immediately I heard the Lord speak these exact words: "If Bruce will honor Me, I will honor him with the transportation package!" I will never forget it. I was dumbfounded as I had no idea as to what those words meant. But I would soon discover the meaning of the Lord's instruction when I ran into Bruce on the way to my office.

Bruce gave me a two-page remonstrance for review. He planned to read it that morning on the floor of the House during legislative business. It was Bruce's counterattack to defend himself and discredit the lobbyist from the House floor. It's the worst nightmare for a high-powered lobbyist. Now I understood the meaning of the Lord's words that morning. Bruce would need to decide.

Bruce asked me for my opinion regarding his floor speech. I then shared what the Lord told me and what I thought it meant. His pause was brief. The political payback was quickly forgotten as we both went to legislative counsel to draft his legislation. Bruce would later become the celebrated "hero" of that legislative session, praised by his colleagues and political foes alike. Even the governor believed the historic legislation was a miracle!

God was true to His word, for the Lord did indeed honor Bruce with passage of the transportation package! We both knew, without a doubt, God had worked this miracle. But more importantly, it happened because Bruce made the right choice. That choice was predicated on one dynamic—to honor the Lord by doing His will! It is this preeminent truth that guides, defines, and describes the all-important look and lifestyle of the eternal house God promised to build for David!

We have now come to the centerpiece as to what it means to have a heart after God's heart. It was the very pulse of David that sustained and caused him to become the most effective ruler in Israel's history. So significant is this truth, a thousand years later, the apostle

Paul in one of his sermons, while referring to Israel's history, offered a summation of David's life regarding this central dynamic: "He (the Lord) raised up David to be their king, of whom he (the Lord) testified and said, 'I have found in David the son of Jesse, a man after My heart, *who will do all My will*" (Acts 13:22).

Paul underscores that it is the Lord Himself who provides the definitive and qualitative meaning to having a heart after His own heart. To honor God means to do what God wants. This is how God illustrated the meaning of David's love for Him. And that is how Paul described David's life. David did God's will. David learned there was nothing more important than doing what God wanted done. Indeed, it was David's pulse and passion to honor God with his life!

Then again, we must also not forget the other part to the eternal principle in honoring God. God also says He will honor those who honor Him! But what does that mean and what does that look like?

It simply means God will bless a person with his extraordinary goodness. The incident with Bruce illustrates the practical reality of such. God wanted to bless Bruce. God desired to honor Bruce. But before that could happen, God wanted Bruce to serve Him in the way that reflected the nature and character of God. God wanted Bruce to discover that when one is attacked unfairly and unjustifiably, there is a better way to respond—God's way. There is no honor for God when the Lord is misrepresented through personal attacks or withdrawal or both actions, which occur most often in our various relationships.

God wanted Bruce to be gracious, kind, and merciful, just as God is toward us. Bruce had to make a choice. Would he do it God's way, or would Bruce do it his way? Bruce chose to honor God rather than follow his natural inclination. Bruce chose to honor God by reflecting God's character and doing His will by *not* reading the remonstrance! Bruce made his decision, and then *God did what He likes to do, He blessed Bruce!*

Now we begin to gain a glimpse of the look and livability of this eternal house. There is also something more deeply significant God wants us to learn in honoring Him with our lives. We learn what this dynamic means as we consider the social interactions of the Father to the Son, the Son to the Father, and the Holy Spirit to both of them. So we must revisit that momentous occasion between God and David. For in that exchange between them, therein lies a deeper message, a message that informs us regarding how we can learn to honor God with our entire being!

A Reflection of the Trinity

As we visit again the text of 2 Samuel chapter 7, we recall David wants to honor God by building a Temple. But God declines by saying no to David's plans. Instead, God tells David what He plans to do for him. In this scene between God and David, we gain a glimpse of the Trinity. How? Everything God does flows from His character—selfless love. It is natural for God to want to honor David, for that is the ethos of the Trinity. David is a pre-figure of Jesus Christ, a partial reflection or a preview, if you will.

Now we want to consider these important questions: Did God characterize David as a "man after My own heart" for the simple purpose of commending him? Or did God have a greater purpose regarding such an inscription of David? We must keep in mind everything God does has a purpose, and God is teaching us invaluable truths regarding His nature. It is not mere coincidence God chose to make a covenant with David. His life is recorded so we may learn what is important to God relationally, because God desires for every one of us to have a heart after God's own heart. God's priority is for us to know Him, resulting in cultivating a heart like His own. This is what God wants us to learn from David's life, even in spite of his missteps.

David not only fulfilled God's purpose for his life, but also was a preview of someone greater, who would embody the quintessence of God's own heart!

Jesus is at the center of God's Promise to David, for He is the descendant of David's house. It would be through the "Root of David," the Anointed One of Israel, God would ultimately reveal and teach us how to have a heart after His own! It is for this very reason God chose to make His covenant with David as God wanted someone who would similarly reflect His appointed Savior for the world—His own Beloved Son!

With this background, we can now discover how a picture of the Trinity is revealed in the exchange between David and the Lord. David originates the idea to build God a house. It will be an extraordinary house, a house of worship, and one worthy of the Lord. God commended David by saying, "Whereas it was in your heart to build a house for My name, you did well that it was in your heart" (1 Kings 8:18). In other words God was delighted David had considered Him and that he wanted to honor God in this way.

So instead of David building a house for God, the Lord wanted to honor David by building him a house that will "endure forever." This is a picture of Trinitarian relationship in which One desires to honor the other. But what is most important to understand is the interactions of both are generated by their love for the other!

This scene is only a "limited window" into the relationships of the Trinity. It is not the Trinity. The exchange between David and the Lord is only a reflection that mirrors the Trinity. But we do gain a glimpse of the relationships we have been invited to participate through this scene. So in order to more fully realize what the *house* is designed to look like, we must take a closer look into the relationships of the Trinity—between the Father, His Beloved Son Jesus, and the Holy Spirit. For it is from their relationship we will discover the deeper meaning and understanding of how God's house is to look and live with those who are the community of God's sons and daughters. As we know, it is how we live (look) that will determine our effectiveness in bringing honor to God, the honor for which He is worthy!

Someone has said, "Try to explain the Trinity and you'll lose your mind; try to deny it and you'll lose your soul."[1] There will always be a mystery regarding the Triune Godhead. As much as we may try, we can never put the infinite God into a "box." Stephen Seamands, in his wonderful book *Ministry in the Image of God*, qualifies this truth in describing the Trinity:

> The Trinity reminds us that our highest most profound logical categories will never penetrate or fully comprehend, explain or contain, resolve reasoning powers and or remove the mystery of God. Our finest words about God are feeble, faltering attempts to express what can never fully or adequately be conveyed in any human language...So we need to be reminded that God can't be completely contained and imprisoned in any of our categories. He breaks out of all our carefully constructed boxes.[2]

Well said. There will always be an ineffable mystery regarding the Trinity. This does not mean God would not want us to understand the nature of their relationship to the other. It is one of the reasons God sent Jesus into our world, which was to reveal the character of the Father (John 14:9). Though limited, God was teaching, through His Son Jesus, the nature of their relationships. God would not have presented the emphases of the Trinity throughout His written Word unless He wanted to provide some insight into their relationship. It's my conviction, the primary purpose He has revealed the nature of the Triune Godhead is so their relationship will be reproduced in the ongoing life of the community of believers known as the Church. For this community, or *house*, if you will, is designed to "look" like them in the way we live and interact with one another. This is the meaning of the livability of the *house* God has originally intended.

The "Living Mark" of the House of God!

The "living mark" of this extraordinary community is to be distinguished by the greatest commandment Jesus gave to anyone who would decide to follow Him and become His student. On the night before Jesus would go to the Cross, He stated, "A new commandment I give to you, that you love one another, just as I have loved you, you also are to love one another. By this all people will know that you are My disciples, if you have love for one another" (John 13:34–35).

Today, more than ever, we live in a culture that attempts to tell people everywhere what God's love is like, all in the name of inclusion. Nothing could be further from the truth when it comes to the accuracy and authenticity of God's love. Based on His new commandment, Jesus has commissioned His Church to be the defining essence of God's love. The Church is to have the look and livability of God's love. God's House—the community of His "many sons"—is to be clearly identified by the same kind of love Jesus demonstrated and expressed to His Father with every precious and holy drop of His blood. This is the same love poured out into His disciples during the three years He spent investing in them for the ministry He called them to do. This love God demonstrated for us is to be the same love mirrored in our lives for each other. For it is the Trinitarian life of God that is to be reproduced in the *House* of God!

Such an expression of God's love for each other will mark us to the world as distinct and extraordinary. Why? Because Jesus was saying, such love, which is not of this world but of God, will mark you as Mine! Jesus effectively said as much, "By this my Father is glorified, that you bear much fruit and so prove to be my disciples" (John 15:8). It is through the mark of loving one another in the same way Jesus loved us, the world will then learn and discover the Savior, Jesus Christ.

The world is desperately looking for authentic love. Such love, expressed among true followers of Jesus, will attract others to God. This is what Jesus meant when He said, "You are the light of the world, like a city on a hill that cannot be hidden" (Matt. 5:14). It is not coincidental Jesus occasioned a similar metaphorical self-description, "I am the light of the world" (John 8:12). It is intentional by Jesus to make the same comparison with those who decide to be His followers since we are to be a mirror image or reflection of His Character. This marking, if you will, is what makes the House of God look and live like Christ. For a house well-lighted is a house that is warm and welcoming to all those who enter!

Now if we are realistic and pragmatic, we must honestly acknowledge Jesus has set the bar very high. Some might even believe such a standard is unlikely to be attained, if not impossible to actualize. However, if anyone has a fundamental understanding of God's word, they would realize Jesus would not have established this standard if it was not possible to authenticate such a lifestyle! This is true, particularly for anyone who is serious in honoring God with their life. After all, do you believe a city on a hill can be hidden from view?

We must begin with this premise. Even though it may seem impossible to love others as Christ loved us, it is possible, for all things are possible to those who will allow the Holy Spirit to do in us what we cannot do for ourselves. We must remember, it is always about the indispensable grace of God that enables one to do what is inconceivable or unimaginable according to the Holy Spirit who works in us (Eph. 3:20). How will we become such a "living mark" by exemplifying we are not our own but owned by Jesus?

The Mystery Unveiled in Part!

To answer such a question, we must begin with Trinitarian life. They are our model. More importantly, it is from them we will learn *how* we can truly honor the Lord in every aspect of our lives. We subsequently gain insights through the relational lens of the Trinity, from the Father to the Son. One of the great windows into the life of the Trinity is the longest prayer ever recorded in the life of Jesus found in chapter 17 of the gospel of John. (Please note the passage is referenced periodically in this chapter.)

Before Jesus began His public ministry and had performed one miracle or provided one teaching, He hears from His Father these words: "You are My Beloved Son; with You I am well pleased" (Luke 3:22). This announcement provides an insight into the Father's relationship with the Son. The word meaning for *pleased* is to have delight in or pleasure with someone. *Enjoy* also works. The Father was telling Jesus, by tenderly referring to Him as His, "Beloved, I very much enjoy You, for You!" Therefore, an overall translation would be: "This is My Beloved Son, for He is Mine and gives Me great joy!" In fact, God spoke this same truth prophetically through the prophet Isaiah over seven hundred years before the Incarnate birth of Jesus: "Behold My servant whom I uphold, My chosen, in whom My soul delights" (Isa. 42:1). This reveals the kind of relationship they both enjoyed with the other even before Jesus became flesh (John 1:14).

Their relationship is further qualified later in another New Testament passage recorded by a different writer: "For in Him (Jesus) the fullness of God was pleased to dwell" (Col. 1:19). Think about it.

This means it *pleased* the Father to give Himself—the full indwelling embodiment of His divine nature—to Jesus and remains as Father. God's divine nature is His wisdom, power, Spirit, and His glory.[4] It was *pleasing* to the Father to give Himself fully to His Son in such a way. In fact, this is further amplified in the prayer of Jesus as the past and present verb tenses of *gave, give,* and *given* are used fourteen times regarding all Jesus acknowledges the Father has given to Him.

The same is true of Jesus as this selfless love is also the driving impulse for Jesus to do what He was sent to do by the Father. Listen to His own words: "And He (the Father) who sent Me is with Me. He has not left Me alone, for I always do the things that are pleasing to Him" (John 8:29).

We must remember this kind of mutual relationship between the Father and the Son was an eternal one—it always existed. Jesus experienced such a life with the Father before the Father sent Jesus into our world for His eternal mission—the Cross. This is captured effectively by Dr. Seamands:

> John, the beloved disciple, conveys this intimacy at both the beginning and end of the prologue to his Gospel, "In the beginning was the Word," he says, "and the Word was with God" (John 1:1). The Greek preposition *pros* (translated "*with*") suggests both nearness and movement toward God. "Face to face with God" is a literal translation. From all eternity, says John, the Son (the Word) and the Father have existed not merely like side-by-side acquaintances, causally chatting with one another, but like face-to-face lovers, intently gazing into each other's eyes, engaged in joyful communion and intimate dialogue with each other.[5]

This magnifies the relationship of the Father toward Jesus as He expresses the pleasure and enjoyment Jesus gives Him. And Jesus conveys the same toward the Father as He describes the driving force and power that sustains Him to do what He does as the Son. Jesus lived for the Father and desired above everything to please Him in every aspect of His life. This *natural* desire to please the other is the ontology or character of the Trinity and is a natural outflow of their selfless love for the other.

God's Love Is Creative!

Since everything about God has to do with His character, love, it is important to define and describe the characteristic nature of God's love. As we know, Scripture tells us, "God is love" (1 John 4:16). This basically describes God's Person—He is not about love, He is love. The Greek word that characterizes such love is *agape*. This can be best explained and understood through the purpose of God's motivation in creating the entire cosmos as offered by the theologian Clark Pinnock:

> He creates in a way that is consistent with His loving nature as a relational being. Not narcissistic or self-enclosed, God is inwardly and outwardly self-communicating, a gracious being. Creation arises from loving relationships in the divine nature. God creates out of His own abundant interpersonal love—it is the expression of His generosity. No outside force compels it; no need drove the decision.[6]

We understand then, God did not create out of personal need but the generosity of His love. This is very important. God creates out of love, not need. His desire to create flows from His nature to share Himself, and this dynamic comprises what is known as "His generosity." Such an action commences from His being—a selfless love that by nature enjoys giving—since it is His preference. God is relational and is reflected in the interpersonal relationships of the Trinity, as further explained by Dr. Pinnock:

> God's nature is overflowing, and creation is a fruit of it. God loves relationships, not solitariness. He is not at all Aristotle's god, thinking only about thinking. God is pure ecstasy—each Person exists in loving relationship with the other Persons, and the joyous fellowship spills over into giving life to the creature. God does not hoard His interpersonal life but gives it away, and His Spirit fosters communion both with God and between creatures.[7]

Now we understand it is God's very nature to give, and He can give even without reciprocation. In so doing, He creates, to share His life, by giving Himself. It is this natural tendency of God to create that is also consonant with His act of redemption. God desires to redeem, rescue, recover, and restore humankind because it naturally fits His very disposition to create. Yes, He even creates through death. This is the power of His selfless love!

Hence, the Cross! The atonement Christ provides is forgiveness of sins, but as great a gift this is, there is much more God offers. Central to God's plan for mankind's redemption is the *re-creation* of a new human family the *House* God promised to build for David. The heart of the gospel message, at least it should be, is transformation.

God desires many sons—a new family to have the same character as Jesus, selfless love. This explains how the Cross was always in God's eternal view even before the creation of humankind. To give Himself through His Beloved Son, Jesus—to self-sacrifice in order to reconcile His highest of all creation, mankind, to Himself, was a natural fit for His character. And the same is true of Jesus, the personified, expressed selfless love and wisdom of God. Therefore, we can say, God's creative nature flows from His love, which is His natural preference of giving generously Himself!

God's Preference to Deference!

Now just as the Cross attracts us to the distinct nature of God's selfless love, it also gives us another window into the relationships of the Trinity. Someone has said, "Self-giving love is the Trinity's signature!"[8] The nature of each Person of the Godhead is to give fully to the other. This intimate exchange is the very pulse of the eternal Cross. It is as Seamands offers "glad submission" and "mutual deference"—qualities that characterize the relationships between the Father, Son, and Holy Spirit. He further elaborates regarding these traits of self-giving love: "Each divine person is always denying himself for the sake of the others and deferring to the others. The Father gives up His only son for the sake of the world (John 3:16, Rom. 8:32). The Son never seeks to do His own will but only the will of the Father (John 4:34, 5:19, 6:38). The Spirit, in turn, seeks only to glorify the Son and the Father (John 16:13–15)."[9]

The lifestyle and intimate interaction between the Triune Godhead is exemplified in the prayer of Jesus as He prays to the Father: "I glorified You on earth, having accomplished the work that You gave Me to do. And now, Father, glorify Me in Your presence with the glory that I had with You before the world existed"

(John 17:4–5). Jesus would not pray such a request if it was not what He had known, experienced, and enjoyed in relationship with His Father. This is the kind of love He knew from the Father, and it was also the same love He gave to His Father by doing the Father's will. This is how Jesus glorified the Father by doing His will. Their love enjoys and prefers giving honor to the other through what is known as mutual deference! They prefer to defer to the other!

But what is most important to discover from their relationships is the reason they love the way they do is because it is who they are. It is their nature to prefer the other by fully giving themselves to the other because that is selfless love. Everything they do is based on the ontology of such character.

The Righteous Love of God!

God's love is also a "right love" because He knows how to love rightly in all that He is and does! The apostle Paul says as much in regard to the primary theme in his letter to the church in Rome: "For I am not ashamed of the gospel, for it is the power of God for salvation to everyone who believes, to the Jew first and also to the Greek. For in it (the gospel) the *righteousness* of God is revealed from faith for faith" (Rom. 1:16–17).

Paul is referring to the "rightness of God's love" that is displayed on the Cross. This can also be viewed as the justice of God. It is natural for God's love to redeem and restore that which is broken and need of rescue, but not at the expense of compromising the integrity of His character. So God adjudicates sin justly by giving it the right sentence—death. This means God's judgment or rightness flows from His love. God, who is love, makes the right judgment by providing the right payment for sin—selfless love! Sin or self-centeredness does not belong in God's world because it is incompatible (does not fit) with the selfless love of the Triune Godhead. This is the meaning of the righteousness of God revealed in the gospel of Jesus Christ. God's love always makes right determinations because of His goodness. This is the *rightness* of God's love!

The Heart after God's Heart!

Another essential reason God sent Jesus is so we would have a model or reference point to learn from for our own lives. God wanted to give us One who would not only be the most effective teacher we could ever have in the grand classroom of life, but a living demonstration of the ultimate man after God's own heart! We must therefore realize this significant truth, since everything God does is good. Doing God's will is good for us to do and is inseparable from His love. It is important to understand God's will is a benevolent will, meaning God's will is always good and beneficial to those who want Him.

There is no greater illustrative model to learn this truth from than Jesus. On occasion Jesus offered those self-descriptive references that defined His Person and the purpose of His ministry: "Truly, truly, I say to you the Son can do nothing of His own accord, but only what He sees the Father doing. For whatever the Father does, that the Son does likewise. For the Father loves the Son and shows Him all that He himself is doing" (John 5:19–20). Jesus did the Father's will because it was His identity. It was natural for Jesus to live for the Father's will because that was how He loved the Father, selflessly. It was not hard work for Him but simply His natural bent.

Clearly, Jesus is giving us insight in which His ministry is really the Father's ministry at work through Him, for He is only doing what the Father wants Him to do, nothing more and nothing less. Jesus explained the reason the Father showed Him what to do is because of the Father's love for Him. And Jesus shows His love for the Father by doing His Father's work, according to the Father's direction. This was the work Jesus was committed to do as He declared to His Father in prayer: "I glorified You on earth, having accomplished the work that You gave Me to do" (John 17:4). Mutual deference!

Elsewhere, Jesus said, "My food is to do the will of Him who sent Me and to accomplish His work" (John 4:34). Jesus emphasized doing the Father's will not only sustained Him, but it gave Him pleasure in doing the Father's will and work. We again see this mutual desire to please the other in which the Father reveals to His Son what He wants Jesus to do and the Son desires to do it because Jesus wants only to please the Father. This is the selfless love of Jesus expressed in wanting only to honor His Father by doing the Father's will. Jesus knows the Father's will is always good! That includes the purpose of the Cross!

Another truth is Jesus would not have a ministry separate from the Father. This is what Jesus meant when He said, "The Son can do nothing of His own accord." And more importantly, Jesus wouldn't want it any other way. Jesus demonstrated His humility in being fully dependent upon the Father so that the Son would do only the Father's will, which was always beneficial.

Central to the ministry of Jesus by doing His Father's will was His identification. Jesus's identity as God's Son is inseparable from doing His Father's will. Doing the Father's will is Jesus's identification as His Son since He knows the Father is good. A "son" wants to do what the Father wants. Jesus stated as much when He said, "For I have come down from heaven, not to do My own will but the will of Him who sent Me" (John 6:38). Jesus revealed to us, doing God's will is inseparable from loving God. One reason Jesus did this was to give us a living example of what it means to love Father-God, as He so stated, "But I do as the Father has commanded me, so that the world may know that I love the Father" (John 14:31). Jesus's love for the Father drove Him with a divine passion to the Cross.

For Jesus, to honor His Father defined His life. This was and is like for Him as breathing. Doing the Father's will for Jesus was His sustenance, His food. Jesus only wanted to honor His Father in all that He did. A. W. Tozer stated as much in regarding this priority of Jesus: "He sought not His own honor, but the honor of God who sent Him."[10]

This passion of Jesus is His desire for us also. On the night before He went to the Cross, He said, "If you love Me, you will keep My commandments" (John 14:15). Jesus underscored, doing God's will is inseparable from our love for Him. Just as this is the identity of Jesus's relationship to the Father, it must be our identity to Him as well. To do the will of the Father, we must want the same thing the Father wants. This is what it means to have a heart after God's own heart. When we want what the Father desires, we will do what He wants us to do. This is the expressed meaning of loving God "with all our heart, with all our soul, with all our mind, and with all our strength" (Mark 12:30). And this is what God desires to produce in all our lives: the same heart, with the same desire to do only the Father's will, as Jesus personified. This what it means to honor God with our life. And such is the pursuit of God's own heart!

Honoring the Father was the priority of Jesus, and it is the ontology of the Trinity. Jesus knew this reality because it was the life He always knew before He came into our world: "If I honor Myself, My honor is nothing; it is My Father that honors Me" (John 8:54). Throughout His ministry, Jesus demonstrated His love for the Father as inseparable from doing the Father's will.

The Unity of God's Love!

This dynamic of the inseparability of loving God and doing His will is the meaningfulness of Trinitarian Oneness. Jesus referred to this dynamic in His prayer: "That they may be one, even as we are one" (John 17:11). The Oneness of the Trinity is their will being consonant with the other. The Father wants to honor the Son, and the Son wants to honor the Father. And the Holy Spirit wants to honor both. They want the same for the other. They have the same heart. There is no breach in such correspondence because they all love the same selflessly. Therefore, their will is the same for each other because their love is of the same character. Each prefers to give to the other. This is the *unity* of God's love that causes the desire to honor the other!

Now this same relational unity of God is what Jesus prayed would be reproduced in us. Listen to His words: "That they may all be one, just as You, Father are in Me, and I in You, that they also may be in us so that the world may believe that You have sent Me. The glory that You have given Me I have given to them, that they may be one even as we are one. I in them and You in Me, that they may become perfectly one, so that the world may know that You sent Me and have loved them even as You loved Me" (John 17:21–23).

Let's look at this reality for a moment. Jesus prayed that we would be one in the same way the Father, Son, and Holy Spirit are one. This is a vital demonstration of God's love as the psalmist under-scores, "Behold, how good and pleasant it is when the brothers dwell in unity!" (Ps. 133:1). This is how we are to live with one another. This is how the house is to look! So how are we currently doing in living out Jesus's petition? Unfortunately, not very well!

We Miss the Mark...Badly!

It is interesting to realize there is a direct correlation with the unity Jesus prayed and the new commandment Jesus gave us. Jesus says in His prayer, such unity and the way we love each other serve as a witness to the world and that we would be known as Jesus's students! The unity of the Godhead is the same love and unity we are to have for each other in the Body of Christ—selfless love. Is that the look and livability of God's house today? Tragically, we must be honest and concede, we fall short!

We must take a brief moment and have a reality check, as painful as it is. There seems to be a great disconnect among the Body of Christ. At the risk of appearing disrespectful to some and disdainful to others, it is certainly not my intention. However, it is compelling to make some pointed statements. I believe some issues must be acknowledged because of the representation of the character of God and His love for His Church is at stake. After all, the world has been watching, and continues to observe.

Before I delineate some of the symptoms that fracture us, let me set up the context with these important words from one of Paul's letters to a group of New Testament believers:

> *Walk in a manner worthy of the calling to which you have been called, with all humility and gentleness, with patience, bearing with one another in love, eager to maintain the unity of the Spirit in the bond of peace. There is one body and one Spirit—just as you were called to the one hope that belongs to your call—one Lord, one faith, one baptism, one God and Father of all, who is over all and through all and in all...Let no corrupting talk come out of your mouths, but only such as is*

good for building up, as fits the occasion, that it may give grace to hear. And do not grieve the Holy Spirit of God. (Eph. 4:1–6, 29–30)

Paul is emphasizing we should walk with the Lord in a manner that corresponds accurately with His life by being humble, gentle, and with patience, bearing with one another in love—agape. The result of such a *walk* is one that will maintain the unity of the Spirit. So again, we see a definite correlation between unity of the Spirit and the oneness of God's love.

We also see a severe warning: "Do not grieve the Holy Spirit of God!" We know to grieve someone means to cause sorrow. But in this context, it also means to "give pain to or to pain" the Holy Spirit.[11] This should be a sobering consideration in our walk with the Lord, realizing we can cause His Spirit pain, injury, and sorrow with certain behaviors and attitudes. This is a significant matter that begs serious examination for all who consider themselves to be followers of Jesus. It is evident we can grieve the Holy Spirit by the way and manner we speak regarding fellow believers. One way we do this is by denigrating the ministry of others. Paul qualifies corrupt and corrosive speech as bitter, critical, slander, gossip, malice, and contemptuous communication—communication that obviously does not build up the Body of Christ.

There are two main reasons this grieves the Holy Spirit. First, such communication is dissonant to God's love. It does not express God's love. Secondly, corrupt or corrosive speech causes deep injury by tearing the Body of Christ. This grieves the Holy Spirit because it runs counter to the Spirit's work of building-up Christ's Body. We must not forget, as Paul enunciates in the same letter to the Ephesians, there is only "one body, one Spirit, one Lord, one faith, one baptism, one God and Father of all" (Eph. 4:4–5).

Now it is very well possible the Holy Spirit is grieved with the Church-at-large in America. The issue cannot be avoided since divisiveness causes its anemic spiritual condition with the outcome of being marginalized by the culture. The breadth and scope of dissension is unfathomable. Only the Lord knows the depth of such corrupt speech that occurs throughout the Body of Christ. But one can gain insight with only a brief glimpse of the internet. People are denigrating and discrediting other Christian leaders, purportedly under the guise of exposing false teachers. It is disturbing and should grieve anyone who professes Christ because it is antithetical to the character of the Trinity.

It's been my unfortunate experience to observe prominent ministers using an entire service to denigrate by name a fellow minister. The motives are alleged to be the exposing of false teaching, doctrinal error, greed, financial impropriety, and hypocrisy. Such pseudo-ministries consider themselves to be self-appointed caretakers of God's House. Some may be sincere but are seriously and egregiously misguided. They should be avoided.

I've been grieved when inadvertently stumbling upon corrosive hostility from one minister to another. The display of virulent toxicity was effectively profane, coming from those who profess Christ. Webster's dictionary defines *profane* as "to treat (a holy place or object) with great disrespect."[12] Not only is it disrespectful, but it devalues a brother in Christ. It saddens me deeply for those devalued and for those tearing down. Please understand it is not from a condescending perspective I express this position, but rather from a burdened wound satiated in grief. If such conduct grieves the Holy Spirit based on the word of God, then should we not be able to identify with His grief?

Tragically, there are those who rationalize such conduct in the name of truth while even going to the extent of demonizing fellow believers in Christ. This does violence to the unity of the Body of

Christ and grieves the Holy Spirit because this hostile behavior runs counter to being an effective witness for Christ to an unbelieving world. It makes the Church live impotently and looking understandably ineffective. The only distinctive living mark is contradiction.

A Fresh Revelation of God's Love

There are many factors contributing to this severe spiritual malady, but most of it can be attributed to *not* walking in humility, gentleness, patience—all of which flows from agape. Sadly, I sense, there will remain those unconvinced to change their paradigm as the purported personal caretaker of God's Church, continuing business as usual. However, for those who take seriously the passion of cultivating a heart after God's heart, let me offer some suggestions consonant with the ethos of the Triune Godhead:

- Realize God is quite able to take care of those who perpetrate false doctrine—It is His Church, His Body.
- Recognize the fundamental tenets of our faith to be the priority emphasized by Paul in this scriptural passage of Ephesians that we can focus and agree.
- Acknowledge the Holy Spirit is doing a "new work" through the erosion of denominational barriers that have divided the Body of Christ and have made the church irrelevant to contemporary culture.
- When encountering egregious doctrinal error, go to the individual in private, speaking the truth in love.
- Above all, do not name people publicly, instead give deference by treating the person the way you would want to be treated—that's humility.

- Make it a preeminent priority to honor God in every aspect of your life, including your speech by building up, not by tearing apart the Body of Christ.
- Pray much more for the individual(s) than criticize, as well for a heart of brokenness, so God can continue to "form Christ" within the person, as well as yourself (Gal. 4:19).
- Go to the Lord in prayer with an open heart and mind, asking Him if you have grieved His Spirit—He will always answer such a request.

Only a "personal disconnect" with Christ would cause such division among His body. This divisiveness and its destructive power compromises the testimony of Jesus and inflicts deep injury to the Body of Christ. Such injurious conduct to a brother is an injury to Christ. We must see beyond ourselves, realizing the repercussions of how we treat one another is a deep spiritual principle that not only reflects on the Trinity but affects the Trinity. Until we understand more deeply the Oneness of the Trinity, which is the unity of God's love and will, we cannot fathom the depth of injury to the individual and, more importantly, to Christ Himself.

We must understand, if the Holy Spirit is grieved, so is Jesus. And if Jesus is grieved, so is the Father. It is imperative we identify with their grief through intercessory prayer. The Holy Spirit remains committed to building the House of God to "look and live" as the Trinity. This distinct task is assigned to Him by Jesus. But when we refuse to cooperate with His holy work, He is grieved. And if He is grieved, we should be also, that is, if we truly want to cultivate a heart after God's heart. We must stop for a moment and seek a new fresh revelation of the Trinitarian Oneness they enjoy so their life may be reproduced in the Body of Christ, just as Jesus prayed.

Dr. Dallas Willard provides for us the mind-set he had developed in his relationship to Christ, and I know it would help each of us immensely if we would assimilate such an attitude in our interactions with fellow Christians:

> Among those who live as Jesus's apprentices there are no relationships that omit the presence and actions of Jesus. We never go "one on one"…all relationships are mediated through Him. I never think simply of what I am going to do with you, to you, or for you. I think of what we, Jesus and I, are going to do with you, to you, and for you. Likewise, I never think of what you are going to do with me, to me, and for me, but of what will be done by you and Jesus with me, to me, and for me.[13]

It is evident Dr. Willard gained an understanding of Trinitarian community and their selfless love for each other as he realized we are invited to participate in their "circle of love." This is captured in the invitation by Jesus to each of us: "If anyone loves Me, he will keep My word, and My Father will love him, and we will come to him and make our home with him" (John 14:23). With Christ dwelling in us, we never go it alone. Therefore, we cannot afford to act cavalier or recklessly with someone who professes a commitment to Jesus Christ. It is only the lack of humility one could treat another with such disregard and devaluation.

We must recognize the greater problem is a lack of understanding and knowing the love of Christ. There are many who profess Christ but don't understand and know, truly know, the love of God. It is not an isolated circumstance, evidenced by Paul's prayer for a new church he had planted in Ephesus: *"That Christ may dwell in your hearts through faith—that you being rooted and grounded in love, may have strength to comprehend with all the saints what is the breadth and length and height and depth, and to know the love of Christ that surpasses knowledge, that you may be filled with all the fullness of God" (Eph. 3:17–19).*

Paul's prayer indicates the people had experienced God's love in a real way, having been "grounded in love." However, he continues asking God to reveal His love to them in a deeper way so that they may comprehend better the love of God by "knowing" (intimately experiencing) the reality of Christ's love, which surpasses their human ability and limitations. This should be the daily prayer of every believer. That we will grow in our love for God.

Dr. Seamands shares the story of a young woman who had a burden for India. While on a group ministry trip to the nation with Dr. Seamands, the young seminary student witnessed the severe poverty and squalor, especially for the children, in the urban areas. The woman was overwhelmed by the spiritual darkness she encountered. Knowing her human limitations, she desperately cried out to God, "Lord, give me Your heart for India." Then one day while praying she heard the Lord say to her, "How can I give you My heart for India, when you don't even know My heart for you?"[14] Later, the young missionary did indeed receive a fresh revelation of God's love for her.

We need to understand this preeminent truth. We will not be able to love one another in the same way Jesus loves us until we come into an experiential knowledge of God's love. We must experience His love more deeply. This is where everything starts for the Christian journey. It cannot be mere extrinsic knowledge. It must be an intimate, interactive knowledge of God's love. This is what Jesus prayed for in the very last words of His prayer prior to going to the Cross: "I made known to them Your name, and I will continue to make it known, that the love with which You have loved Me may be *in* them, and I in them" (John 17:26). We can only fulfill Jesus's commandment by allowing God's love to dwell in our hearts, not only in the inauguration of our salvation experience but through a continual abiding in Christ, which will allow His love to grow in our lives.

Think about it, my friend. Jesus prayed the same love the Father has for Him would also be *in* us. Isn't that amazing? That we can be loved by God in the same way He loves Jesus, well, it should overwhelm us with gratitude and worship. This should become our conscious awareness every day as students of Christ. This truth is beyond human words. When this becomes our experiential reality, we will then know how to truly honor God in every aspect of our lives, including how we love one another. Such will be the outcome in which our want will then become conformed to the same will as the Trinity. Then, and only then, will we know the unity or Oneness of the Trinity. For this is the "look and livability" of the house God promised to build for David—"the House that will be made sure forever before Him!"

By the way, remember Bruce? The story continues as he later became appointed to a prominent national position, the National Council of State Legislators, primarily due to his success with the transportation legislation in his state. Just as God promised that day, "I will honor Bruce, if He will honor Me," the Lord continues to bless Bruce! God is just like that.

God enjoys giving His life, and all He enjoys, God gives to others. God desires to honor those who honor Him. Such is the look and livability of God's house, a community like the Trinity, by preferring only to do God's will. This can and will only happen when we learn to want the same thing God wants. It will be to our benefit. We will never do wrong to give Him such honor in our lives! Look what happened to David!

To the degree this reality becomes a part of our lives is determined largely by those attending to the care of God's house. Like David, such caretakers of God's house, need to have a heart after God. God has intended to use David's narrative to instruct the shepherds entrusted with the care of His House: "And I will give you shepherds after my own heart" (Jer. 3:15). Let's now discover the requirements for such a sacred responsibility.

The Passionate Care of David's House!

Part I: The Heart of Humility

And I will give you shepherds after My own heart, who
will feed you with knowledge and understanding.
—*Jeremiah 3:15*

I have never forgotten that meeting with Mark. It was over twenty years ago, after ministering in a large church. He was a young associate pastor who invited me to have breakfast with him the next day. It was unusual because typically such an invitation would come from the senior pastor. However, the lead pastor had another commitment, so I accepted.

When we met I could sense Mark was distressed. He began to pour out his heart, sharing he was on the threshold of leaving the ministry, perhaps for good. He was searching for answers. He soon offered what he felt was the heart of the problem: "John, when I first was hired, the pastor informed me, 'I've hired you to do a job. I'm not into relationships. I just want you to fulfill your responsibilities, and do your job!' That was it. It was all he said. I've spent five years navigating the best I know how. I feel so alone, and now I'm considering getting out of the ministry!"

I must admit, my initial response was somewhat facetious, as I offered, "Isn't that what Jesus said, Mark? Go into all the nations and make hirelings!" However, I tried to encourage him. But when I left that meeting, I was very burdened, not only for Mark but for God's House. Somehow, I knew this was not an isolated incident in the Body of Christ. Let me explain.

Years later, in graduate school, I was given an assignment to interview two lead pastors with a questionnaire prepared by the professor. The two churches I selected had similar demographics. They had about a thousand in attendance. One was in an urban environment, and the other was a rural setting. There were two significant questions of which the answers from both pastors were memorable. One question was "How do you train your teachers?" Independent of the other, both replied, "Well, we don't do a very good job in that area!" The other question was "How do you train leaders in your church?" Again, both pastors offered, "We don't do very well. We need to work on improving in that area also!"

Like Mark's church, these two churches had large staffs. But after those interviews, I couldn't help but wonder, how many pastors on staffs could identify with Mark? How many were left alone, merely hired to do a job, and navigating the best they could with the ultimate objective of expanding church growth? Were they being taught the dynamics of ministry regarding discipleship? More importantly, how many leave the ministry due to this lack of mentoring?

There's plenty of data that supports the severity of this spiritual deficiency. One such survey of 1,050 pastors ten years ago conducted by Dr. Richard J. Krejcir and sponsored by the well-known Francis A. Schaeffer Institute revealed an ominous statistic: "Eighty-one percent of the pastors said there was no regular discipleship program or effective effort of mentoring their people or teaching them to deepen their Christian formation at their church."[1]

Later, I heard Mark left the ministry within a year following our meeting. Tragically, there are many causalities much like him. Numbers today vary regarding the "exodus" of ministers from pastoral ministry, and reasons are variant. However, in my view, the single most vital cause can be attributed to the greatest disaster throughout the history of the Church. It is God's shepherds neglecting or ignoring the directive of Jesus: "Go *make disciples*…teaching them to observe all that I have commanded you" (Matt. 28:19–20).

Pastors can only reproduce in their flock what they know or don't know. The survey as well as my interview indicate most church leaders do not know how to mentor or produce "students" of Jesus. Or perhaps apparently convinced, we can be arbitrary and negligent in doing what Jesus wants done without incurring severe and deep spiritual repercussions reflected in the high pastoral burnout.

Jesus has always wanted followers who would be His students. The deficiency or dysfunction of discipleship in the Body of Christ can be remedied, if we would only learn from David's life as well as the "template" Jesus provided through His life and ministry. In fact, Father-God gave the qualifications for those who would be entrusted to the care of His flock. In a promise God made to Israel through the prophet Jeremiah and with the backdrop of divine judgment, the Lord spoke these words, *"And I will give you shepherds after my own heart, who will feed you with knowledge and understanding" (Jer. 3:15).* Again, the characterization similar to David shows up but now applies to shepherds of God's flock. This promise applies to our contemporary pastor of today who is responsible for the spiritual well-being of God's flock.

Now we must consider some primary questions regarding the theme of this chapter: What does it mean to be a shepherd after God's own heart? What does that look like? Does it parallel David's life as a king or shepherd of Israel? What does it mean for such shepherds to feed God's flock with knowledge and understanding? What kind of knowledge is that to be? Answers to such questions will provide a clear and accurate portrait of what it means for those who are entrusted with the awesome privilege and passionate care of God's House. (Please note, since issues of the heart are significant, the aspect regarding "knowledge" is in Part 2, the next chapter.)

An important scriptural passage written by Peter is a good place to find answers to these questions, as it describes how God wants His House cared for by His shepherds:

> *Shepherd the flock of God that is among you, exercising oversight, not under compulsion, but willingly, as God would have you; not shameful gain, but eagerly; not domineering over those in your charge, but being examples to the flock...Clothe yourselves, all of you, with humility toward one another, for God opposes the proud but gives grace to the humble. Humble yourselves, therefore, under the mighty hand of God so that at the proper time He may exalt you. (1 Pet. 5:2–3, 5–6)*

Peter emphasizes the shepherd should care for God's flock with the right motives and attitude. The shepherd should serve with a willing and glad heart, knowing it is a privilege to serve God's people. Peter further qualifies, to serve God's people, it must not be for personal gain, power, or position. In effect, God's House should not be cared for with hubris or a demanding attitude, leaving people buried under guilt, condemnation, and hyperbole. But rather, God's flock should be nurtured by a shepherd, as Peter instructs, who is "clothed with humility!" This is the priority of God's heart in caring for His people. To be effective, it must be done with the right heart, a heart of humility. Just as humility was foundational to David's success as a king of Israel, it is tantamount to the effectiveness of any pastor who desires to serve God as a shepherd of His people. Why? Because the antithesis of love is pride, and pride is the root cause for self-navigation.

The subject of humility is one many Christians believe they understand and know the meaning. Yet I think there is much to learn regarding this Godly attribute. You see, humility is the key to God's own heart because it is an attribute of the Trinity, as emphasized in the previous chapter. God is humble! That may be a shock to some because we are readily able to believe Jesus is humble, but the Father? Let's remember Jesus said, "Whoever has seen Me has seen the Father (John14:9)." They are One and the same when it comes to their character! Consider the attributes of the Holy Spirit, emphasized in Galatians chapter 5, verses 22–23. The eighth attribute listed is gentleness, and the Greek word *prautes* is associated with humility.[3] Also, in describing the characteristic quality of God's love (agape), Scripture says, "Love is not arrogant" (1 Cor. 13:4). God's love is humble. A shepherd of God should have the same heart!

Now if humility is so important to Father-God and David's success was determined primarily by this attribute, then it is incumbent upon us as followers of Christ, and particularly all leaders of God's House, to learn its definitive meaning and to cultivate this attribute. Humility is what constitutes a shepherd having a heart after God's own heart and will determine which kind of "knowledge and understanding" a shepherd will transmit to God's people! People everywhere are yearning and looking for the reality of God. It is by God's design He planned for people to find and know Him through the shepherds He has entrusted to care for His House. God desires shepherds after His own heart who will care for His flock with the right attitude as well as right motives according to Peter's instruction.

Traits of Humility

Another significant scriptural passage constitutes a worthwhile definition and living application of humility. Paul, in writing to the Philippian church, was instructing them to have "the same mind as Jesus." He described how Jesus had a heart of humility by the way He lived as a human being and then challenged his readers to think, act, and live with the same heart as Jesus toward one another. So let's consider the descriptive traits that construct a clear definition of humility in this passage:

> *Do nothing from selfish ambition or conceit, but in humility count others more significant than yourselves. Let each of you look not only to his own interests, but also to the interests of others. Have this mind among yourselves, which is yours in Christ Jesus, who, though He was in the form of God, did not count equality with God a thing to be grasped, but made Himself nothing, by taking the form of a servant, being born in the likeness of men. And being found in human form, He humbled Himself by becoming obedient to the point of death, even death on a cross. (Phil. 2:3–8)*

Paul clearly enunciates, Jesus Christ is not only the quintessential model of humility but He is the embodiment of humility. Such is the first trait of humility:

1) A shepherd does nothing from selfish ambition or arrogance!

A shepherd after God's heart is one who is Christ-centered rather than self-centered. This person is more interested in God's interests. But what does that look like?

A good illustration is the exchange that ensued between Peter and Jesus right after Peter hit his "grand slam," in response to Jesus's inquiry, "Who do you say I am?" Peter replied, "You are the Christ, the Son of the living God" (Matt. 16:15–16). As soon as that conversation was completed, Jesus began explaining His imminent journey to Jerusalem and His ultimate mission of the Cross. But Peter would have none of it, so much so, Scripture tells us, "He took Jesus aside and rebuked Jesus, saying, 'Far be it from you, Lord!'" (Matt. 16:22).

Jesus was pleased with Peter's accurate identification of Him as God's Son, the long-awaited Messiah. Then in a complete pivot, Peter is found correcting the Son of God because he thinks Jesus needs help in truly understanding His mission and destiny! Perhaps Jesus's commendation of Peter was too much for him to handle: "For flesh and blood has not revealed this to you, but My Father who is in heaven" (Matt. 16:17). Notwithstanding Peter's intent, Jesus firmly responds to Peter, "Get behind Me, Satan! You are a hindrance to Me. For you are not setting your mind on the things of God, but on the things of man" (Matt. 16:23).

Wow! How would you like to be described as one associated with Satan? And if that was not enough, to be told by Jesus, "You are a hindrance to Me!" Talk about wanting to find the nearest rock to hide under! However, Jesus does not give up on Peter but desires for him to learn from his serious misstep by emphasizing the importance of becoming "God-centered" rather than remaining "man-centered"! We know Peter learned his lesson well, as he later instructs shepherds to cultivate a heart of humility by becoming interested in the interests of God!

Peter also draws a correlation between arrogance and selfish ambition. He refers to "avoid shameful gain." This is an aspect of humility that cannot be neglected if one wants a heart after God's own heart. "Shameful gain" is about greed, and greed is about personal gain. Humility does not afford extravagance because the two are incompatible. Extravagance is nothing more than selfish indulgence, which is antithetical to humility.

A leader who is truly humble is interested in God's will and purpose in every ministry endeavor. Just as Jesus taught Peter, if a pastor is going to have a heart after God's own heart, it is essential to be interested in the things of God. It was the key to David's effective reign, and ultimately, the personal intimate relationship he developed with the Lord.

The second and "huge" characteristic that marks humility:

2) You consider others more significant than yourself!

This characteristic is like Trinitarian life in which they prefer to defer to the other. There are four qualities expressed in this trait of humility. The first is cultivating a heart to serve others: "Let each of you look not only to his own interests, but also to the interests of others" (v. 4). It does not mean you do not consider your personal interests and responsibilities, such as your family, job, and other obligations. And of course, this does not merely apply to shepherds, but everyone who wants to be a student and servant of Christ.

The genesis of a true servant is becoming more concerned with the interests of God first. This is very important. We are called to serve God and His agenda, not the reverse. Too often in ministry, and may be an unintended consequence, is the tendency to rubber stamp God's name on our agendas with the effect of God serving my interests rather than me serving God. We must remember always, God initiates the calling. Therefore, it is His ministry and not our own. That is the mind-set of a servant. This priority will then flow naturally the desire to serve the interests and well-being of others. It would be impossible to begin to engender "others more significant" than yourself without this God-centered priority being intact.

Jesus desired to teach the disciples this truth with an object-lesson by washing their feet at the "last meal" the night before He died.

However, one of them resisted; and it was not Judas, but Peter, who challenged the Lord for doing such a menial task—a common practice exercised by the servant of the house—when he asked, "Lord, do you wash my feet?" Jesus replied, "What I am doing you do not understand now, but afterward you will understand." Peter said to Him, "You shall not wash my feet." Then Jesus said, "If I do not wash you, you have no share with me" (John 13:6–8).

What was Jesus trying to teach His disciples, or us for that matter, by washing dirty feet? And why did Peter resist? Peter resisted because he knew Jesus was the Son of God and this was not something Jesus should be doing. Peter thought he was being respectful and considerate of Jesus. But Jesus tried to persuade him gently by reassuring him, "You don't understand now, but later you will!" However, Peter persisted in resisting, provoking a strong rebuke from Jesus, "If you don't let me do this, you have no part of me!"

Jesus was revealing to His disciples, and particularly Peter, the lifelike nature within the Triune Godhead: mutual deference. They enjoy deferring to the other because the Father, the Son, and the Holy Spirit are humble. They prefer to defer! Hence, Jesus's sharp rebuke. Peter could not participate in their union of love if he did not want to identify with their "heart of humility."

Humility impels a heart to willingly serve and to give self to others. Humility gladly submits to others, even if such submission seems to be unfair or unjust. Humility creates the desire to serve and to serve others with a joyful heart. Jesus stated as much: "No one takes it from Me, but I lay it down of My own accord. I have authority to lay it down, and I have authority to take it up again. This charge I have received from My Father" (John 10:18). Jesus willingly gave His life. It was His choice, and He did it with humility and joy (Heb. 12:2).

The second trait of this aspect of humility has everything to do with one's worldview. A worldview basically involves how one views and values life. Paul states how we should value every human being: "From now on, therefore, we regard no one according to the flesh," or another translation offers, "We regard no one from a worldly point of view" (2 Cor. 5:16, NIV). This means we do not merely see people according to the standards or values of the world. Such a standard is limited, shallow, and superficial. Instead, God wants us to see people as He sees each person. He wants us to learn to value people in the same way He does. To do this, we are going to have to experience a reorientation of how we view people in the daily interactions of our lives.

Remember what God told Samuel when the prophet was considering David's oldest brother to be king: "Do not look on his appearance or on the height of his stature, because I have rejected him. For the Lord sees not as man sees: man, looks on the outward appearance, but the Lord looks on the heart" (1 Sam. 16:7). We are not able to know what is in a person's heart, so why should we make a quick and premature judgment?

How different would the church culture be if we would view every person the way God does? If we could see the intrinsic worth of each individual as priceless and meaningful with purpose. It would not only change how we interact with others but would also transform how each person views their own life. We would avoid making premature or harsh judgments in dismissing people from our lives based on superficial shortcomings, such as their appearance and stature. Perhaps it would keep us from measuring and accepting people based on what they could do to benefit our lives?

We've all been guilty of considering people from such a worldly view. Typically, we tend to evaluate people or size one another up, determining if one is qualified for our attention or time investment. However, the good news is we don't have to live with such a shallow view of people. We can change not only our thinking, but our hearts toward people, but we must allow God's Word to instruct and transform us.

Over ten years ago, before I did volunteer work at a local homeless shelter, the Lord began to teach me this principle. One warm spring day, after a haircut, I walked onto the downtown sidewalk and encountered a homeless man asking a young couple for money. I could barely get around them to "escape" into my vehicle, which I did, while hearing myself say, "Praise the Lord!" A short distance later I found myself at a stoplight, and who would be walking slowly in the crosswalk directly in front of my car? Yes, the elderly, homeless man who appeared to be in his seventies and possessing nothing but a child-size backpack. Suddenly, I heard that still, small voice say to me, "You know, John, I made him in My image and died for him too!" Immediately, with tears stinging my eyes, I asked the Lord to forgive me, before turning my vehicle around to place a gift in the man's leather-worn hand.

The incident led me to change how I viewed people. The purpose in sharing this real-life moment is to underscore that our view of people must not simply be an intellectual consent. That is a good start. But what is needed is actualizing God's truth, combined with prayer. I assure you, if you will simply ask the Lord to see people through the "lens" of His Holy Spirit, it is a prayer He will answer. Daily the Lord will remind you of this priority as you encounter people from different walks of life. This dynamic would not be advocated in Scripture if this attitude was not possible to realize in our lives. It is the only way we can cultivate a servant's heart, and the means by which one will learn to "count" others more significant than oneself!

A third quality is being teachable. If you are going to be a student of Jesus, one must be teachable—hungry to learn more from Jesus, from others in leadership, as well as those members in the Body of Christ. The Lord has been gracious to me in providing a foundational knowledge and understanding of His Word. However, I persist in wanting to learn and grow in my knowledge of the Lord. I am constantly learning from other ministers because I consider myself to be a student of Jesus first and foremost.

Becoming a mentor to others is the fourth quality of this humility trait. By engaging and becoming involved in the lives of others on a personal level, you learn how to minister more effectively on a collective level. Nowhere can this trait become enlivened more than when a pastor or a fellow Christian takes the time to invest in the life of another, particularly those new in their journey with Christ. To actualize this priority as leaders in a very practical way requires an investment of one's time. The very essence of discipleship or mentoring is investing your life into the lives of others in a personal way. This is what Mark and many others like him have desired.

As we know, the term *disciple* is a biblical word used during ancient times and the Greek meaning is to be a "student or learner."[2] Jesus invited anyone who wanted to follow Him to become His student. It was His great directive to His shepherds to make this happen: "Go and make disciples of all nations," which includes all ethnicities. Tragically, it has been the greatest disaster in Church history. Listen to this ominous description by Dallas Willard, regarding this spiritual malady:

> Non-discipleship is the elephant in the church. It is not the much discussed moral failures, financial abuses, or the amazing general similarity between Christians and non-Christians... The division of professing Christians into those for whom it is a matter of whole-life devotion to God and those who maintain a consumer, or client, relationship to the church has now been an accepted reality for over 1500 years.[4]

Normally, a pastor offers to their people what they know, as well as what they don't know. If one has never been discipled, then the pastor will most likely reproduce such lack of knowledge. This is evidenced by the Schaeffer Institute survey indicating many pastors do not know how to mentor. The lack of knowledge is not a viable option however. It is Jesus's directive "to make disciples." There are thousands and thousands of Marks who have left the ministry disillusioned and disheartened. It is imperative we listen to the Holy Spirit, who is recovering this dynamic function in the Body of Christ today. After all, it is the preeminent invitation Jesus offers to anyone who would want to follow Him (Matt. 16:24–26). This subject is discussed in more detail in chapter 13 as to how this dynamic should be practically walked out.

Before we move on, please consider these important aspects regarding this biblical dynamic. To truly be a shepherd after God's own heart, a pastor should be mentoring at least one individual, if not several during any given week. It would only take a couple of hours each week, and such an investment is priceless. This applies to any pastor of any size church. A thirty-minute corporate teaching on Sunday morning is not going to suffice. Can you imagine Jesus doing one day a week for three years with His disciples?

My friend, please hear my heart. If you are too busy to disciple someone each week, then you are just too busy! It is much easier to love a nameless collective group of people called congregation. But that is not true, authentic love. It takes humility to "consider others more significant than yourself." Giving one's time to invest in others does just that. Nothing is costlier than giving your time and pouring your life into another.

Consider this: When you take the time to purchase a card for a loved one or a dear friend, and you write a note in the card, you are saying, "You matter to me." When you arrange time in your schedule to mentor someone, you are saying to them, "You matter to me. You are a priority to me. I value you!" That is what Jesus did with His disciples, and it is what He has commanded us to do for others, that is, if you want a heart like God's. Otherwise, this Philippian passage is merely poetic language and an ideal never reached!

Mentoring others requires this third characteristic of humility:

3) Humility is being vulnerable!

There are three main aspects to this trait. The first is that humility does not need to defend itself. Let's face it. No one enjoys being misunderstood, misrepresented, or maligned unfairly when it comes to one's character, especially publicly. When one is falsely accused or subjected to ad hominem attacks, one feels compelled to fix the wrongdoing. Humility does not desire to fight for self. Humility does not have to prove one is right when self has been wronged.

Let's consider this spiritual reality. How often do we see God defending Himself or explaining His actions to us? Has He been maligned, misrepresented, or questioned by us? Absolutely. In fact, today many people say God does not exist, therefore, should be ignored. And if that isn't good enough, to obtain answers to our doubts and dilemmas about His character, we feel entitled to reshape His character into our limited viewpoint and understanding.

The greater truth is we do not hear God defending nor explaining His actions to us very often throughout the Bible. The book of Job is a marvelous illustration of this reality in which it is an account of the tragic misfortunes of a human being and how Job navigates his relationship with God in trying to understand the purpose to his life. But it is more than that. God is actually on trial throughout this narrative of Job and his friends. It is full of presuppositions and presumptuous ideas of what these characters in this book think or believe about God and purport to know regarding His nature, His ways and, most importantly, His motives. Indeed, God is on trial! This is not a new thing as it is widespread in our culture today.

Briefly listen to God's response to Job regarding this reality of life: *"Will you even put me in the wrong? Will you condemn me that you may be in the right?" (Job 40:8)*. Job appears arrogant and self-righteous because of his presumptions about God. This is not a new thing for humankind. Job is an example recorded for our instruction; but many people, including professing Christians, make the same mistake today. We attempt to fashion God into our neat, compact, formulaic presuppositions. The Lord is bigger than anyone's formula since He is relational. Love wants to be known. God desires to be sought. He wants to be pursued and experienced because He will not go where He is not wanted! David pursued after God, and this is our greatest need too!

Not once did God explain or defend Himself to Job and his friends. God did not explain to Job what caused the occurrences of loss and suffering in his life. Humility does not need to defend itself when accused falsely. If this is good enough for God who does no wrong, well, it should be good enough for us too! The next time you incur mistreatment or someone maligns your character, be humble as the Lord is humble!

Similar is the second quality, being vulnerable, enduring rejection with kindness and mercy. God not only doesn't need to defend Himself, He willingly endures rejection. This is God's nature as Jesus describes, "But love your enemies, and do good, and lend, expecting nothing in return, and your reward will be great, and you will be sons of the Most High, for He is kind to the ungrateful and the evil" (Luke 6:35). This means God is kind and merciful to those who are not only ungrateful, but who really don't like Him or want anything to do with Him.

Consider, God created mankind knowing full well He would be rejected by us because we would have a bent on going our own way (Isa. 53:6). It's the nature of God's love to create man with the capacity of free will, even with the risk involved. We do not understand such love and humility. One of the most sacred aspects of God creating man in His image is *choice*. God created man to be free, with freedom to choose. God's kind of love, selfless love, inherently requires choice. This is what Jesus meant when He said, "For this reason the Father loves me, because I lay down my life that I may take it up again. No one takes it from me, but I lay it down of my own accord. I have authority to lay it down, and I have authority to take it up again. This charge I have received from my Father" (John 10:17–18). Jesus was saying, the Father loves Him by giving Him the choice to go to the Cross. In the same way, the apostle Paul describes God's love: "It (agape) does not insist on its own way" (1 Cor. 13:5). The power of selfless love (agape) is giving the individual person the freedom to make their own choice, even if it may be the wrong one.

Such is humility. Humility pursues reconciliation with God's highest creation, even though God is rejected and wronged without cause. It is the vulnerability of humility that is willing to endure such horrific betrayal and grief. And despite the depth of injury to God, it does not stop Him from giving up His Beloved Son in order to reconcile us to Himself. This, of course, reiterates how the Cross fits naturally into the character of God. Humility causes God to give up His Son for us. Humility compels Jesus to give up His life for the Father. This is the most powerful display regarding the vulnerability of humility—the choice to give, regardless.

This naturally evolves into a third aspect of a vulnerability, but has a human quality. It has such a distinction because it not only applies to when we have been wronged, but when we have committed wrongdoing. This quality refers to the earlier emphasis that "humility breeds reconciliation, and reconciliation bleeds humility."

When one has committed wrongdoing, humility takes complete ownership without condition or explanation. This is a very important aspect because we don't do reconciliation very well as human beings. To acknowledge one has made a mistake or offended someone seems to be almost an impossible task for some. People don't like to become vulnerable. Perhaps this gives some explanation to the prevalence of unforgiveness in the Body of Christ. People seem to struggle with the words "I am sorry!" This aspect of humility is foundational to one's relationship with the Lord, as evidenced by David's life. David knew how to repent or change course by simply acknowledging to the Lord, "I am wrong...I did it...I am to blame...I am the man, and I am responsible!" It is such humility that produces reconciliation, which, of course, allowed God to heal and restore David in relationship to Him.

It is also foundational to all relationships. How wholesome would it be if more parents would apologize to their children when they make a mistake? After all, parents are not infallible. As a school principal, I emphasized to the students, staff, and parents the importance of what I described as the seven most powerful words in the human vocabulary: "I am sorry...will you forgive me?" I learned the significance of such words as a young father. When Brian was just a little guy, I made the mistake of disciplining him with the wrong attitude. The Lord spoke to me clearly, telling me, "You can fix it." Father-God, in that most tender of moments, showed me it was not merely enough to express my regret but I was to ask Brian for his forgiveness. I did, and he did. Children will learn to respect parents more when they see such vulnerability. To this day, we have a very close and solid relationship.

Humility requires one to be vulnerable by taking ownership without excuse or condition. The Lord taught me this personal truth, and He is more than willing to teach you, even if you did not see such vulnerability in your home growing up. Those seven words are so powerful because they are the most difficult for many people to express. You should have seen the students squirm in my office when I asked them to extend those words to reconcile with their classmate. You would think I was a dentist!

Those words are so powerful because the human condition naturally resists such vulnerability. But please don't misunderstand me, for I'm not implying they will bring immediate healing to the most severe wrongs committed. But they are a great start to generating reconciliation, even in the most painful of hurts incurred. Trust me, if you will ask the Lord to help you in any relationship that has been or becomes broken, He will. Humility does that. Just ask Jesus what He thinks about forgiveness!

Now we have come to the fourth and perhaps the most vitally important traits of humility and directly associated with Jesus in our Philippian passage, "Though He was in the form of God, did not count equality with God a thing to be grasped, but made Himself nothing, by taking the form of a servant, being born in the likeness of men" (vv. 6–7):

4) Humility acknowledges I am nothing without God!

No, this has nothing to do with commiserating in self-pity. It has nothing to do with such a mind-set because that is not the expression of God's goodness in my life. Humility is the deep cry of the soul that acknowledges one's need for God. This means, I know I am nothing because I am incomplete or inadequate without God to do in my life what I need Him to do of which I cannot do by myself!

Too often, believers commonly presume, since Jesus was the Son of God, He could arbitrarily do all He wanted to do. But notice what it says about Jesus: "But made Himself nothing, by taking the form of a servant, being born in the likeness of men." This means Jesus was willing to become less than He was by emptying Himself of His divine prerogatives by being born a human being. By becoming human, Jesus was limited. Therefore, to do the Father's work, He had to be dependent upon the Father. Jesus gives us the template for humility by His living example when He states, "Truly, truly, I say to you, the Son *can do nothing* of His own accord, but only what He sees the Father doing. For whatever the Father does that the Son does likewise" (John 5:19).

Jesus showed up in our world to reflect what God was like. Scripture underscores this truth: "He is the image of the invisible God" (Col. 1:15). Jesus came to give us a model for how to live with and for God as He emptied Himself while becoming a fully yielded vessel and being poured out as a living sacrifice to fulfill the Father's work He delighted to do. Fulfilling the Father's will was Jesus's sustenance: "My food is to do the will of Him who sent Me and to accomplish His work" (John 4:34).

God gives us another example how a man learned to cultivate this godly attribute in his life, the apostle Paul. Most of us are familiar with Paul's self-descriptions of personal inadequacy: "I am the least of the saints" (Eph. 3:8) or "I am the least of the apostles, unworthy to be called an apostle" (1 Cor. 15:9), and "Of whom (sinners) I am chief" (1 Tim. 1:15). Paul not only sincerely believed he was the least of the apostles and the worst of sinners, but he also believed he was nothing!

On one occasion, Paul defended his ministry to the church at Corinth, so he stated, "For I was not at all inferior to these super-apostles, even though *I am nothing"* (1 Cor. 12:11). But more importantly, not only was this his self-view, he instructed others to acknowledge or discover this truth about themselves: "For if anyone thinks he is something, when *he is nothing*, he deceives himself" (Gal. 6:3).

How did Paul learn to actualize humility in his character? We get a good indication as he shared an experience of how the Lord taught him an eternal truth. Paul explained, "That a thorn was given me in the flesh, a messenger of Satan to harass me" and how "three times he pleaded with the Lord about this" (2 Cor. 12:7–8).

Whatever the "thorn" was, it caused Paul to beg the Lord on three different occasions to be free from it! Paul shared the Lord's response to his desperate request, "My grace is sufficient for you, for My power is made perfect in weakness" (2 Cor. 12:9). Paul's reaction to the Lord's answer was profound and powerful. It provides a window into understanding Paul's declaration, "I am nothing!" Subsequently, Paul responded, "Therefore I will boast all the more gladly of my weaknesses, so that the power of Christ may rest upon me. For the sake of Christ then, I am content with my weaknesses, insults, hardships, persecutions, and calamities. For when I am weak, then I am strong" (2 Cor. 12:9–10).

Amazingly, Paul responds with joyful exuberance and a passionate exclamation to a wonderful and powerful discovery he wants to share with anyone who will listen. It is almost like he has been given the map to a secret treasure or been told he has won the lottery! Again, listen to his words: "I will boast...gladly...and will be content in my weaknesses!" And if that is not enough, he then lists some of those weaknesses he has experienced: "Insults, hardships, persecutions, and calamities" to name a few. But we must ask ourselves, is Paul clearheaded in his understanding? "Boasting and content in my weaknesses?" Who does that? Someone who has discovered "strength" in humility!

Paul gets Jesus! Paul understood the eternal truth Jesus gave to him. For you see, in this letter to the Corinthians, Paul shared the explicit reason he was given this thorn in the flesh in verse 7: "So to keep me from becoming conceited because of the surpassing greatness of the revelations." Paul had been blessed with a vision of heaven, which understandably most people never experience in this life. Therefore, to keep him from becoming arrogant about such a blessing and the manifestation of God's power in his ministry, he was given "a thorn in the flesh" to keep him Christ-dependent.

Jesus wanted Paul to learn it would be his personal acknowledgment he was inadequate, causing him to be fully dependent upon God to do what he could not do for himself. In fact, again, the Greek word used in this context for *perfect* means "to become complete or be fulfilled."[5] Therefore, one can ascertain the meaning of Jesus's words to be: "My grace is sufficient, for My power completes in you, what you cannot do on your own!"

It's not that Paul enjoyed the hardships; he didn't. Instead, he discovered and learned the importance of being Christ-dependent always, because such dependency gave opportunity for God's grace and power to show up in his life. This produced contentment in the midst of, at times, great personal suffering. If the exchange of physical comforts for the power of Christ would advance the reality of Jesus Christ and His gospel, Paul would not only be content and glad, he would be fulfilled, knowing the experiential reality of God's Presence was at work in his life for the benefit of others! That, my friend, is not only the mark of humility, it is the defining essence of humility: The personal realization I am nothing, incomplete, or inadequate, without full dependence upon God to do what I cannot do! Translation: "I'm no good without God!"

The fifth humility trait found in the Philippian passage can be described as the motif of a shepherd after God's own heart:

5) Humility honors God!

"He humbled Himself by becoming obedient to the point of death, even death on a cross" (v. 8). In this verse, the key word, and often lost in the contemporary Church today: obedience! For whatever reason, believers tend to have a negative view of obedience. Various factors contribute, but probably the single most important factor causing such a distorted view is pride. We tend to believe "we know a better way!"

However, obedience should have a positive constitution in our lives as "adopted sons of God." Obedience simply means to want the same thing God wants. When we want the same as God wants, we will love Him as He loves us! This is the heart of honoring God with our lives. This verse is saying because of Jesus's humility, He honored the Father. It was our Lord's humility that compelled Him to accept the inhumanity and humiliation of the Cross. It was Jesus's humility that drove Him to fulfill the very purpose the Father sent Him into the world to accomplish: "To give His life a ransom for many" (Mark 10:45).

Jesus could not do what He did alone or independent of the Father. More importantly, He would not have wanted to! We need to understand it was Jesus's full surrender and complete dependence upon the Father to do what was humanly impossible. Remember, an angel was sent "to strengthen Him" to complete His mission. And what was Jesus doing at the time? Praying. Jesus had to decide: His will or the Father's will?

The reality that Jesus could not do the Father's will alone is underscored by the writer of Hebrews: "Although He was a son, He learned obedience through what He suffered" (Heb. 5:8). This speaks of Jesus's humanity. When Jesus became a human being, He entered our world of brokenness. He had never known, physically, what it was like to encounter human suffering. Jesus discovered what it was like to experience all types of human suffering, such as fatigue, rejection, unbelief, abandonment, betrayal, hatred, and excruciating physical pain. It is through His humanity, Jesus learned what it was like to be obedient through such circumstances.

This doesn't mean Jesus had to suffer in order to learn obedience. But rather it was Jesus's willingness to endure suffering and to be obedient despite it, which qualified Him to be the Savior for mankind. This truth is underscored in Scripture: "For it was fitting that He (the Father), for whom and by whom all things exist, in bringing many sons to glory, should make the founder (Jesus) of their salvation perfect through suffering" (Heb. 2:10). Jesus is the "perfect" or qualified Savior because He not only can identify with and have great compassion for our temptations as human beings, but most importantly, He was obedient regardless of such great anguish and sufferings He incurred for our sake. This makes Jesus the perfect Savior because He fulfilled His Father's ultimate purpose in producing "many sons." This is what it means to honor God with a heart of humility!

For Jesus, nothing was comparable to the importance of being obedient throughout His life by doing the Father's will. Truly, Jesus is our consummate model of humility to learn from and to emulate, as Paul instructs us: *"Therefore God has highly exalted Him and bestowed on Him the name that is above every name" (Phil. 2:9).* How fitting, only Jesus could be worthy of such honor and glory!

Clothe Yourself with Christ: The Humility of God!

Humility is vitally important since it has everything to do with how we begin our journey with Christ as well as how we finish. Humility is important to God because He is humble and He desires for us to be like Him. Again, listen to the words of Andrew Murray:

> Christ is the humility of God embodied in human nature: The Eternal Love humbling itself, clothing itself in the garb of meekness and gentleness, to win and serve and save us. As the love and condescension of God makes Him the benefactor and helper and servant of all, so Jesus of necessity was the Incarnate Humility. And so He is still in the midst of the throne, the meek and lowly Lamb of God.[6]

Think about it. The Creator of the entire cosmos, is humble! I know it can be difficult to wrap your head around, but it is true!

Furthermore, Murray underscores Jesus still remains humble even now while on His throne. Humility is an attribute of Trinitarian life. It is their nature. God's humility causes Him to redeem brokenness. It is God's nature to pursue after that which is lost. It is God's humility to redeem, rescue, restore, and to recover mankind for a relationship with Him. Humility does that because it flows from His selfless love! We must never forget, it is God's humility that causes His movement toward us, even though He did nothing wrong.

But again, God will not go where He is not wanted. Only the same, kindred humility can extend a personal invitation from you and me to Him. We must make a choice. Consider what God said to the prophet Isaiah in this regard:

> Thus says the Lord: "Heaven is my throne, and the earth is my footstool; what is the house that you would build for me, and what is the place of my rest? All these things my hand has made, and so all these things came to be, declares the Lord. But this is the one to whom I will look: he who is humble and contrite in spirit and trembles at my word." (Isa. 66:1–2)

Humility is our expressed invitation we want Him. The person who recognizes their need for Him is humility. The person who realizes they cannot live without Him is humility. The person who reveres and values what God has to say and trusts their life on it is humility. That is the person God desires to visit. That is the person with whom God wants to manifest His presence, not a house made with human hands. This is the House God promised David He would build, a house comprised of a people of humility!

Humility has such critical importance because it is foundational to one becoming a mature adopted son of God. David learned and actualized this godly attribute in his life as he suggests in one of his psalms: "He leads the humble in what is right, and teaches the humble His way" (Ps. 25:9). David learned the magnitude of this truth as God prepared him to rule Israel. This attribute led him to become the most effective king in Israel's history. As God's appointed shepherd for His people, David was the most successful because there was nothing he desired more than to learn God's heart and to know His way in life. Humility does that.

Actualizing this attribute is a total work of the Holy Spirit. He does such work in the classroom of life and through the occasional "tests" in our daily circumstances. The only thing we can do is surrender to the Lord's will by listening and allowing Him to do only what He can do in our lives. This is the work of God's grace and is only realized through the decisive responsiveness to becoming a student of Jesus. If this work of God was true for David's life, should it be any different for those who are today's pastors and leaders of God's House? If anyone should know and understand the heart of God, it should be His shepherds.

These words from Andrew Murray should encase the living constitution of every shepherd's heart entrusted with the care of God's flock, as well as those who profess the name of Jesus Christ: "When we see, that humility is something infinitely deeper than contrition, and accept it as our participation in the life of Jesus, we shall begin to learn that it is our true nobility, and that to prove it in being servants of all is the highest fulfillment of our destiny, as men created in the image of God."[7] Indeed, humility, the entrance to participation of life in Christ!

The Passionate Care of David's House!

Part II: Preparing and Presenting the Meal for God's Flock

*Who then is the faithful and wise servant, whom his master has set
over his household, to give them their food at the proper time? Blessed
is that servant whom his master will find so doing when he comes
—Matthew 24:45–46*

We've come to understand the passionate care for God's
House begins with humility. Now we must attend to
the second important aspect, the type of spiritual food
God desires to provide His people: "Who (shepherds) will feed you
with knowledge and understanding." What kind of knowledge and
what understanding?

Since God values His people with such a deep love, those who
are entrusted with the care of His House have an awesome responsibility. We should understand, anytime we have an opportunity to
teach God's people, it should be approached with the same mind-set
as if one is preparing and presenting a delicious meal for important
guests in one's home. The only difference, this meal is prepared for

God's House—God's people. This should explain the reason more meticulous attention is required and should be invested accordingly.

We should never be sloppy or reckless in our preparation and planning of such a meal for God's people. And since God has specifically emphasized the kind of food to be fed to His flock, we must carefully consider what should be on the menu through critical thinking, diligent study, guidance, and prayer, as well the importance of how it should be presented.

It is from such a prism, we must acknowledge a dilemma for the shepherds who are feeding God's flock and the food that is being provided. We gain a snapshot of the problem in the previously mentioned Schaeffer Institute survey, offering an ominous revelation regarding pastors and their personal relationship to the Lord: "Seventy-two percent of the pastors only studied the Bible when they were preparing for sermons or lessons. Only 28 percent read the Bible for devotions or personal study."[8]

If this is true, wouldn't this be an alarming trend reflecting a serious spiritual malady? Even though the survey of 1,050 pastors is a small number, it is representative, perhaps a microcosm, of something more significant in the Church-at-large. It provokes these thoughts: What is the knowledge and understanding God's shepherds are feeding His flock? What kind of meal is being prepared and presented to God's house? Of which then other questions ensue: Could this explain why the Church, according to some leaders, appears irrelevant to contemporary culture? Or perhaps provides perspective to the anemic, impotent condition of God's house? Is there a correlation to this malady and the high burnout rate of pastors in ministry?

I believe there are answers to these questions and others that can be found in the spoken words of God's prophet Hosea, who predicted the impending divine judgment of Northern Israel: "My people are destroyed for lack of knowledge; because you have rejected knowledge, I reject you from being a priest to Me" (Hos. 4:6). What knowledge was lacking that caused an entire nation's destruction? For Israel, the answer is the knowledge of God: His law, His Word, the revelation of His character, His will, and His ways for their lives!

Israel no longer knew the Lord due to the generational progression of rejecting God. The knowledge of God in Israel had become corroded and, consequently, deteriorated rapidly in time, largely due to the leadership. It was this lack of knowing God that ultimately resulted in their destruction as a nation. This is the meaning of Hosea's prophetic words for Israel then, but can it also apply to God's House today? The simple answer is yes.

This great spiritual malignancy is not new. Obviously, Israel was faced with this challenge throughout her history. And so it has been for the Church throughout the ages, as evidenced by the pastors who appear to be neglecting the development of their own personal relationship with the Lord. This is cause for serious concern regarding the kind of meals prepared and provided to feed God's flock today, simply because if it is not the right food or nourishment, it will lead to spiritual immaturity, impotency, and even spiritual death!

The kind of knowledge that is God's priority is found in the second sentence of the longest recorded prayer in the life of Jesus when He declares the definition of eternal life: "And this is eternal life, that they know you the only true God, and Jesus Christ whom you have sent" (John 17:3). This is the preeminent knowledge that is the priority of God's heart—people will come to know Jesus, His nature, and cultivate a personal interactive understanding of Him in their daily lives. This is the assigned task of every shepherd: to transmit the heartbeat of God, accurately and authentically, to God's people, His flock.

In Jesus's prayer, He offers the defining essence of eternal life that is centered in one key word: *know*. The Greek word is *ginosko*, which in its basic meaning denotes "To learn to know, to understand, perceive, to have knowledge of."[9] But it means more than simply a mental or extrinsic type of knowledge. Often, the word was used as a Jewish idiom, referring to the most intimate union experienced between a husband and wife. Jesus is praying that people will know God intimately. This means a shared experience or experiential knowledge of the Lord. Such knowledge means to personally experience God through an intimate, interactive relationship with Him in our life daily. Jesus is describing such a relationship with Him and with Father-God as eternal life!

Such experiential knowledge of God caused David to say, "Oh, taste and see that the Lord is good!" (Ps. 34:8). The verb *taste* was also a common Hebrew metaphor in the Old Testament and meant "to personally experience."[10] David had come to know in his relationship with God that when you actually experience Him, you realize God is good!

David had experienced a lifetime of God's Presence because God's Spirit had touched him in a very real and tangible way. The Lord's Spirit had affected all his physical senses and saturated his entire being. David occasioned moments of total immersion in God's Presence. So much so, he compared such an experience to that of a feast, which sustained him throughout his day, and had overtaken him before sleep, late into the evening, saying, "My soul will be satisfied as with fat and rich food, and my mouth will praise you with joyful lips, when I remember you upon my bed, and meditate on you in the watches of the night" (Ps. 63:5–6). This is the distinction between heart and head knowledge!

Incredible! David is so filled with God's love, his final thoughts before falling asleep were not the concerns of the affairs of a nation, but all the marvelous works and blessings the Lord had provided throughout his life. Perhaps, during the late night changing of the guard ("the night watches"), David reviewed the time Samuel anointed him and his wonderful encounter with the Spirit of God for the first time in his young life or his reminiscence of the Goliath victory! Whatever David's thoughts, we know his journal reflects a personal, intimate interaction with the God he has come to know and love much!

This is the kind of knowledge and understanding God desires His shepherds to provide His flock. God desires for those who are His shepherds to convey His true nature—the knowledge of who He is and what He is like and how He desires for us to live with Him and our fellow man. But what does this involve?

The Bible states, "God is love" (1 John 4:16). The Greek word for love, *agape*, is a noun.[11] God is not about love; He is love. Love is His Personhood, His being, His nature! As established previously, God is relational. Love always wants to be known. God desires to share Himself. The Lord desires for us to know and understand His will, His ways, His nature, and His purpose for our lives—a constant strand throughout the Old Testament.

Such was God's initial call to Israel at Mt. Sinai as He formed them into a nation: "You shall be to Me a kingdom of priests and a holy nation" (Exod. 19:6). The call was the same for David: "The Lord has sought out a man after His own heart" (1 Sam. 13:14). God desired Israel and David to know Him and to know His heart. This was the highest calling for the nation and for David! Today, it's our highest calling: to know God's heart, to know His love, to taste Him!

The Spiritual Malady!

The Schaeffer Institute Survey offers a disconcerting narrative regarding leaders who appear to be negligent in cultivating their personal relationship with the Lord, indicating only 28 percent maintain regular devotions. This leads to a serious question: what is being offered to God's flock? But perhaps there is a more important question, such as what are the unintended effects of this type of misaligned priority? If ministry in and of itself surpasses the importance of one's devotional life to God, it is a spiritual malady of unimaginable consequences. There are damaging repercussions for the individual leader as well as for those entrusted to the shepherd's oversight and care.

Before we look at the adverse ramifications for the individual leader, let's first consider the community of believers. Probably more than at any other time in human history people are searching for the reality of God. People are looking for God's authenticity. It is a natural inclination because God has created us to know Him. He is relational, and so are we, since we're made in His image. We have an inherent aspiration and hunger for God. It is in our DNA, so to speak. This is one reason there are so many different religions. People have self-navigated in their search to "find" God for their lives. The human condition has a proclivity to be religious.

Consequently, people are largely depending upon leaders in God's House to transmit accurately and authentically the knowledge of God—who He is, His character and nature as well as insight into His purpose for their lives! Without such knowledge, people will die spiritually. They become distracted and discouraged in their pursuit of God's own heart.

This is the central meaning of Hosea's warning to the nation of Israel. Israel's downfall could be summed up in one word—*idolatry*. Idolatry can be defined as anything or anyone that requires more attentive importance and value than God, which effectively displaces God to a secondary role, and replaces Him with self. Is it possible that ministry itself can become one's idol? Yes, especially if the pastor's life is devoid of a personal, intimate relationship with the Lord. Tragically, if the mind-set is ministry rather than the One who has ordained the ministry, the result is self-navigation!

The tendency for ministry to become the priority and a surpassing importance in one's relationship with the Lord is a need for validation. We have all been susceptible to such error. Stephen Seamands offers this insight regarding this prevalent misstep in ministry:

> Too often persons enter ministry without this proper foundation firmly established. Consequently they make their achievement, their work for God, the foundation of their ministry, rather than their acceptance and approval by God. Wanting to do something in order to be someone, they view themselves, in Mike Bickel's words, as "loving workers" instead of as God intends, as "working lovers."[12]

The compelling distinction of a "working lover" rather than the deficient "loving worker" is our focal point. The difference is found in being a shepherd, whose sole interest, passion, and love is in doing what God wants done. Jesus said it another way: "Whoever abides in Me and I in him, he it is that bears much fruit, for apart from Me you can do nothing" (John 15:5). Again, the emphasis of humility is paramount to effective ministry. To do Father-God's will, and thereby honor Him, is the true measurement of success regarding ministry.

Another significant misstep is a "performance-oriented" mindset. Rather than present the meal, our tendency is to make a good impression. We are always trying to outdo the last sermon or hit another home run. Or we become ensnared into the self-comparison game. Frequently, the disastrous effect of the need to perform is the messenger will surpass the message. Instead of people being captured by the message or Person of Jesus Christ, they will instead become captivated by a personality. This is not the kind of foundation that will construct growth in the life of the believer that will be durable and long lasting.

The third fallacy is the role-reversal of being a servant. This can be a subtle and unintentional development, but one that too often results in God serving our agenda rather than us serving the Lord's agenda. We all must consider this question: Whose gifts are they that He has given to you and me? Are they yours? Are they mine? Can we just use them arbitrarily without any sense of accountability to Him for their use? They are God's gifts to be used for His purpose, for that is the message in the parable of talents (Luke 19:11–27).

Therefore, we must remember this important truth: It is not *my* ministry! It is Father-God's ministry working through each of us, to the degree of our surrender. Jesus gave us such an example when He said, "My teaching is not Mine, but His who sent Me" (John 7:16). Jesus acknowledged the Father sent Him into the world for a mission and to do His work: "I glorified You on earth, having accomplished the work you gave Me to do" (John 17:4). The Father's work was what Jesus wanted to do, no more, no less. Jesus further qualified this dynamic by saying, "For I have come down from heaven, not to do My will but the will of Him who sent Me" (John 6:38).

This is the focus Jesus emphasized as priority in His Vine-branch analogy in chapter 15 of John, which I refer as the "constitution" for Christian living and ministry. What constitutes effective ministry is doing God's will, determined by our full dependency upon Jesus to do what we cannot do. This is the character that qualifies the shepherd who has a heart after God's own heart.

The Necessary Spiritual Food for God's Flock

Yet there must be something more. It's essential for a shepherd to know the Presence and power of God in their own personal life. No one knew this reality better than the apostle Paul. He stated as much in his letter to the church in Rome: "For I will not venture to speak anything except what Christ has accomplished through me, to bring the Gentiles to obedience—by word and deed, by the power of signs and wonders, by the power of the Spirit of God" (Rom. 15:18–19).

Paul would only preach those truths God had taught him and worked out through his own life. This truth is foundational for effective ministry. Let's face it. It is difficult, if not impossible, to teach about prayer, if one does not have an active vibrant prayer life. This is the very point of Paul's emphasis in this scriptural passage. Again, it is the same emphasis Jesus stated that constitutes effective ministry. It is about our abiding relationship in Christ, which only can produce fruitfulness in ministry.

There is no question the miraculous occurred in Paul's ministry because the power of God was present. And yet Paul did not remain satisfied with the status quo. Paul passionately pursued a "higher" priority, as he so stated, "That I may know Him and the power of His resurrection, and may share His sufferings" (Phil. 3:10). To know Christ, to experience Him, personally, intimately—to grow and increase in knowledge of God—was Paul's greatest desire. In fact, this priority surpassed the value and vitality of his powerful ministry. His greatest passion was to know Christ, and if one is going to have a heart after God's own heart, the same must be true for anyone who is called pastor and holds the position as a shepherd of God.

The kind of knowledge Jesus invites anyone to experience from Him is based on His own self-description: "I am the living bread that came down from heaven. If anyone eats of this bread, he will live forever" (John 6:51). And He qualified this truth further: "As the living Father sent Me, and I live because of the Father, so whoever feeds on Me, he also will live because of Me" (John 6:57). This is the personal knowledge and understanding God wants fed to His flock through His shepherds. But the shepherds themselves must be willing to take the personal time to feed on the Bread of Life, first and foremost.

Let's recognize to "eat" of the Bread of Life or to "feed" on Jesus has the same strong and comparable meaning of the OT metaphor to "taste and see the Lord is good." We are called to feed or experience Christ daily and to allow Him to satisfy us. And trust me, my friend, once you taste of Him, you will be satisfied, but then earnestly desiring to know Him more. Like Paul, Jesus will germinate an insatiable appetite for more of Him. Your hunger to study God's word diligently will be the evidence of such, and not merely for constructing a message!

This brings us naturally to the all-important subject of prayer. What do we offer God's flock as His shepherds, if we don't have much of a prayer or devotional life? Remember, people are hungering for the authenticity and reality of God. They are depending on you to be dependent upon Christ by "feeding" on Him through prayer. The theologian Gordon Fee underscores the vital importance of such a priority:

> Prayer, therefore, is not simply our cry of desperation or our grocery list of requests that we bring before our heavenly Abba; prayer is an activity inspired by God Himself, through His Holy Spirit. It is God siding with His people and by His own empowering presence, the Spirit of God Himself, bringing forth prayer that is in keeping with His will and His ways.[13]

If we are struggling in our prayer life, we can ask for the Holy Spirit to assist us. We cannot pray effectively alone. Effectual prayer must be facilitated by the Holy Spirit. This is reiterated by two prominent pastors Henry and Richard Blackaby in their book *Spiritual Leadership*: "While all Christians have the Holy Spirit's presence in their lives, the condition of being filled by the Holy Spirit comes through concentrated, fervent, sanctified prayer."[14]

There is no substitute for God's Presence and power in prayer. Through the assistance of the Holy Spirit, only prayer, saturated with God's Presence, is truly satisfying and will sustain effective ministry. This is what Jesus meant when He said, "I am the bread of life; whoever comes to Me shall not hunger" (John 6:35). This is necessary to transform a prayer life that has grown stagnate and dry. For this to happen, we must want Christ more than anything else in our lives—more than any activity, other relationships, and more than ministry.

If we do not spend time with Him, we then must ask ourselves a vitally important question: How do we realize God's agenda or will for the ministry He has called us to do? Too often, God's leaders have the wrong mind-set because their focus is on the latest trend of ministry or the next best marketing method. This is done all in the name of relevance to a postmodern culture. Please don't misunderstand. I'm not saying such approaches do not have some value. It is about priorities. It is about a mind-set or philosophy of ministry. Becoming "seeker sensitive" in the truest biblical meaning is encapsulated in Jesus's teaching in His longest recorded sermon: "Seek first the kingdom of God and His righteousness" (Matt. 6:33).

There is no substitute for the Presence and power of God's Holy Spirit, but He must be welcome in our meetings. The true, genuine manifestation of God's Holy Spirit will always satisfy and quench the driest, most hardened heart of any human being who desperately desires Jesus! But, there must always be more time spent seeking the Lord and experiencing Him than anything else in our life.

You would think, based on our misguided priorities and that which we offer people, we should apologize on behalf of Jesus. I'm not saying all or everyone, but a good majority of leaders act like He is not enough or somehow He is just not relevant enough for our contemporary culture! So our tendency is to look for other methods, techniques, or promotional strategies to attract people to the Church. The problem is we are looking in the wrong direction, seeking the wrong sources. Sadly, people can see through it for what it offers—spiritual bankruptcy!

There is good news though because we can turn it around. We just need to do a radical pivot in our ministry mind-set. Again remember, people are hungering for the authenticity of God. When we present to them the bona fide Person of the Holy Spirit, through God's word and His works, He will be more than relatable to their hearts.

We must be decisive—that is, if we want to be a shepherd after God's heart—and determine that Christ is very much enough! Such a determination must be made in one's prayer time with God alone. The Lord waits to be wanted, but He will not go where He is not welcome. The Holy Spirit is gentle and humble and does not want to intrude on the practices and priorities of which shepherds have placed more importance and value.

The Lord stands patiently, knocking at our door, waiting for someone to open it and invite Him in to fellowship with them (Rev. 3:20). By the way, the church door Jesus is knocking on is described as "I am rich, I have prospered, and I need nothing" (Rev. 3:17). Oh, dear friend, I can't help wondering if we would see tears streaming down His face when we do open the door. No, not tears of sorrow, but tears of joy! He waits to be wanted more than anything!

The Final Moments of God's House!

The kind of meal prepared and presented by God's shepherds is critical. We are living in the most pivotal moment in Church history. Time spent on this truth is so important, Jesus refers to feeding His flock "properly" against the backdrop of the disciples' inquiry regarding a "sign" that will mark His return and the end of this age (Matt. 24:3).

Jesus proceeds to describe many negative and adverse "signs" in the world that will mark His imminent return. But one singular positive sign is regarding those true shepherds after His own heart who will be found doing His work: *"Who then is the faithful and wise servant, whom his master has set over his household, to give them their food at the proper time? Blessed is that servant whom his master will find so doing when he comes" (Matt. 24:45–46).*

The faithful and wise servant is the shepherd who is diligent in fulfilling their calling by "properly feeding" the people in the household of God. Such a shepherd, Jesus says, is blessed because the servant is "faithful and wise" by taking care of God's House according to the purpose for which they have been called by the Lord. How vitally important are the shepherds who are feeding God's flock according to the provisions of God's own heart—the knowledge and understanding of His Beloved Son, Jesus Christ! Let it be, our Father, let it be!

CHAPTER 13

The Invitation to Be God's House!

If anyone would come after Me let him deny himself and take up his cross and follow Me. For whoever would save his life will lose it, but whoever loses his life for My sake will find it
—Matthew 16:24–25

The story of David's life, like many Old Testament characters, such as Abraham, Jacob, Joseph, and Moses, all began with divine pursuit. Such pursuit is simply God showing up in one's life. For each of them, their encounter with the Lord produced a life-changing transformation, dependent upon the person's individual response to God's overtures.

There are two major principles we can glean from David's narrative. God always makes the first move. God initiated pursuit of David and anointed him with His Holy Spirit. Secondly, then is the response of David to God's movement toward him. The Old Testament is filled with such initiatives by God, all of them, a preview to the most incomparable and incomprehensible timeless movement of God toward all humankind—the Cross!

But now it is our move. We have a choice to make, and it will prove to be the most profound decision as well as the greatest opportunity one will ever determine for their course in life. God has extended to us His invitation to be a part of His House. God's invitation is unique. It begins with a cross. What will we do? Will we accept or reject His offer? After all, the offer is extraordinary. It is an offer filled with eternal life—an invitation to be a part of His eternal family, and to rule with His Beloved Son, Jesus, for eternity! Who would not want that?

However, tragically, some people can't get beyond the invitation. Remember the rich young ruler who asked Jesus, "What must I do to have eternal life?" (Matt. 19:16). He turned down Jesus's offer because for him it was too costly to "give up all he possessed" to follow Jesus (Matt. 19:21). The problem for him is the same for many today. They look through their "God-filter"—those presuppositions, ideas, and preconceived expectations of who they think God is or should be as well as act.

An Unattractive Invitation?

More than likely, it also may have everything to do with the invitation not being too attractive or, in fact, may very well appear harsh and confusing. The offer to become a pursuer of God's heart is from Jesus: *"If anyone comes to Me and does not hate his own father and mother and wife and children and brothers and sisters, yes, and even his own life, he cannot be My disciple. Whoever does not bear his own cross and come after Me cannot be My disciple" (Luke 14:26–27).*

To understand this invitation, we must consider the meaning of *hate* in this context because it has a different meaning in Jewish culture than our literal English meaning. It means to "love less."[1] Jesus was not saying one must literally hate his family or oneself—that would be a contradiction of His other teachings. The theologian J. Dwight Pentecost provides further clarity: "The use of 'hate' in terms of Jewish idiom, did not refer to emotion, but rather to the will."[2]

Jesus was saying it comes down to the *will* regarding what one values as most important. Who's *will* do you love more? Who's will do you love less? The authority of Christ is the issue in the Lord's invitation, and of "whose will" shall an individual value more is the central question. Will you value the *will* of your father, mother, your family, or even your own will, more than God's? Each of us must make that decision. Like the rich young ruler, Jesus is offering the invitation to give up one's natural bent to self-govern and, instead, to decisively surrender to the Lord's benevolent rule of goodness! Such a decision determines if you will be a student, a truly devoted student of Jesus. This decision is the most pivotal, for it will determine your course in life!

The Exchanged Life—Transformation!

We should understand the invitation from Jesus involves an exchange. This truth is amplified in the statement by Jesus: "For what will it profit a man if he gains the whole world and forfeits his soul? Or what shall a man give in return for his soul?" (Matt. 16:26). The "exchange" revolves around "What shall a man...*give*...in return for his soul?" The answer for the person who desires to be a student of Jesus is found in the exchange of one who gives up their will to the Lord's willful goodness, thereby allowing God to govern one's life. An exchanged life is the essential journey of the Christian life!

Such an exchange is qualified by Dr. Dallas Willard regarding the meaning and reality of such a decision:

Being His apprentice is, therefore, not a matter of religious activities, but an orientation and quality of my entire existence. This is what is meant by Jesus when He says those who do not forsake all cannot be His disciple (Luke 14:26&33). The emphasis is upon the all. There must be nothing held of greater value than Jesus and His kingdom. He must be clearly seen as the most important thing in human life, and being His apprentice as the greatest opportunity any human being ever has.[3] (Note: Dr. Willard preferred the term *apprentice*, which is synonymous with "student" or "disciple.")

There are three words that capture my attention regarding Dr. Willard's applied meaning of becoming a student or apprentice of Jesus and what is involved, as well as those benefits of such a commitment. They are *orientation*, *all*, and *opportunity*.

Let's first consider the word *orientation*. This applies to one's "quality of existence." As an apprentice or learner of Jesus, the Lord will provide a new orientation or paradigm regarding one's entire purpose in life. One who takes Jesus up on His offer will discover the very reason they were created, much like David did. The offer is an exchanged life for anyone willing to give up (surrender) their life and exchange it for the willful goodness and reign of God in their life. This is the meaningfulness of "deny, to gain; lose, to find; or die, to live"—the centerpiece to the invitation. More about this in a moment.

Is the Invitation Worth the Cost?

Then there is the important emphasis of *all*. This is best explained in a corollary passage in the gospel of Matthew in which Jesus is again qualifying His invitation to follow Him: *"Whoever loves father or mother more than Me is not worthy of Me, and whoever loves son or daughter more than Me is not worthy of Me. And whoever does not take his cross and follow Me is not worthy of Me. Whoever finds his life will lose it, and whoever loses his life for My sake will find it"* (Matt. 10:37–39). To love and esteem one's parents was one of the highest duties taught in Judaism.[4] Jesus is emphasizing that following Him must even surpass the value of their family because He is worth such complete devotion.

The *all* is defined by Jesus on an occasion when a religious leader desired to entrap the Lord by asking Him, "Which commandment is the most important of all?" Jesus answered, "Hear, O Israel: The Lord our God, the Lord is one. And you shall love the Lord your God with all your heart and with all your soul and with all your mind and with all your strength" (Mark 12:28–30). Yes, the *all* is one's entire being—the heart, soul, mind, and body (strength). It must be the entire human being that gives *all* to Christ, out of complete love for Him, in order to follow Him and become His student.

Hear me, my friend, we must understand very carefully how such a decision is pivotal for the Christian life. It is the most powerful decision one can make since it will determine one's course for their entire life. To form such a decision is an active demonstration of love and a pursuit for the one who wants Christ more than life itself—giving up one's own life—is the person who wants to spend time with Him, to learn from Him, and, most importantly, to do what He wants done.

Jesus shares two stories to illustrate this wonderful dynamic truth. In one parable He compares such an opportunity to finding an invaluable treasure: "The kingdom of heaven is like treasure hidden in a field, which a man found and covered up. Then in his joy he goes and sells all that he has and buys that field" (Matt. 13:44). Similarly, in the other story the opportunity is comparable to a priceless pearl: "The kingdom of heaven is like a merchant in search of fine pearls, who, on finding one pearl of great value, went and sold all that he had and bought it" (Matt. 13:45). Both illustrations focus on a great discovery that is deemed of priceless value, and that discovery is the Person of Jesus Christ.

In both stories such discovery produced two major effects. The first is the decision by both men "to sell *all* that they had" in order to obtain the invaluable treasure. Such a decision produces the second effect, which is great joy! Ecstatic happiness!

There is a direct relationship between these two parables and the invitation by Jesus. There is a cost to obtain the hidden treasure or the priceless pearl. Both men sold everything. They gave up everything. They gave their all in exchange for the hidden treasure. Yes, an exchange did transpire. But more importantly, when the exchange occurred, what was the response of the men? Was there disappointment or despair? Were they disillusioned or depressed with the cost to invest? Were they miserable for such a cost? Was there resentment or a grudging regret in their purchase? No, instead, they had great *joy* in making such a life-changing decision. Through both illustrations, Jesus is giving every indication that if you decide to follow Him—to become His student—you will not be disappointed!

This leads us to the third term, *opportunity*. The invitation by Jesus to be His student should be viewed as the greatest opportunity in life, and there is probably no better Scripture that underlines such a truth than this one spoken by Jesus: *"Unless a grain of wheat falls into the earth and dies, it remains alone; but if it dies, it bears much fruit. Whoever loves his life loses it, and whoever hates his life in this world will keep it for eternal life. If anyone serves me, he must follow me; and where I am, there will my servant be also (John 12:24-26). If anyone serves me, the Father will honor him."*

Similar to the other invitations extended by Jesus, the theme of loving God's will more than one's own will is again the major emphasis. The distinction of this invitation as life's greatest opportunity is determined by the ability to bear fruit, that is, if one decides to become a student of Jesus. But what does that mean you may ask?

As the Master-teacher, it is interesting the analogy Jesus used regarding a "grain of wheat." Jesus conveyed, if the "seed" would do what it was created to do—to be sown in the ground—it would produce a crop. The grain of wheat would be fruitful based on its designed purpose. But if it did not do what it was designed to do, it would die, becoming of no use to anyone. The outcome is the same for any individual who wants to remain self-willed, resulting in missing out on God's designed purpose for one's life. To fulfill the very purpose for which one is created is why such a decision should be viewed as the greatest opportunity in one's life.

Furthermore, Jesus provides the template for such a momentous decision. Scripture tells us, "Who, though He was in the form of God, did not count equality with God a thing to be grasped, but emptied Himself, by taking the form of a servant, being born in the likeness of men" (Phil. 2:6–7). As mentioned previously on the subject of humility, Jesus willingly gave up His divine prerogatives in order to serve His Father's purpose. He humbled Himself on a cross to die that we might live. And as He taught, there is no greater love demonstrated than when you lay your life down for others.

Therefore, ultimately, the message is, if we are going to be useful, if we are going to bear fruit, if we are going to fulfill God's original design for our life, we must follow Jesus's example of "losing our life for His sake" so we can be where Jesus is right now, learning what He presently wants done while working in cooperation with Him by being involved with what He is doing on earth as it is in heaven.

Serving with this same mind-set of Jesus will lead us to be where He is in our world and enable us to do what He wants done. And most importantly, Jesus lets us know, the Father will inevitably honor us because we have served Jesus in such a way!

The Joyful Priceless Possession

There is definitely another reward that is found in surrendering our will to God's will as illustrated by the two parables: joy. *Joy* is an interestingly unique and simple word and yet carries significant meaning, especially in our world. A common definition offered, "A strong feeling of happiness arising from the expectation of some good, or from its realization....A state of contentment or satisfaction, and anything that causes delight or gladness!"[5]

The definition emphasizes the prominent relationship of a "strong feeling of happiness" with the "realization of something good." This corresponds with the reaction of the two men when they discover the "priceless possession" of the kingdom of heaven. We can easily conclude they are delighted and very happy with their discovery! But why should we be surprised? Consider this spiritual insight of God's nature as described by Dr. Willard: "Undoubtedly He is the most joyous being in the universe. The abundance of His love and generosity is inseparable from His infinite joy."[6]

Often joy or happiness is spoken of throughout Scripture as a personal characteristic of God and is associated with another quality of God: His goodness. The creation account in Genesis indicates God was very happy as He created our world, concluding, "It's good." It was good, because what God does is always good. Joy is also an attribute of the Holy Spirit (Gal. 5:22–23). Elsewhere the Bible says, "The joy of the Lord is your strength" (Neh. 8:10). As Jesus prepared His disciples for His impending death, He offered them the consolation of His joy: "These things I have spoken to you, that My joy may be in you, and that your joy may be full" (John 15:11).

Someone else knew about the joy that comes from God: David. On one occasion David declared, "You make known to me the path of life; in your presence, there is fullness of joy" (Ps. 16:11). When David sought forgiveness and restoration from God, we hear him speak these words: "Let me hear joy and gladness; let the bones that You have broken rejoice...Restore to me the joy of Your salvation" (Ps. 51:8, 12).

David discovered there was a relationship between his salvation and God's joy! David knew God was delighted David wanted to know Him. And he recognized it made God very happy to reveal who He was to David. David's salvation and knowing God's joy were inseparable as far as David was concerned. To know true joy was to experience God. To experience God's Presence was pure joy. Dr. Willard further enhances this truth: "Joy is our portion in His fellowship. Joy goes with confidence and creativity. It is His joy, and that is not a small joy or a repressed joy."[7] Yes, it is a great, big joy that affects us to know and experience the goodness of God, no matter what our circumstances may be in life.

Unfortunately, millions of people who profess a belief in Jesus have missed the great opportunity to be a student of Jesus. Perhaps, it is due to the lack of attractiveness to such an invitation. Or they do not know about such an invitation, because after all, in today's Church, the preferred message would be something deemed more pleasant or positive—not realizing this invitation by Christ is the most positive and greatest opportunity He extends to anyone. I recall approaching a friend of mine years ago who was very successful in business and had become a millionaire in his mid-thirties. I asked him to consider this invitation from Jesus. I have not forgotten his response. He simply said, "No, I'm not ready for that!"

I'm not certain of his reason, and I'm not sure he knew what "that" offered. Maybe he thought God would want him to give up all his money and give it to the poor or he would be asked to serve in some uncomfortable capacity. I don't know. But what I do know, he was not ready to give up his will—his all—to the will of Christ. Sadly, this is not an isolated incident. It happens a lot today in the culture of the Church.

What Does It Mean to be a "Learner or Student" of Jesus?

The invitation to be Jesus's disciple means to spend time with Him so as to learn from Him. Subsequently, it is worth repeating. The word *disciple* comes from the Greek word *mathetes*, meaning a learner, a pupil, a student.[8] Jesus's invitation is about a personal relationship with Him. It's about spending time with Him, to be where He is, learning from Him, and growing into the person He desires us to become. An exchanged life is what Jesus offers! When you experience Him, truly experience Jesus, you can never remain the same person!

As a school principal, I would emphasize to the children that learning is growing and growing is changing and one could never learn if they were not listening to their teacher. To add emphasis to my message, I would remind the children, "Just because you sleep in a garage, doesn't make you a car!" After their laughter subsided, they realized, just because they were in a classroom, with a desk, books, pencils, and the environment to learn, did not make them a student. They would need to make the decision if they wanted to learn, even if their friends or peers wanted to play when it was not the time to play.

So it is the same in God's House today, in which many profess Christ but have not made the determination to become a student of Christ. It exists for many reasons. Before Jesus ascended into heaven, He gave instructions to His disciples: "Go therefore and make disciples of all nations (peoples)…teaching them to observe all that I have commanded you" (Matt. 28:19–20). This means the disciples were to replicate in all people what they learned and applied in their lives from time spent with Jesus. They were to lead others to Christ by investing their knowledge of Christ into others, which would produce more students of Jesus.

For whatever reason, this biblical mandate has not been done with diligence or intentional purpose. A leader is going to reproduce what he/she knows or does not know with the congregations they are entrusted to shepherd. If many leaders were not discipled, the effects will be reproduced. Keep in mind, the instruction by Jesus was not an option but a directive. God still expects leaders in His Church to "make learners" of His Beloved Son, Jesus. But how are we to do something we ourselves have never experienced, one may legitimately ask.

The Design for Discipleship

I believe the answer has three parts. The first is that we begin with the model of Jesus. He gave His disciples the blueprint for His directive, which was based on how Jesus personally invested in their lives. Although there were large crowds that followed His ministry, Jesus spent most of His time investing in twelve men. Jesus demonstrated to them how valuable every one of them was to Him. Jesus started with a small, limited group to invest His time and truths. This is the first important principle of mentoring. Today's pastor should do the same.

The next question would be, what did He teach them? We learn much of this from the type of questions they asked Him: "How should we pray?" (Luke 11). That is a great place to start—by teaching people how to cultivate a conversation with Father-God or how to seek and spend alone time with God. This is essential, particularly in our cultural context of social media and technology. On another occasion, they asked Jesus to teach them, "How to do the works (miracles) He did?" (John 6:28). Another time they asked, "How many times were they supposed to forgive?" (Matt. 18:21). Or He taught them how to serve against their backdrop of self-promotion with the goal of sitting at the right hand of Jesus (Mark 10:43–45). He taught them humility, both by words and example.

What would the Church look like if every pastor personally invested their time and knowledge of the Lord, as well as His word into the lives of young believers? Have you ever noticed how many questions new converts have? How many people need to be taught how to read and study the Word of God or how to memorize Scripture? And yes, it needs to be a small group so people can interact with their mentor, just as the disciples did with Jesus. Who knows where the Church-at-large would be, particularly regarding spiritual maturity, if we would only follow Jesus's directive!

It is important leaders model the blueprint of Jesus and begin mentoring as He directed. In fact, Jesus taught the disciples how to disciple others. On one occasion Jesus said, *"Therefore every scribe who has been trained for the kingdom of heaven is like a master of a house, who brings out of his treasure what is new and what is old" (Matt. 13:52).* Jesus is emphasizing that a leader who is trained in the principles of kingdom living should be training others how to live for Christ. This is the second most important dynamic for mentoring. It is from our own experiences—past and present—in our personal walk with the Lord that we draw from to teach others how to pray or fast, how to worship, or how to study. We need to move from just a one-time weekly message of telling people what to do or not to do, without telling them how to apply and live the truth of God's word in their lives.

When it came to His disciples, it was not just their questions He answered. He taught them how to effectively minister by telling them what to say, where to go, how to go, and what to do (Matt. 10). And more importantly, He taught them how to love people by the way He loved them. He taught them so many things. In fact one of His disciples stated, "Were every one of them to be written, I suppose that the world itself could not contain the books that would be written" (John 21:25).

The third most important dynamic of mentoring believers is you direct and guide them in cultivating their relationship with Jesus but without coercion. Sadly, not everyone wants to be a student of Jesus. The person must be given the choice to make such a determination. It is important the dignity (free will) of the individual is always respected and maintained since this sacred ability has been created in every person by God. A. W. Tozer underscores this dynamic truth:

> God has made us in His likeness, and one mark of that likeness is our free will. We hear God say, 'Whoever will, let him come.' We know by bitter experience the woe of an unsurrendered will and the blessedness or terror which may hang upon our human choice. But back of all this and preceding it is the sovereign right of God to call saints and determine human destinies. The master choice is His, the secondary choice is ours. Salvation is from our side a choice, from the divine side it is a seizing upon, an apprehending, a conquest of the Most High God. Our 'accepting' and 'willing' are reactions rather

than actions. The right of determination must
always remain with God.[9]

Again, God first moves through the Person of Jesus and the
invitation to be His student. The next move is ours. This should
amplify why this invitation by Jesus is the "greatest opportunity ever
extended to any human being." It is the greatest opportunity because
you will realize the very purpose for your existence and the plan God
has designed for your life. It is the most pivotal decision because it
is also the most difficult to make due to the persistent self-will to
self-navigate. However, the greater pain is missing out in not fulfilling God's will and purpose for your life.

Consider David. Do you think, when he was but a shepherd
boy, David dreamed about becoming the second king of Israel? Do
you think he intended to slay a ten-foot giant of a warrior at the age
of seventeen? Or do you believe David desired to be a fugitive for
ten years of his life, merely trying to survive against insurmountable odds? Though speculative, I believe he planned to marry, raise a
family, and follow the footsteps of his dad, which was the inevitable
pattern of many young Jewish men. David was probably looking forward to a simple, quiet family life on the farm.

But God had other plans for David. Tozer asserts it is the divine
pursuit that compels one to say yes to God's invitation. It is the "seiz-
ing upon and apprehending" of David that compelled the young
shepherd boy to say yes to God. No matter what David incurred, he
knew the cost would be worthwhile! David was just as human as you
and me. Even as a fugitive for ten years, while enduring those times
of bewilderment and confusion, he was yet willing to pay whatever
price to fulfill God's plan and purpose for his life. From the wilderness to the palace, David was willing to endure no matter what!

Think about it, my friend, and consider how strong and powerful the natural inclination is regarding self-determination. It requires

something or someone greater than one's self to come to such a realization, "My life is not my own, and I would do better, giving myself to Another!" Jesus tenderly waits for such a powerful awakening and personal decision today.

And there is of course something more. Jesus promised for the one who would follow and serve Him, "The Father would also honor!" Does that sound familiar? It was God's statement to a prophet at the introduction of Israel's monarchy: "For those who honor Me I will honor" (1 Sam. 2:30). God has not changed. Jesus also emphasized this eternal truth that makes it all the worthwhile to follow Him and become His student.

David's Discipleship Training

This is precisely what God described, David would well discover in his pursuit of God's own heart. David learned the priority of God's heart through a personal intimate relationship. David would learn what matters most to God. To value God through knowing Him and realizing the most important response to Him is doing what He wants you to do. But this could never happen without David first becoming the man God wanted him to become. Having a heart after God's own heart caused him to want to do what God wanted done as the "shepherd of Israel." This is what it means to honor God.

We should now have a better understanding of how David became the man God said he would become—"A man after My own heart." God was certainly not looking for a man that was perfect, just a man who was interested in the interests of God. A man who, above all else, would desire to "honor God" by doing what *would benefit* God!

From David's first classroom, the surrounding hills and obscure fields of Bethlehem while tending sheep, he learned to pen heartfelt songs of praise to the Lord he was getting to know and growing to love. There in the still, quiet, and fresh open air, the Lord taught the young shepherd the meaningfulness of worship in the natural beauty of God's created environment. I can't but wonder if later in life, during the busyness and demands of royal life, David looked into his rearview mirror longing for those quiet, uninterrupted moments with the sheep as they grazed. But, regardless, in looking back, David knew without a doubt, *his life was not his own.* And he would not have wanted it any other way.

The foundation for David was progressively and firmly laid as he graduated to the battlefield, and then to a lonely wilderness, learning from his Teacher how to be dependent upon God while developing a servant's heart. Each step of the way the Lord was teaching David Who He was, what He was like—His nature, His heart, and His purpose for his life. At the same time, David was learning who he was, especially when he stumbled periodically. But then doing a complete pivot toward God's grace, with a humility and repentant heart, he learned from the Lord. Such truth David realized throughout his life, all of which caused him to say, "I say to the Lord, 'You are my Lord; I have no good apart from You!'" (Ps. 16:2).

David had discovered, for him, life did not fit, it did not work, without full surrender and dependency upon the Lord. David indeed became a diligent, eager, and faithful student of the Lord, confirmed by his own words: "Make me to know your ways, O Lord; teach me Your paths. Lead me in Your truth and teach me" (Ps. 25:4–5). David continued to be hungry and thirsty to know the Lord, even in the classroom of a palace with all the luxuries afforded a king. Even with such privilege, power, and position, David could not *taste* enough of God. David stayed hungry for God by remaining teachable!

There was a price to be a student of the Lord—a cost to learn the ways of God— particularly during those dark seasons in his life. There were the ten years in the desert as a fugitive. Also, those tragic losses of his first four sons, one of which he suffered betrayal. The Lord taught him not to waste life's misfortunes with resentment but to use them for God's honor by remaining humble. David was indeed learning an important aspect of God's nature: "All things work together for good, for those who are called according to His purpose" (Rom. 8:28). David was learning, God was good, no matter his circumstances in life. David knew sorrows, but he also knew the joy of the Lord that surpassed anything this world could possibly offer him. David knew the cost to serve God was *not a miserable one, but more than worthwhile.* David realized the reward incredibly surpassed the cost to be a student of the Lord and was incomparable to anything in this life, as his words echo endlessly throughout time: "Because Your steadfast love is better than life, my lips will praise You!" (Ps. 63:3).

David was a joyful king and a fine student of the Lord, but he became something much more. Though God was fashioning a man to be a "prince of Israel, a shepherd of God's people," the Lord wanted more. The Lord was framing and forming a heart, a heart that would be just like God's own heart! And David did indeed become that man!

David died at the age of seventy. His reign endured forty years (1 Kings 2:11). No king in Israel's history secured and extended the borders of the nation as much as David. None were comparable in effectiveness and success like David's rule. David's reputation was such that over a thousand years later, another Jewish man, Paul, would say of David: "He (God) raised up David to be their (Israel's) king, of whom God testified and said, 'I have found in David the son of Jesse a man after My heart, who will do all My will'" (Acts 13:22).

We should never forget this all-important truth. David became the man God said he would become because he gave all to obtain the priceless pearl, the hidden treasure, which is God Himself! God searched and found a man who would respond to God's movement toward him. David seized the opportunity of a lifetime by listening and learning from the Lord he loved. This was David's pursuit of God's own heart. The result was an exchanged life—a transformed heart. David's life should underscore for us today the significance and meaning of Jesus's words: "If anyone serves Me, the Father will honor him" (John 12:26).

CHAPTER 14

The Destiny of David's House!

The one who conquers, I will grant him to sit with Me on My throne,
as I also conquered and sat down with My Father on His throne.
—Revelations 3:21

God's metanarrative refers to the larger or grand story of the entire Bible. It is the overarching narrative, His-Story, throughout the Old and New Testaments. God's metanarrative, like a long and winding river, runs its course, consistently, throughout all sixty-six books of the Bible, from Genesis to Revelation. And the central Person of every book is the Beloved Son of God, Jesus Christ!

Though the Old and New Testaments are distinguished by each Covenant, they are not inseparable from the other. Instead they should be read as one unified narrative. It is the "New enfolded in the Old, and the Old unfolded in the New," in a constant remarkable way! All the stories and individuals are subplots to God's metanarrative, which provide extraordinary consistency, transcending diverse cultures and personalities over thousands of years, convincing us of a compelling, singular Author! (2 Tim. 3:16).

For example, Israel's narrative, which we will discuss more in this chapter, is a part of God's metanarrative. The same is true regarding David's biography. You cannot really understand David's purpose unless you know something about Israel's destiny. Each story is an integral part to the progressive unveiling of God's metanarrative. Both are complementary for this purpose because they lead us to the Main Character of God's plot in His grand narrative. This reality alone, when understood from this perspective, should offer further credibility to the veracity, as well as to the consistency of Scripture.

All of this brings us to the important question: What is the metanarrative of God? It can be summed up in one sentence: *"Before the foundation of the world, God desired to have many sons (non-gender) to be just like His Beloved, and to rule with Jesus for all of eternity!" (Eph. 1:5).*

This grand story reveals God had a plan for our existence before He even created the world. That plan had everything to do with the very purpose for which God created you and me. In this chapter, we will discuss the first part of God's plan involving the destiny of the house God promised to build for David. The destiny: to reign with Jesus Christ for all of eternity.

God always purposed to have an eternal family that would rule with His Beloved throughout eternity. We gain our first glimpse through God's own words in the creation account: *"Let us make man in our image, after our likeness. And let them have dominion...over all the earth" (Gen. 1:26).* By giving mankind such an important responsibility of governing the earth, it reveals God's desire to share His rule of the universe with His highest of all creation. This is an amazing reality when you think about it. Man's original destiny was co-rulership with God!

On one occasion, perhaps while attending his sheep, David made such a discovery while gazing at the evening sky. He began thinking about God, and while worshiping Him, he expressed his contemplative thoughts regarding God's creative handiworks and His original purpose for mankind. It was only through the Holy Spirit's assistance, David could receive such a powerful revelation of man's purpose in relationship to God's creation. He later recorded this truth in one of his psalms:

> *When I look at your heavens, the work of your fingers, the moon and the stars, which you have set in place, what is man that you are mindful of him, and the son of man that you care for him? Yet you have made him a little lower than the heavenly beings and crowned him with glory and honor. You have given him dominion over the works of your hands; you have put all things under his feet. (Ps. 8:3–6)*

Let me share with you my translation of this powerful revelation and spiritual insight David received from God regarding humanity's original purpose: "Why do you Lord, give man such honor, and value him with such significance in your vast world you have created? You have given mankind the position in life, a little lower than You, and crowned him with your glory! What is your purpose in caring about mankind in such a way?" The word for heavenly beings is *Elohiym*, the plural meaning for God, referring to the Triune Godhead.

As the psalm reflects, man was created to rule, which is the meaning of "given dominion over the works" of God's hands. This is further validated through the word *honor* in this passage. It's an honor God gave to man—the position to rule with Him over His creation. But notice it is not to be done alone. Anytime we see the word *glory* in Scripture, it typically refers to God's Presence. Such is the meaning of man being "crowned with glory." Man was destined to rule with God but not independent from God. God is to be ever-present, alongside, if you will.

Remember we discussed in chapter 5, after Adam and Eve sinned, they felt "naked and hid themselves." Their nakedness not only referred to their physical condition, but their spiritual connectivity to God. When they sinned, God's glory or His Presence departed from them. Sin alienates as it informs God, He is no longer welcome.

We were never destined to rule without Him. We cannot have one without the other. Both dynamics are inseparable, and why not? Why would we want it any other way? Why would we want to go it alone? For this is the ultimate truth we must realize—we were never created to be separated from God. Instead, we were created to rule with His Presence, complementing and empowering our lives!

A small, but profound, book *Destined for the Throne*, authored by Paul Billheimer over forty years ago, amplifies the eternal plan and purpose God has had throughout human history:

> This royalty and rulership is no hollow, empty,
> figurative, symbolical, or emblematic thing. It is
> not a figment of the imagination. The Church,
> the Bride, the Eternal Companion is to sit with
> Him on His throne. If His throne represents
> reality, then heirs is no fantasy. Neither joint heir
> can do anything alone (Rom. 8:17). We may
> not know why it pleases the Father to give the
> kingdom to the little flock. We may not know
> why Christ chooses to share His throne and His
> glory with the redeemed. We only know that
> He has chosen to do so and that it gives Him
> pleasure.[1]

Mr. Billheimer underscores the most important aspect regarding our enthronement "to rule with Christ." We will not be alone or on our own. We have seen, throughout centuries of mankind's existence, the catastrophic consequences of going it alone. Never again.

Another time this truth of man's eternal destiny is underscored. The incident involves an exchange between a young wealthy ruler and Jesus. It ensues from the young ruler's inquiry of Jesus: "Teacher, what good deed must I do to have eternal life?"

Jesus responded, "If you would enter life, keep the commandments."

The young man then asked Jesus, "Which ones?"

And Jesus said, "You shall not murder, you shall not commit adultery, you shall not steal, you shall not bear false witness, honor your father and mother, and you shall love your neighbor as yourself."

The young man then said, "All these I have kept. What do I still lack?"

Jesus then said to him, "If you would be perfect, go, sell what you possess and give to the poor, and you will have treasure in heaven; and come, follow Me" (Matt. 19:16–21).

We are told the scene concludes with the young man walking away "sorrowful, because he was a man of great wealth." As the young man walks away, Jesus continues teaching his disciples by saying, "It is easier for a camel to go through the eye of a needle than for a rich person to enter the kingdom of heaven."

The disciples were stunned by the statement, so they questioned Jesus: "Who then can be saved?"

Jesus then said, "With man this is impossible, but with God all things are possible" (Matt. 19:24–26).

We can learn much from this account regarding God's eternal destiny for us, especially in the reaction of the disciples. For there are two main themes in this exchange: eternal life and rewards (treasures). The disciples are astonished with Jesus's teaching regarding a person of wealth. Why? Simply because they were impressed with the young man! This young ruler had kept Torah—the Law. The disciples were impressed with the young man's pedigree. And so their reaction was confusion and bewilderment: "If this man doesn't measure up, if he can't enter the kingdom of heaven, well then, who can?" Their basic assumption was, "Who can possibly qualify for acquirement of eternal life?"

Fulfilled by Him Alone

They did not realize, Jesus, the Master Teacher, cut precisely to the core issue by offering an invitation to the young man's question, "What do I still lack?" Jesus offered to him, "If you would be perfect, go, sell to the poor, and you will have treasure in heaven, and come, follow Me."

For the young man to follow Jesus, he had to give up what was most important to him—himself! The money is not the issue with Jesus. It was the condition of the young man's heart. Jesus wanted the man's heart—his self-governing will. But, in reading this passage, we tend to get stuck on the money issue. So did the young man and the disciples as evidenced by their reactions to the challenge made by Jesus.

Don't misunderstand me. This young man's wealth was an issue, but it was not *the* issue. People who are poor can miss God's purpose for their lives, just as much as people of wealth. Jesus was emphasizing the young man had a heart issue. The heart is always the priority with God, as Jesus emphasized while teaching this eternal truth in His Sermon on the Mount: *"Do not lay up for yourselves treasures on earth, where moth and rust destroy and where thieves break in and steal, but lay up for yourselves treasures in heaven, where neither moth nor rust destroys and where thieves do not break in and steal. For where your treasure is there your heart will be also" (Matt. 6:19–21).*

291

Jesus inserted the word *treasure* in the discussion because Jesus knew the young man's heart and what he valued most. What did the young man treasure most in life? What do you and I value most? Is it our possessions or position in life? Is it about our performance in life that validates or defines us? Is it our career, according to the world's definition of success, or how we perform well to impress others? These are issues of the heart, and the heart is the defining issue with God.

Why? Why is the heart of man so important to the Lord? We know when Saul failed to follow God, Samuel was told by the Lord in searching for Saul's replacement, "I have sought out a man after My own heart" (1 Sam. 13:14). Later then, during the selection process, God told Samuel, "For the Lord sees not as man sees...but the Lord looks on the heart" (1 Sam. 16:7).

The heart is vitally important to the Lord because it is the "core center" of the human will. Dr. Dallas Willard underscores this truth in his incisive book *Renovation of the Heart*: "The human heart, will, or spirit is the executive center of human life. The heart is where decisions and choices are made for the whole person. That is its function."[2] The heart determines one's course in life, as Scripture reflects: "Keep your heart with all vigilance, for from it flow the springs of life" (Prov. 4:23).

Jesus gave the young man an invitation that hinged on a preposition *if* and has everything to do with the young man's heart condition. Jesus offered, "If you would be perfect" (v. 21). Now we tend to get hung-up on the word *perfect* anytime we see it in Scripture. But in most translations, the Greek word origin for perfect is *teleios* and in this context means, "to complete or fulfill."[3] Therefore, a better understanding of this exchange would read regarding the young man's inquiry of what he still lacked, "If you want to be *complete* (fulfilled), go and sell, and give...and come, follow Me." Jesus was telling him the way to receive eternal life, "If you want to be *complete,* if you want that for which you were created and to know what will fulfill your life, give to Me, your heart…give to Me…yourself!" Jesus was telling him eternal life was about a personal, intimate, life-giving relationship with Him. It is the *only* way to be fulfilled in life. It is for this very reason each of us were created.

The only singular scriptural passage in all the New Testament, Jesus defines eternal life and is found in the longest recorded prayer of Jesus. It is in the gospel of John, chapter 17. How appropriate, and not merely coincidental, the definition comes to us in the form of a prayer: "And this is eternal *life*, that they know you the only true God, and Jesus Christ Whom You have sent" (John 17:3).

The eternal life Jesus was offering to the young man was a personal, interactive relationship with Father-God and His Son, Jesus Christ, in which he could know them intimately. This is the *life* they provide that would complete him. Jesus had said on another occasion, "For as the Father has life in Himself, so He has granted the Son also to have life in Himself" (John 5:26).

It was this gift of life Jesus desired to give to the young man. If only the young ruler would make the choice to give himself to Jesus and follow Him. It was the only way for the young man to be truly fulfilled. Jesus offers the same invitation He gave to the rich young ruler to you and me. Jesus invites each of us to become His student!

However, there are too many people who are like the young wealthy ruler. We all have the tendency to fill the void in our lives through other means. We self-navigate the best we know how: through the "riches" of various resources, such as relationships, sex, possessions, positions, and performances, including pseudo-induced highs (drugs)—all of which leave the person still wanting. People are not realizing, it is our heart that yearns for the very reason we were created. And nothing less than Jesus can complete us. For that void or vacuum in our hearts is reserved for only One Person—God and God alone!

Unfortunately, millions upon millions of people tragically spend a lifetime in their search looking for that which will fill the vacuum in their hearts, not discovering the eternal plan and purpose God has for every human being. Sadly, the young ruler was numbered among them as he turned away sorrowfully from the priceless offer Jesus gave him.

Destined to Rule with Christ!

As we know, the scene did not end there because, as only Peter could, he seized the moment by making the obvious comparison, underscoring the stark contrast between the decision of the disciples and the rich young ruler: "See, we have left everything and followed you. What then will we have?" Jesus said to them, "Truly, I say to you, in the new world, when the Son of Man will sit on His glorious throne, you who have followed Me will also sit on twelve thrones, judging the twelve tribes of Israel" (Matt. 19:27–28).

If you are like me, you can't help being amused with this conversation, especially if you are acquainted with Peter's history. Don't think for a moment the others were not asking themselves the same question—they were, indeed. It's just that Peter was the likely candidate they could coax and cajole to state and therefore ask the obvious! Ah yes, our courageous Peter!

Nevertheless, Jesus did not disappoint because He knew the Father's eternal plan for humankind. It was the very purpose Jesus was sent by the Father (John 7:29). So Jesus shared with them a glimpse of their reward. Jesus tells them, "Where I am enthroned, you will be enthroned with Me!" Jesus also indicates in the conclusion of this scene the destiny to rule with Him is not only for His disciples but "for everyone" (v. 29) who follows Him and accepts His invitation to be His disciple.

Is it any wonder David would be so amazed in this discovery of God's purpose for mankind? Later in his life he would again be overwhelmed with the majestic graciousness of God, when he is given the promise of God to build him a house and a throne that would last forever. We should not forget David's initial response to God's covenant with him: "Who am I, O Lord God, and what is my house, that You have brought me thus far?" (2 Sam. 7:18).

This entire plan and purpose of God is all due, as Paul says, "According to the riches of His grace, which He lavished upon us" (Eph. 1:7–8). It is all about God, His desire and destiny for His most beloved of all creation—you, I, and everyone who will decide to accept the invitation by Jesus to follow Him. Furthermore, this is exactly what the apostle Paul meant in his letter to the Ephesians when he declared, "By grace you have been saved—and raised us up with Him and seated us with Him in the heavenly places in Christ Jesus" (Eph. 2:5–6). Our destiny is to be enthroned with Jesus Christ and to reign with Him forever and ever. This wonderful destiny planned by the Father is also the promise of Jesus as He declares, *"The one who conquers, I will grant him to sit with Me on My throne, as I also conquered and sat down with My Father on His throne!" (Rev. 3:21).*

A Price to be Paid

As we conclude this aspect of God's metanarrative, I would be negligent if I did not emphasize the opening words of our Lord's declaration, "The one who conquers." Another translation also says, "The one who overcomes." This refers to the one who completes their training. It speaks of one who decisively became a student of Jesus and persevered in their training. The tendency of the human condition is to desire the blessings of God and the honor without investing a personal cost. Paul told Timothy, "If we endure, we will also reign with Him" (2 Tim. 2:12). To overcome means for us to finish our course of training. We must realize our destiny is determined by our willingness to be prepared. This is accepting the Lord's invitation to be His student. There is a price to be paid, and it is not a miserable one. Paul gave Timothy such instruction: "Rather train yourself for godliness; for while bodily training is of some value, godliness is of value in every way, as it holds promise for the present life and also for the life to come" (1 Tim. 4:7–8).

The world is God's classroom; and Jesus, our Teacher. We must rely on Christ to become like Him; therefore, we must choose to respond to His invitation: "Come to Me, all who labor and are heavy laden, and I will give you rest. Take My yoke upon you, and *learn from Me*, for I am gentle and lowly in heart, and you will find rest for your souls. For My yoke is easy, and My burden is light" (Matt. 11:28–30).

It is our choice to decide to become Jesus's student, and when we do, we will learn from Jesus how to become like Him every day and in every aspect of our lives. And most importantly, we will then discover His way will be "tailor-made" for us because His yoke is *easy*, which does actually mean "fit for use."[5] Indeed, His yoke is "well-fitting" because we were never designed to carry the load alone. It is His work and is reliable since we were originally designed for life with the Trinity—the Father, Son, and Holy Spirit—so as to fit naturally within the ethos of their community: selfless love!

Thus, it is our destiny for which God is preparing us for rulership with His Beloved for all of eternity. The world revolves around such training and preparation of the eternal companion for God's Beloved. Such preparation is predesigned to lead us to God's ultimate destination. It is the final piece to the magnificent metanarrative of God!

CHAPTER 15

Our Pursuit of God's Heart and Ultimate Destination for David's House!

For the creation waits with eager longing for
the revealing of the sons of God.
—Romans 8:19

M any people who believe in God, think our ultimate destination is heaven. It is not. Do not misunderstand me, heaven will be an indescribable reward because God's throne is there. To see Him, words will of course fail those who gain such an experience. It will be a wonder beyond our comprehension or imagination!

But, as tremendous heaven will be, it is not God's ultimate destination for the "house" He promised to build for David. Heaven is our reward. It has nothing to do with our purpose in this life. However, our ultimate destination does. Our ultimate destination, planned by God before the world was created, is such: *"And we know that for those who love God all things work together for good, for those who are called according to His purpose. For those whom He (Father-*

God) foreknew, He also predestined to be conformed to the image of His Son in order that He (Jesus) might be the firstborn among many brothers" (Rom. 8:28–29).

God's ultimate purpose for each of us is to fashion us into the character of His Son, Jesus, which is a very good thing. This means God will transcend our daily circumstances, which includes "all things" good or bad, and will use all such resources to ensure we reach His ultimate destination for our lives—Christlikeness. Our pursuit of God's heart is to allow Him to do what only He can do—transform us into the characteristic qualities of Jesus.

Three Levels of Spiritual Growth

Now it must be emphasized there are primarily three distinct levels of development in our journey of the Christian life. We all begin as "infants," which Paul describes as "feeding with milk, not solid food, for you were not ready for it" (2 Cor. 3:2). Then there are those who are "children, who should not remain children, tossed to and fro by the waves and carried by every wind of doctrine" (Eph. 4:14). Many believers tend to be in this category and should be challenged to grow up and "not to remain as children." In the same passage, Paul subsequently instructs the need to move on to "mature manhood (sonship), to the measure of the stature of the fullness of Christ" (Eph. 4:13). Sonship usually refers to becoming a son (or daughter) of Father-God, involving the progressive development of growing in our knowledge of God, resulting in the "fullness of Christ" or that which is known as spiritual maturity or Christlikeness.

Spiritual maturity is what God is seeking, the essence of becoming an "adopted son" of God. This journey is a time of training and spiritual development to become prepared to rule with Jesus. God wants to trust us with such a leadership responsibility for eternity.

God is not going to be arbitrary in entrusting those with such an honor and reward. So there will be a price to be paid, one that is very worthwhile, as we learned in chapter 13. The cost is allowing one to be shaped in the character of Jesus Christ, the ultimate destination for every follower who decides to become a student of Jesus! So if a cost is involved in our journey leading us to conformity to Jesus's character, this naturally provokes such questions: What does the price involve? Or what does the journey look like and what ensures we will reach God's ultimate destination for each of us?

Our Pursuit of God's Heart—Sanctification

You may recall, as a sixteen-year old, I asked God "to be a Father to me." Without a doubt, I knew the Lord had spoken to me in that moment. But I had a problem as a young Christian man. God knew how to be a Father to me, but I did not know *how* to be a son! It would be some years later, during a season of brokenness and early prayer at the track field, the Lord would speak to me, through His still, small voice, these words: "I have ordained this path you are on, a path of consecration!"

To be honest, I wasn't certain what the word *consecration* even meant. When I got home I asked my wife the meaning because I had not heard the word used very often in church. I then did a quick study in my concordance. I learned *consecration* carries the basic meaning, "to be set apart or separated to God." The word is also synonymous with *sanctify*, and both are associated with the term *holiness*.

To consecrate captures this fuller meaning, "Dedicate to service and loyalty to God; make holy, sanctify, to cause one to have the quality of holiness."[1] To be holy, according to the literal Greek, also includes the definition, "to be set apart or separated to God."[2] But what does that mean? Yes, there is a deeper meaning that we will discuss in a moment.

The words *consecrate, sanctify,* and *holiness* were at the time used infrequently in my experience as a young Christian. They were unfamiliar to me, not only in their meaning but practical application. I believe the same is even truer today for many believers.

Now I considered, if God took the time in prayer to personally emphasize the value of this "pathway" He had planned for me, then it must be very important to Him and I should give it the same weight of value. The Lord constitutes tremendous significance to this character attribute, according to just a few selected scriptures:

- *As obedient children, do not be conformed to the passions of your former ignorance, but as He who called you is holy, you also be holy in all your conduct, since it is written, You shall be holy, for I am holy. (1 Pet. 1:14–16)*
- *For God has not called us for impurity, but in holiness. Therefore, whoever disregards this, disregards not man but God, who gives His Holy Spirit to you. (1 Thess. 4:7–8)*
- *Now may the God of peace Himself sanctify you completely and may your whole spirit and soul and body be kept blameless at the coming of our Lord Jesus Christ. (1 Thess. 5:23)*
- *Even as He chose us in Him before the foundation of the world, that we should be holy and blameless before Him. (Eph. 1:4)*

Clearly, holiness is important to God. It is noteworthy the apostle Peter cites the scripture recorded in the book of Leviticus, which was God's initial call to Israel at Mt. Sinai: "Consecrate yourselves therefore, and be holy, for I am holy" (Lev. 11:44). This corresponds to God wanting to give the Israelites their new identity: "God's treasured possession...a kingdom of priests, a holy nation" (Exod. 19:5–6). This was how God specifically defined Israel. God wanted the nation to be unique and distinct from all the nations of the world. God desired Israel to be a "treasured possession" set apart to Him and to no other. God wanted a people who would want Him the same way He wanted them. God desired they would have a heart after His own heart.

Holiness is important to God because He is Holy! And if it is important to God, it should be important to us. If He wants us to be holy, as He is holy, then it must be for our best interest and well-being. We should realize it is for our benefit to become what God wants us to be since God is good, wanting only His beneficial goodness for us!

If that is true, and Scripture insists it is, then why is it not emphasized more often in God's house today? Is it because of a misconception of holiness? Is it because it is not that popular a message for people to hear? Do some believe it may be an irrelevant message, particularly for a culture that seemingly has license to be self-indulgent or entitled? Or do we think it may be a lifestyle that is not only impractical but unrealistic to actualize in daily living? Most of these factors contribute to some extent for the lack of emphasis regarding holiness. Certainly, the lack of understanding, as well as not realizing the importance of this Godly attribute, contributes to the dilemma.

Unfortunately, much of the misconception can be attributed to a distorted meaning of the Christian life. For example, in the past, a holiness emphasis was on the external behavior. Much attention was given to how one dressed, particularly for women, involving "no makeup, no jewelry" clauses, as well as rules for hairstyles and fashion. You could not attend movies, go to dances, or play cards. These were labeled as "things of the world" and must be avoided in order to maintain a lifestyle of holiness. Consequently, holiness comprised an extrinsic emphasis of rules. And, though the standards of conduct may have changed due to our culture, the misconception of holiness has not to a large extent. David Kinnaman provides a recent survey how the perception of the Christian life remains to be a list of do's and don'ts in the following summary:

> We explored the perspectives of those who attend church in a typical month. More than four out of every five agreed that the Christian life is well described as "trying hard to do what God commands." Two-thirds of churchgoers said, "Rigid rules and strict standards are an important part of the life and teaching of my church." Three out of every five churchgoers in America feel that they 'do not measure up to God's standards." And one-quarter admitted that they serve God out of a sense of 'guilt and obligation rather than joy and gratitude." These are the actual phrases we used in our surveys, which makes it quite startling to see how much these terms resonate with church attenders.[3]

There are plenty of surveys that indicate this perception persists among millennials (eighteen to twenty-nine) today and is a leading factor for repelling people toward organized religion. Although church leadership in the past may have been well intentioned, the emphasis has been sorely misguided by focusing on the outward behavior or things we do not do. As a result, we have a brief and fragmented glimpse of what holiness is not!

However, despite past misguided emphasis, our conduct and lifestyle is important to God. But it is not the starting point. Holiness does not begin with what we do or don't do. Rather the emphasis should begin with our personal identity. The human heart is always the starting point with God. Outward behavior is always determined by the heart. And if we are going to better understand the journey leading us to our ultimate destination, holiness must be defined and described based upon God's Word, starting with the human heart.

What Is Holiness?

There are two known distinctions: the positional and progressive qualities. Both are complementary to the other. The latter cannot be attained without the former. Let's discuss first the positional status. This understanding begins with the knowledge God is holy. God by His very presence affects holiness. When God touches anything, He makes the article holy by His very presence. When the Lord appeared to Moses in the burning bush, God instructed Moses to take off his sandals because "he was standing on holy ground" (Exod. 3:5).

When we surrender our life to Christ, salvation is inaugurated through the Holy Spirit becoming resident in our heart. Since the Spirit of God is Holy, He makes us holy. Holiness comes from the life of God, and it must begin with God's highest priority—the human heart!

As God introduced Himself to Israel, He had Moses construct an altar for sacrifices and a Tent of Meeting from which He would speak to Moses and Israel. Listen to His instruction: "There I will meet with the people of Israel, and it shall be sanctified by My glory. I will consecrate the tent of meeting and the altar. Aaron also and his sons I will consecrate to serve Me as priests" (Exod. 29:43–44).

Glory always refers to God's Presence. God was informing Moses when He showed up and touched the various articles, He sanctified them. In fact, when Moses met with the Lord, the countenance of the Lord's glory was so brilliant on Moses's face, he had to wear a veil (Exod. 34:35). The same occurs when Christ comes into our hearts.

God initiates His holiness into our lives through the infusion of His Indwelling Presence.

Now then if this is true, and it is, why would Peter also instruct people to become holy in all their conduct (1 Pet. 1:15)? Or consider Paul's exhortation: "Beloved, let us cleanse ourselves from every defilement of body and spirit, bringing holiness to completion in the fear of God" (2 Cor. 7:1). Because there is a second distinction involving a specific goal determined by God. Holiness is a progressive work also of the Holy Spirit. It has everything to do with our journey and an ultimate destination God has in mind for our lives.

Pastor Jack Hayford, in his wonderful book *Rebuilding the Real You*, offers an incisive view regarding this work of the Holy Spirit:

> The word *holy* is derived from the medieval English "hal," an eleventh-century word that is the root to such contemporary words as health, hale, whole, and holy. Obviously, therefore, holiness is more than an esoteric spiritual attribute, and it relates to more than merely the invisible. Holiness involves the completion in all your parts of the human being. That's what holiness is really about—wholeness.[4]

It is unfortunate holiness has been viewed as something unattainable or merely a religious construct of extrinsic rules and regulations. Pastor Hayford's insight informs us, holiness is a good thing. God has called us to be whole, as He is whole. Complete, as He is complete. And we will never be made holy or become complete without God.

We should never forget, God is the One who completes us. It is His work and involves the entire human being—our heart, soul, mind, and body. Scripture says as much: *"But when one turns to the*

Lord, the veil is removed. Now the Lord is the Spirit and where the Spirit of the Lord is, there is freedom. And we all, with unveiled face, beholding the glory of the Lord, are being transformed into the same image from one degree of glory to another. For this comes from the Lord who is the Spirit" (2 Cor. 3:16–18). This is God's work: to transform us into the image of His Son from one level to the next.

So we should understand holiness to be a two-fold work of the Holy Spirit. Holiness begins with the human heart, the residence of the human will. This is the positional distinction. It is from this position, the Holy Spirit begins to lead us so that we may grow into maturity and we may reach our ultimate destination, which is to have a heart like Jesus. This is the journey of sanctification; and it will affect our entire being, as Paul says, including our outward behaviors toward God and others. Such a journey is our pursuit of God's own heart.

Now we are ready to answer the original question: What does a journey of consecration look like and what does it involve? Initially, I didn't know. But eventually I learned some important insights through my study of God's word, as well as what He taught me in my personal walk, which was transformative. During a season of brokenness, the Lord apprehended two significant areas of concern. He emphasized the need to attend my prayer life with more regularity and to gain a better knowledge of His Word. The Lord revealed to me these two functions needed to become a solid foundation in my relationship with Him if I really wanted to know Him. As I allowed the Lord to construct such a foundation in my life, I would soon discover the reality I would not be alone since He would be interacting with me daily.

Prayer That Transforms

It was during prayer in the early morning hours at the track field, the Lord began to teach me some important dynamics regarding prayer. The Lord taught me how to listen to Him—how to become familiar with His voice. When we learn this, I promise, prayer does become the most exciting, enriching, and enjoyable experience in one's life. Too often, prayer becomes mundane and boring because we are doing all the talking. Prayer was never intended to be a one-way conversation.

Our times of prayer should evolve and expand into becoming interested in the interests of God. Have you ever considered posing this heart-stirring question: How are *you* doing today, Father-God? What are you up to, and how can I be a part of it? Please don't misunderstand, I know God is all-sufficient. He doesn't need us to accomplish His purpose. However, He has chosen such a method as the means in training us for rulership throughout eternity. This is what it means to be a "co-laborer or fellow worker with God" (1 Cor. 3:9).

Isn't this one of the great discoveries David learned in his life? David was interested in God and what concerned the Lord. He writes as much: "The secret of the Lord is with those who fear Him; and He will show them His covenant" (Ps. 25:14, NKJV).[5] Another translation says, "The Lord confides in those who fear Him."[6] This is a powerful truth regarding prayer. David desired to know the mind of the Lord in his prayer life. It's as if David was asking, "Lord, what are you desiring to do today in Israel? What are your plans, Lord?" This became David's concern. As the Lord taught and revealed to David His will and plans, David learned to become more interested in what benefits God.

This was exemplified in David's desire to build the Lord a house. Remember the tender words of God that Solomon reviewed while dedicating the newly built Temple: "But the Lord said to David my father, 'Whereas it was in your heart to build a house for My name, you did well that it was in your heart'" (1 Kings 8:18). It was, as if God said, "Thank you, David, for thinking of Me. You have done well, David, to consider Me!" That is a heart after God's own heart, and this dynamic truth has everything to do with holiness!

We are becoming more mature as a son and daughter of God when our prayer life is evolving into more of an interest toward the concerns of God. This is precisely what Jesus meant as He compared our relationship to Him through the Vine-branch analogy: "If you abide in Me, and My words abide in you, ask whatever you wish, and it will be done for you" (John 15:7). It is through such a connection with the Lord we learn what He wants, and then our want becomes what He wants! This is true, effectual prayer, and it is exciting when you experience such answers of prayer!

All of us are on a different level of faith in our journey with the Lord, and our prayer life is a leading indicator how we are growing in Christ. It's simply about becoming more interested in what benefits God. You become more interested in doing what God wants. Dr. Willard articulates this powerful truth from his perspective: "To love God with all your heart is to have your will and your spirit entirely set on the accomplishment of what is good for God."[7] I like that. We become more interested in doing what God wants rather than what we want. Such is the pursuit of God's own heart. Becoming more like an adopted son of God by growing in holiness and being formed more in the image of Jesus is the heart of holiness!

Another important transformative aspect of prayer is the Lord revealing those issues that hinder us from reaching God's destination He planned for us. A scriptural passage that captures this truth is the following:

But that is not the way you learned Christ—
assuming that you have heard about Him and

were taught in Him, as the truth is in Jesus, to put off your old self, which belongs to your former manner of life and is corrupt through deceitful desires, and to be renewed in the spirit of your minds, and to put on the new self, created after the likeness of God in true righteousness and holiness. (Eph. 4:20–24)

The journey of sanctification, as Paul instructs, through guidance and direction of the Holy Spirit, is the displacement of the "old self" and the replacement with the "new self." The old self is described further, "We walked in the futility of our minds...alienated from the life of God" (Eph. 4:17–18). Because we were estranged from a relationship with God, we once walked in the futility of self-navigation. Therefore, we are called to do away with such practices, putting off the old self. We then put on the new self as we *learn Christ*. Learning Christ is the gradual process of being transformed into the likeness of Jesus. Such is the progressive work of holiness in our lives.

Let me share a practical illustration. On one occasion, I purchased a designer sport coat, which cost several hundred dollars. It was a custom fit and became a favorite. During the first visit to the dry cleaners, it was ruined by a disgruntled employee. Unfortunately, the owner was going through a difficult time and did not have insurance. We agreed to her arrangement of $50 payments each week. Nevertheless, I was frustrated!

Soon after my coat's collision with the mad employee, I was reading the following teaching by Jesus in His Sermon on the Mount during my devotions:

If you love those who love you, what benefit is that to you? For even sinners love those who love them. And if you do good to those who do good to you, what benefit is that to you? For even sinners do the same. And if you lend to those from whom you expect to receive, what credit is that to you? Even sinners lend to sinners, to get back the same amount. But love your enemies, and do good, and lend, expecting nothing in return, and your reward will be great, and you will be sons of the Most High, for He is kind to the ungrateful and the evil. Be merciful, even as your Father is merciful. (Luke 6:32–36).

As I finished reading this passage, I clearly heard the Lord speak to me, "John, I want you to forgive this debt!" Immediately, tears welled up in my eyes, because for the first time I understood the "reward" Jesus was talking about. The reward is, "You will be sons of the Most High!" Jesus was teaching, "If you love and live in this radical new way, you will become like your Father, who is kind and merciful to those who don't deserve it!" Eventually, I forgave the debt. I really liked the coat—a lot. But really, this was the penetrating truth that gripped my heart. It was as if Jesus said to me, "If it was me, I would forgive the debt!"

So the decision came down to what was more important to me? Did I want to become like God's Beloved? This was the teaching point Jesus presented to me, which embodies the process of "putting off the old self, and putting on the new, which is Christ."

God's Word Trains Us

It's important to also emphasize, I was reading God's Word at the time. Through the combination of prayer and study of God's word, I changed course. The Lord spoke by His Spirit to my heart and then to my mind through His written word. The importance of the word of God cannot be overstated. It is another important discipline the Lord uses to cultivate holiness in our lives. Paul reminds us of this truth: "All Scripture is breathed out by God and profitable for teaching, for reproof, for correction, and for *training* in righteousness, that the man of God may be complete, equipped for every good work" (2 Tim. 3:16–17). The pathway of sanctification is God training us for our eternal rulership with Christ.

The reason the word of God is so invaluable to me is because it has changed my life. Although I've had the fortunate opportunity of seminary, I rely heavily on the Lord's assistance with exegetical work. Many of us understand the Bible as the most complex and comprehensive book ever written, primarily due to the Author. Therefore, I never study Scripture alone. In this process, one of the major guidelines I've learned when studying is to read it from God's perspective and not merely from my limited human view. "Father, what are you saying here? Lord, what is the principle you are teaching in this scene?" This helps immensely in gaining a better understanding of God's nature, especially in relationship to people. Studying God's word through the prism of His nature and heart will enable one to see the marvelous consistency and veracity of God's metanarrative, transcending all human history.

We should study God's word and assimilate it into our lives as one of God's greatest priorities. Subsequently, I desire it to become just as important to everyone I may encounter. One of the primary objectives of this book is that people who desire to become true followers of Jesus will fall in love with God's word and discover the enriching value of its irreplaceable purpose. It's my constant hope to inspire others to dig into God's Word and discover the transformative "gems" His word can and does produce in our lives as we get to know Him. It is from such a perspective I share a sobering concern. There seems to be a rapid erosion of valuing God's word in the Church today. The George Barna Group conducted a survey, assessing the spiritual climate of the Church, comparing from 2011 to 1991. One of the most pronounced changes over the twenty-year span was how the Bible was viewed. The Barna Group offered this ominous summary among those who described themselves as Christians: "The largest change in beliefs was the decline in those who firmly believe the Bible is accurate in all of the principles it teaches. Only 43 percent of self-identified Christians have such a strong belief in the Bible."[8]

More recently, a well-known, self-identified Christian leader on a prominent national platform contended the Church would find itself more and more irrelevant in today's culture, if it continued to quote ancient letters from over two thousand years ago. It's saddening to view the growing inclination to diminish the value and importance of God's Word in the life of the believer. Both the Church trend and the leader's commentary are egregious in their misjudgment of the value of God's Word. The repercussions for our society are evident and grievous. Clearly, we see a culture convulsing with blurred boundaries of moral truth, especially in the context of one's pursuit for individual pleasure and happiness. And tragically, this cultural mind-set has invaded the church. Here, we don't have time to spend on the causes, which are various regarding those misguided deductions that place less or little value of God's word. The only thing I would offer is such conclusions have everything to do with one's "God-filter"—a futile attempt to redefine and reduce God to our image based on human circumstance or expectations. People are picking and choosing what they are willing to believe based on their preconceived image of God. And, if God doesn't fit "our" view according to our presuppositions, we then must redefine Him—or worse, displace Him!

To succumb to such grievous deception is a grave condition spiritually. With sadness, all I can say is any person who can reduce

God to their own definition is someone who apparently has no fear of God, meaning, a wrong assertion for the "right worth" of God. Such an individual has a weak constitution of God and will suffer the effects of being "tossed to and fro by every wind of doctrine" (Eph. 4:14), resultant in a severe lack of maturity. A good, wholesome fear—a fear that is awed by His Presence—simply cannot afford such redefinition. Reducing God to our finite understanding is nothing new. It is only a form of idolatry known as self-sufficiency. To view God through such a limited filter, reduced to human understanding, would be, for me, completely boring. I'm thankful God is God, and I am not!

Instead of neglecting the word of God, let us attend carefully the value of those words, "*training* in righteousness" (2 Tim. 3:16). Our preparation to rule depends on it.

This statement by Jesus defines the real value of God's Word: "I am the way, and the truth, and the life" (John 14:6). We must not forget what God taught David when he committed adultery. The cause for David's indiscretion was due to not valuing God's word. To value God's word is to trust what God says is true about Him, about us, and especially about sin. God's truth is not only *a way* of believing but *a way* of living! God's Word provides a framework and a constitution for Christian living, and we should always esteem the veracity and value of it in our pursuit of God's heart!

"I will Honor those who Honor Me." (1 Sam. 2:30)

Now we need to understand a life of holiness has everything to do with love—God's love for us and our love for Him. God wants us whole because of His love for us. Holiness becomes wanting the same thing God wants. True holiness is loving God well.

In today's culture, the word *love* has taken on many meanings. For some, it lacks depth and devotion. But when it comes to loving God, love is inseparable from doing what He wants us to do! Love for God is active, not passive. Jesus defined loving God as such: "Abide in My love. If you keep My commandments, you will abide in My love, just as I have kept My Father's commandments and abide in His love" (John 15:9–10). Jesus equates loving Him with doing what He wants us to do! Let's not forget this is how God described the heart of David: *"I have found in David the son of Jesse a man after My heart, who will do all My will!" (Acts. 13:22)*

Doing God's will for our life is what it means to "honor God." How can we say, we love God and not do what He wants us to do? Such actions contradict the nature of a mature adopted son! Dr. Dallas Willard articulates a passionate and profound summary regarding this spiritual truth:

> Single-minded and joyous devotion to God and His will, to what God wants for us—and do service to Him and to others because of Him—is what the will transformed into Christlikeness looks like. That is the outcome of Christian spiritual formation with reference to the will, heart, or spirit. And this outcome becomes our character when it has become the governing response of every dimension of our being. Then we can truly be said to have "put on Christ."[9]

Let's give close attention to those words: "Single-minded and joyous devotion to God and His will, to what God wants for us…" Dr. Willard's statement corresponds precisely with the relationship described by Jesus with His Father: "For He has not left Me alone, for I always do the things that are pleasing to Him."

We must listen carefully to those words or we will miss the depth of Jesus's statement: *"For I always do the things that are pleasing to Him."* Everything Jesus did was to please the Father. But there, is where most of us fall off the track. It's so pivotal a truth, this core issue will determine whether we will become a student of Jesus. We must ask ourselves: Do we really intend to please our Father in every aspect of our lives? Jesus did.

To be honest with you, I'm not sure how many who profess Christ really believe it's possible. Do we really believe we can live a life wholly and fully dependent upon God in the same way Jesus did? Do we think it possible for one to do only the Father's will for one's life? Do we truly understand one can be holy as God is holy? Do we find it realistically possible or practical for sin to be an "unwelcome stranger" in our life? Do we have confidence we can reach the ultimate destination God has for every believer, which is to be conformed to the character of His Son, Jesus Christ? (Rom. 8:29). The answer will only be yes if we truly discover how God will do such a work.

One + One = Honor for God!

The ultimate outcome of becoming a son like Jesus cannot be actualized through passionate prayer and the study of God's word alone but must also have the intentional assimilation of two prominent principles required to participate in the life of Christ. These should be viewed as the vehicles that will drive each of us to God's ultimate destination for our lives.

The first has everything to do with *trust*. The meaning of this principle is best illustrated in the plight of the Israelites who wandered in the wilderness for forty years. The writer of the book of Hebrews tells us the very reason they did not enter "God's Rest"

(Promised Land): "And to whom did He swear that they would not enter His rest, but to those who were disobedient? So, we see that they were unable to enter because of unbelief" (Heb. 3:18–19).

Many of the two and half million Israelites died in the wilderness because they were unwilling to *trust* God to do for them what they could not do for themselves. Another word for trust is *confidence*. They did not have confidence in God to do what He had promised them. Listen to the words God spoke to Moses: "How long will this people *despise Me*? And how long will they not believe in Me, in spite of all the signs that I have done among them? None of the men who have seen My glory and My signs that I did in Egypt and in the wilderness, and yet have put Me to the test these ten times and have not obeyed My voice, shall see the land that I swore to give to their fathers. And none of those who *despised Me* shall see it" (Num. 14:11, 22–23).

God considers a lack of confidence in Him as a devaluing act personally! That's what it means to despise the Lord. It's personal. Think about it, my friend. When we don't believe Him, we are saying, "We don't trust or have confidence in you, to do what you say you will do!" Ultimately, the Israelites did not believe in God's promise that He would be the One who would give to them the Land He had promised them. So due to their lack of confidence in the God who loved them, they could not enter His rest.

Now because of its significance, we must now ask: What was the specific form of their unbelief? Fear! They were unwilling to fight! Listen to the response of the ten spies that had went in to scout the land in advance, and came back with their own conclusion: "We are not able to go up against the people, for they are stronger than we are" (Num. 13:31). The tragedy was the people agreed with their assertion, "We are not able," resulting in the people wondering and wandering in defeat, never reaching their God-given destination!

The problem was not recognizing they were "not able." God agreed with their assessment. The problem was not acknowledging large fortified cities and a strong people who greatly outnumbered them. The problem was their misguided focus. It was on themselves—their circumstances, their expectations, past and present. Their focus was on their own human limitations, rather than God, who for the past two years had demonstrated what *He was able* and willing to do in their lives if they would *only* surrender to His will for their lives!

God never told the people they would go in and take the land alone. That was never His plan. In fact, God told them He would go with them, according to Moses: "The Lord your God who goes before you will Himself fight for you, just as He did for you in Egypt before your eyes, and in the wilderness, where you have seen how the Lord your God carried you, as a man carries his son, all the way that you went until you came to this place" (Deut. 1:30–31). They would indeed fight, but God would be right there with them, leading the charge and giving them the victory. This was God's promise. It was always God's purpose to have a people who would be known as conquerors. Victors in this world and not victims. The problem was they were too self-absorbed. To be more concrete, they were not willing to surrender their hearts to the Lord. They had to decide to *trust* God to lead them into the Promised Land.

We must remember the human will resides in the heart. Holiness is about the heart and has everything to do with the human will. We can never reach God's ultimate destination for our lives without a surrendered will to His good will. Israel is a portrait of such a tragedy and is a lesson for millions of professing Christians today. Because of Israel's unwillingness to trust God, many of the people died in the wilderness, not arriving to their God-appointed destination. And worse yet, they also missed out on their destiny. Remember God had called them to be His "treasured possession."

Speaking of treasure, this brings us to the second most powerful principle. What does one *treasure* or value most in life? This is life's defining issue. Jesus described it another way: "For where your treasure is, there your heart will be also" (Matt. 7:21). Jesus is saying, what is most important or valuable to a person will determine one's course in life. Just as God wanted Israel to be His treasured possession, He wants the same for you and me today. The goal of Father-God is to have a people who will treasure Him in the same way He treasures us. God wants a people who have "a single-minded and joyous devotion" to His will, which is always good. On our pathway of consecration, we begin to "learn Christ" by wanting the same things He wants. This is the essence of treasuring and valuing God, which is the outcome of becoming a son to the Father.

Such truth is captured by Paul's exhortation: "Walk in a manner worthy of the Lord, fully pleasing to Him, bearing fruit in every good work and increasing in the knowledge of God" (Col. 1:10). There is that key word, *pleasing*, again. When we desire nothing but to please the Lord, we will then want more than anything to live a life that honors God! It simply comes down to what do you want most in life? If we will treasure God more than anything in life and then actualize this purpose in our lives, we can be confident of reaching God's destination for our lives: Christlikeness!

We must understand both dynamics are inextricably connected. One will probably not trust God without treasuring Him most in life. And we will not *treasure* Him most until we learn to *trust* Him more than anything in this world. Both dynamics are interdependent and result in honor for God! Living a consecrated life to God is possible. Jesus would not ask us to become something we are not capable of becoming. He is not that kind of Savior, and God is not that kind of Father. It just comes down to who we *trust* and what do we *treasure* most in life.

There is no reason to stay stagnate in our growth to become an adopted son of God. For God has provided all the necessary resources to ensure we reach His ultimate destination. Peter says as much: "His divine power has granted to us *all things* that pertain to life and godliness, through the knowledge of Him who called us to His own glory and excellence" (2 Pet. 1:3). This tells us of God's unfathomable commitment to get us to our God-appointed destination.

Separated to God!

There is probably no better illustration of this reality than a profound scene involving Peter and Jesus on their way to Gethsemane. Jesus gives Peter an ominous warning: *"Simon, Simon, behold, Satan demanded to have you, that he might sift you like wheat, but I have prayed for you that your faith may not fail. And when you have turned again, strengthen your brothers"* (Luke 22:31–32). Peter responds typically as he always did, with bravado and boldness, insisting he would rather go to prison or die for Jesus than to deny Him. However, Jesus persists in letting Peter know he will not deny Him just once but on three separate occasions.

This incident illustrates what it means to be *separated to God*. To understand the meaning, we must consider the word *sift* as applied to Peter. As we know, to sift is an agricultural process of separating the kernels of wheat from the chaff or what is known as the "worthless seed coverings and other debris." The process is designed to separate the "good from the bad."[10]

Now let's consider again the warning of Jesus to Peter: "Satan has demanded you, to sift you like wheat!" This means Satan wanted to separate Peter from something or someone good. This begs the question, what good is in Peter? The only good in Peter is Jesus! Satan desired to separate Peter from Jesus. But Jesus said no, "Peter is mine!" This is what it means to be "set apart or separated to God." It is the deepest expression of intimacy by becoming a part of God—being indwelt by Him, completed and cared for by Him. It is a sacred union. Inseparable!

This is the powerful and beautiful message for each of us. Jesus knew Peter would fail and informed him as much. However, Jesus also encouraged Peter by telling him, *"But I have prayed for you that your faith may not fail."* Jesus was telling Peter in advance, "I know you are going to fail Me, but I want you to know Peter, I'm not going to give you up to Satan, no matter what!" We don't know exactly how Jesus prayed, but there is some indication, as He prayed to the Father for His disciples: "I have manifested Your name to the people whom you gave Me out of the world. *Yours they were, and You gave them to Me*, and they have kept Your word...I am praying for them. I am not praying for the world but for those whom you have given Me, for they are Yours. *All mine are Yours, and Yours are mine*, and I am glorified in them" (John 17:6, 9–10). Being set apart to God is the spiritual reality, "I am His, and He is mine!"

This should encourage us by realizing, despite our failures and mistakes, much like Peter or David, God does not give up on us. God does not separate from us and leave us alone if we still want Him. God remains committed to us as He leads us to our ultimate destination: Christlikeness. And He will not give you up to the evil schemes of the enemy of your soul. However, our tendency is to remember and focus on our missteps and stumblings rather than the unfathomable grace of God as He refashions us into the image of Jesus.

We must not forget, especially in that moment before Peter's failure, the most important gem Jesus wrapped in hope for him. Let me paraphrase it: "When you pivot back to me, again, teach your brothers what you learned from me, for it will encourage them (Luke 22:32). In effect, Jesus was telling Peter, "When you learn the lesson you needed to learn from your weakness, let everyone else know, how deep my love and commitment is for those who are mine." He taught Peter, His love transcends whatever circumstances we will encounter. God's love and grace is greater than our greatest failure because it is God's intention to use "all things to work together for good who are called according to His purpose" (Rom. 8:28). God is just like that.

Defined by a Father

True holiness is becoming the person God wants us to become. We should think of it as the highest expression of God's love. For to have "Christ formed in you" (Gal. 4:19) should be viewed as the greatest privilege in this life, because it is the greatest blessing and benefit one could ever experience—learning to love as God loves. For holiness is our heart becoming like God's heart. This was God's goal, predetermined for us before the foundation of the world, and He will not be denied His ultimate purpose in creating mankind as He reminds us through the prophet Isaiah: *"Remember the former things of old; for I am God, and there is no other; I am God, and there is none like Me, declaring the end from the beginning and from ancient times things not yet done, saying, 'My counsel shall stand, and I will accomplish all My purpose'"* (Isa. 46:9–10).

A leading indication of our spiritual growth and maturity into the kind of "son" our Father desires is measured by becoming more interested in what is good for Him. Certainly, and without question, God is interested in us becoming uninterested in sin. God wants us to realize how boring and unappealing it is, especially in comparison to who He is and what He offers. But more than that, becoming a son that is more interested in the interests of his Father is a son who only desires to do what is good for his Father. Such is the pursuit of God's own heart!

As we have learned by now, David learned to become such a man. Nothing was more important for David than to know the Lord and to do His will. From the pasture to the palace, God was always teaching David who He was, His will, and His ways. The same is true for us today. God can teach those who are willing to be His student. The student who is willing is that person who wants to arrive to their God-appointed destination no matter the cost. The student who is willing is the one who wants to fulfill their God-given destiny to become the "son" God can trust with rulership... *"For all who are led by the Spirit of God are sons of God" (Rom. 8:14).*

So we now realize this is the "House" God promised to build for David, an eternal family. But greater yet, it has always been God's plan and goal of preparing this "House" for her eternal destiny. The world naturally thinks life revolves around its own course of daily pursuits and the workings of living life. It does not. There is a greater reality and purpose beyond what we can see, and it is not obvious. It's about God's purpose and the building of David's house.

This is the realness of purposeful living in the reality of God's world. The world is God's grand classroom in which He's constantly preparing His eternal family for rulership with His Beloved. The world revolves around this destiny of and for God as He apprehends His eternal sons and daughters, a plan before the ages, and brings them to their well-appointed and scheduled destination: Christlikeness. My friend, this is indeed our inheritance we wait to obtain: "In Him, we have obtained an inheritance, having been predestined according to the purpose of God" (Eph. 1:11). Amazingly, we have been predestined in God's love to become His adopted sons through Jesus Christ! (Eph. 1:5).

Personally, I have found nothing comparable in this life than to hear Him say, "You are mine, and I am yours!" There is no amount of money, position, possessions, or persons that could cause me to sacrifice such a treasure. To be able to know, without any doubt, He is my Father and I can be a son to Him, well, it just doesn't get any better than that! That by itself would be enough, but to consider He desires for each of us to rule with His Son, Jesus, to give us such an honor, it is indeed beyond words!

All these spiritual blessings compel me to view Father-God with such awe, causing me to say, like David, with overwhelming gratitude, "Who am I, that you would give me such purpose? Who am I, that I can call you, Father? Who am I, that I can be called, your son? Who am I, You would frame me for fellowship with You, so I could enjoy you? Who am I, You would give me such an identity, to be Your treasured possession, designed for Your dwelling? Who am I, You would destine me for rule with Your Beloved Son, Jesus? Who am I, You would fashion for me a heart, like Jesus, so I can live a life worthy of You, as well as to know You?" Such is your pursuit, Father-God, of my own heart, as I now pursue yours!

And yet probably the greatest question should be posed with astonished reverence of worship … "Who are You, O God, You would desire and purpose to do all this for me?" Oh, my friend, if we listen, ever so carefully, you and I can hear Him say, *I am Jesus, the root and descendant of David, the Bright Morning Star!*

Yes, it is He who leads us every day to our ultimate destination and provides the unfathomable promise … *"The one who conquers (completes their training) will have this heritage, and I will be His God and he will be My son!" (Rev. 21:7).*

Notes

Preface

1. The ESV Study Bible, *Introduction to The Psalms*, (Wheaton: Crossway, 2008), 935.
2. Walter C. Kaiser, JR. *A History of Israel: From the Bronze Age through The Jewish Wars* (Nashville: B & H Publishing Group, 1998), 266.

Introduction

1. Charles R. Swindoll, *A Man of Passion & Destiny—David*, (Nashville: W Publishing Group, 1997), 137.
2. Walter C. Kaiser, JR. *A History of Israel: From the Bronze Age through The Jewish Wars*, (Nashville: B & H Publishing Group, 1998), 248.
3. Ibid, 232.
4. Ibid, 243.
5. Ibid, 226.
6. I. Howard Marshall, A. R. Millard, J.I. Packer, and D. J. Wiseman, eds., *New Bible Dictionary, 3rd ed.* (Downers Grove: Intervarsity-Press, 1996), 258.

Prologue

1. Michael J. Gorman, *Elements of Biblical Exegesis—Revised and Expanded Edition* (Peabody: Hendrickson Publishers, 2009), 10-11.

Chapter 1: The Divine Pursuit of David!

1. J. Swanson, *Dictionary of Biblical Languages with Semantic Domains: Greek (New Testament)* (electronic ed.), (Oak Harbor: Logos Research Systems, Inc.), 1997.
2. Jane Willard, John Ortberg, and Dallas Willard Center, *Dallas Willard: Living In Christ's Presence—Final Words on Heaven and the Kingdom of God* (Downers Grove: Inter Varsity Press, 2014), 116.

Chapter 4: The Pursuit of God: A Pathway of Prayer!

1. Gordon D. Fee, *Paul, the Spirit, and the People of God* (Peabody: Hendrickson Publishers, Inc., 1996), 149.
2. Brad H. Young, *The Parables—Jewish Tradition and Christian Interpretation*, (Peabody: Hendrickson Publishers, 1998), 42.
3. David Kinnaman and Gabe Lyons, *Unchristian—What a New Generation Really Thinks About Christianity and Why it Matters*, (Grand Rapids: Baker Books, 2007), 31-32.
4. A. W. Tozer, *The Knowledge of the Holy*, (New York: HarperCollins Publishers, 1961), 1.

5. A. W. Tozer, *The Pursuit of God—The Human Thirst for the Divine* (Camp Hill: Wing Spread Publishers, 1982), 84-85.
6. Jack W. Hayford, *Prayer is Invading the Impossible*, (Alachua: Bridge-Logos, 1977), 94.
7. Gordon D. Fee, *Paul, the Spirit, and the People of God*, (Peabody: Hendrickson Publishers, Inc., 1996), 149.
8. Ibid, 148-149.
9. Richard J. Foster, *Prayer—Finding the Heart's True Home*, (New York: HarperCollins Publishers, 1992), 6.

Chapter 5: The Shepherd Boy Becomes King... And a Pivotal Moment!

1. Walter C. Kaiser, Jr. *A History of Israel—From the Bronze Age through the Jewish Wars* (Nashville: B & H Publishing Group, 1998), 240.
2. Ibid, 248.
3. Ibid, 249.
4. Jack W. Hayford, *The Essence of Repentance*, Sermon Series: Luke 3:1-14, Church On the Way, July 20, 1980.
5. John Ortberg, *Soul Keeping, The Most Important Part of You*, (Grand Rapids: Zondervan, 2014), 78.
6. Dallas Willard, *Renovation of the Heart—Putting on the Character of Christ* (Colorado Springs: NavPress, 2002), 60.
7. Jane Willard, John Ortberg, and DallasWillardCenter, *Living In Christ's Presence—Final Words on Heaven and the Kingdom of God* (Downers Grove: InterVarsity Press, 2014), 116.

8. James Strong, *Enhanced Strong's Lexicon*, Woodside Bible Fellowship, 1995.

9. Andrew Murray, *Humility—The Beauty of Holiness*, (Ft. Washington: CLC Publications, 1997), 14-15.

Chapter 6: The Deficiency for David's Derailment

1. A. Scott Moreau, Gary R. Corwin and Gary B. McGee, *Introducing World Missions—A Biblical, Historical, and Practical Survey*, (Grand Rapids: Baker Academic, 2004), 14.

Chapter 7: David: "I Want to Build God a House!"

1. Walter C. Kaiser, Jr. *A History of Israel—From the Bronze Age through The Jewish Wars* (Nashville: B & H Publishing Group, 1998), 248.

2. Ibid.

3. Ibid, 247.

4. Ibid, 248.

5. Jane Willard, John Ortberg, and Dallas Willard Center, Dallas Willard: *Living In Christ's Presence—Final Words on Heaven and the Kingdom of God*, (Downers Grove: InterVarsity Press, 2014), 118.

6. A. W. Tozer, *The Pursuit of God—The Human Thirst for The Divine* (Camp Hill: WingSpread Publishers, 1982), 16.

7. Jack W. Hayford, *Manifest Presence—Expecting A Visitation of God's Grace through Worship* (Kent, England: Sovereign World, 2005), 58.

8. The ESV Study Bible, See Note, John 4:20-21, (Wheaton: Crossway, 2008), 2028.

9. Dallas Willard, *Renovation of The Heart—Putting on the Character of Christ*, (Colorado Springs: NavPress, 2002), 30.

10. Jack W. Hayford, *Manifest Presence—Expecting A Visitation of God's Grace through Worship* (Kent, England: Sovereign World, 2005), 46.

11. A. W. Tozer, *The Pursuit of God—The Human Thirst for the Divine* (Camp Hill: WingSpread Publishers, 1982), 9.

12. Stephen Seamands, *Ministry in the Image of God—The Trinitarian Shape of Christian Service*, (Downers Grove: InterVarsity Press, 2005), 28.

Chapter 8: The Lord: "No, David, I will Build You A House!"

1. Frederick William Danker, *A Greek-English Lexicon of the New Testament and Other Early Christian Literature—Third Edition* (Chicago: The University of Chicago Press, 2000), 698.

2. The ESV Study Bible, *Cited from 1 Chron. 22:9-10*, (Wheaton: Crossway, 2008), 734.

3. James Strong, *Enhanced Strong's Lexicon*, (Bellingham: Logos Bible Software, 2001), #3427.

4. Ibid, #3942.

5. R. B. Hughes and J. C. Laney, *Tyndale Concise Bible Commentary*, (Wheaton: Tyndale House Publishers, 2001).

Chapter 9: The House God Promised David...For Eternity!

1. Walter C. Kaiser Jr., *A History of Israel—From the Bronze Age to the Jewish Wars*, (Nashville: B & H Publishing Group, 1998), 249.

2. Andrew Murray, *The Two Covenants—Your Blessings in Christ, Moving from Promise to Fulfillment*, (FortWashington: CLC Publications, 2005), 84.

3. Walter C. Kaiser, Jr., *A History of Israel—From the Bronze Age through the Jewish Wars*, (Nashville: B & H Publishing Group, 1998), 102.

4. Ibid, 117.

5. Peter Scazzero, *Emotionally Healthy Spirituality—Unleash a Revolution in Your Life in Christ*, (Nashville: Thomas Nelson, 2006), 66.

6. Dr. Larry Crabb, *Effective Biblical Counseling—A Model for Helping Caring Christians Become Capable Counselors*, (Grand Rapids: Zondervan Publishing House, 1977), 61.

7. Dallas Willard, *The Divine Conspiracy—Rediscovering our Hidden Life in God*, (New York: HarperCollins Publishers, 1997), 15.

Chapter 10: The Perfect Plan: A Precious Foundation for David's House!

1. Cornelius Plantinga, Jr., *Not the Way It's Supposed to Be—A Breviary of Sin*, (Grand Rapids: Wm. Eerdmans Publishing Co., 1995), 10.

2. Ibid, 14.

3. Ibid, 12-13.

4. Paul E. Billheimer, *Don't Waste Your Sorrows—A Study in Sainthood and Suffering*, (Fort Washington: Christian Literature Crusade, 1977), 44.

5. W. A. Elwell and P. W. Comfort, *Tyndale Bible Dictionary*, (Wheaton: Tyndale House Publishers, 2001).

6. R. L. Thomas, *New American Standard Hebrew-Aramaic and Greek Dictionaries—Updated Edition*, (Anaheim: Foundation Publications, Inc., 1998).

7. I. Merriam-Webster, *Merriam-Webster's Collegiate Dictionary—10ᵗʰ Edition*, (Springfield: Merriam Webster, 1996).

8. Kenneth S. Wuest, *Wuest's Word Studies in the Greek New Testament*, (Grand Rapids: Wm. Eerdman's Publishing Co., 1997).

Chapter 11: The Design: "Look and Livability" of David's House!

1. Clark H. Pinnock, *Flame of Love—A Theology of the Holy Spirit*, (Downers Grove: InterVarsity Press, 1996), 22.

2. Stephen Seamands, *Ministry in the Image of God—The Trinitarian Shape of Christian Service*, (Downers Grove: InterVarsity Press, 2005), 101.

3. The English Standard Version Study Bible, *For in Him the Fullness of God was Pleased to Dwell--Commentary*, (Wheaton: Crossway, 2008), 2294.

4. The ESV Study Bible, *Another Descriptive Quality Attribute by Jesus of the Holy Spirit--John 16:13*, (Wheaton: Crossway, 2008), 2057.

5. Stephen Seamands, *Ministry in the Image of God—The Trinitarian Shape of Christian Service*, (Downers Grove: InterVarsity Press, 2005), 59.

6. Clark H. Pinnock, *Flame of Love—A Theology of the Holy Spirit*, (Downers Grove: InterVarsity Press, 1996), 55.

7. Ibid, 55.

8. Roderick Leupp, *Knowing the Name of God*, (Downers Grove: InterVarsity Press, 1996), 28.

9. Stephen Seamands, *Ministry in the Image of God—The Trinitarian Shape of Christian Service*, (Downers Grove: InterVarsity Press, 2005), 79.

10. A. W. Tozer, *The Pursuit of God—The Human Thirst for the Divine* (Camp Hill: WingSpread Publishers, 1982), 100.

11. H. G. Liddell, *A Lexicon: Abridged from Liddell and Scott's Greek-English Lexicon*, (Oak Harbor: Logos Research Systems, Public Domain).

12. I. Merriam-Webster, *Merriam-Webster's Collegiate Dictionary—10th ed.*, (Springfield: Merriam-Webster, 1996).

13. Dallas Willard, *The Divine Conspiracy—Rediscovering Our Hidden Life in God*, (New York: HarperCollins Publishers, 1997), 236.

14. Stephen Seamands, *Ministry in the Image of God—The Trinitarian Shape of Christian Service*, (Downers Grove: InterVarsity Press, 2005), 66.

Chapter 12: The Passionate Care of David's House! (Part I)

1. Richard J. Krejcir, *What is Going on with Pastors in America?* (Francis A. Shaeffer Institute of Church Leadership Development: www.churchleadership.org, 2007).

2. J. Strong, *Enhanced Strong's Lexicon*, (Bellingham: Logos Bible Software, 2001).

3. J. Swanson, *Dictionary of Biblical Languages with Semantic Domains: Greek (New Testament) (electronic, ed)*, (Oak Harbor: Logos Research Systems, Inc. 1997).

4. Dallas Willard, *The Divine Conspiracy—Rediscovering Our Hidden Life in God*, (New York: HarperCollins Publishers, 1997), 301.

5. J. Strong, *Enhanced Strong's Lexicon*, (Bellingham: Logos Bible Software, 2001).

6. Andrew Murray, *Humility—The Beauty of Holiness*, (Ft. Washington: CLC Publications, 1997), 21.

7. Andrew Murray, *Humility—The Beauty of Holiness*, (Ft. Washington: CLC Publications, 1997), 9.

Chapter 12: The Passionate Care of David's House! (Part II)

8. Richard J. Krejcir, *What is Going on with Pastors in America?* (Francis A. Shaeffer Institute of Church Leadership Development: www.churchleadership.org, 2007).

9. J. Strong, *Enhanced Strong's Lexicon*, (Bellingham: Logos Bible Software, 2001).

10. The ESV Study Bible, *Psalm 34, A Psalm of Thanksgiving by David*, (Wheaton: Crossway, 2008), 978.

11. J. Strong, *Enhanced Strong's Lexicon*, (Bellingham: Logos, Woodside Bible Edition, 1995).

12. Stephen Seamands, *Ministry in the Image of God—The Trinitarian Shape of Christian Service*, (Downers Grove: InterVarsity Press, 2005), 65.

13. Gordon D. Fee, *Paul, the Spirit, and the People of God*, (Peabody: Hendrickson Publishers, Inc., 1996), 148-149.

14. Henry Blackaby and Richard Blackaby, *Spiritual Leadership—Moving People on to God's Agenda*, (Nashville: B & H Publishing Group, 2001), 149.

Chapter 13: The Invitation to Be God's House!

1. Cleon L. Rogers Jr. and Cleon L. Rogers III, *The New Linguistic and Exegetical Key to the Greek New Testament*, (Grand Rapids: Zondervan Publishing House, 1998), 146.
2. J. Dwight Pentecost, *The Words & Works of Jesus Christ—A Study of the Life of Christ*, (Grand Rapids: Zondervan Corporation, 1981), 332.
3. Dallas Willard, *How Does the Disciple Live?* (Berkley: Radix Magazine, spring, 2009), Vol. 34:3.
4. Craig S. Keener, *The IVP Bible Background Commentary: New Testament*, (Downers Grove: InterVarsity Press, 1993).
5. SidneyI. Landau, Ed., *The Reader's Digest Great Encyclopedia Dictionary*, (Pleasantville: Reader's Digest Assoc., 1966), 731.
6. Dallas Willard, *The Divine Conspiracy—Rediscovering Our Hidden Life in God*, (New York: HarperCollins Publishers, 1997), 62.
7. Ibid, 290.
8. James A Swanson, *Dictionary of Biblical Languages with Semantic Domains: Greek (New Testament) (Electronic ed.)*, (Oak Harbor: Logos Research Systems, Inc., 1997).
9. A. W. Tozer, *God's Pursuit of Man*, (Camp Hill: WingSpread Publishers, 2006), 19.

Chapter 14: The Destiny of David's House!

1. James Strong, *Enhanced Strong's Lexicon*, (Bellingham: Logos, Woodside Bible Edition, 1995).

2. Paul E. Billheimer, *Destined for The Throne—A Remarkable New Perspective on the Eternal Destiny of The Bride of Christ*, (Minneapolis: Bethany House Publishers, 1975), 27.

3. Dallas Willard, *Renovation of the Heart—Putting on the Character of Christ*, (Colorado Springs: NavPress, 2002), 30.

4. Cleon L. Rogers Jr. and Cleon L. Rogers III, *The New Linguistic and Exegetical Key to the Greek New Testament*, (Grand Rapids: Zondervan Publishing House, 1998), 43.

5. James Strong, *Enhanced Strong's Lexicon*, (Woodside Bible Fellowship, 1995).

Chapter 15: Our Pursuit of God's Heart & Ultimate Destination for David's House!

1. James A Swanson, *Dictionary of Biblical Languages with Semantic Domains: Greek (New Testament) (Electronic ed.)*, (Oak Harbor: Logos Research Systems, Inc., 1997).

2. K. S. Wuest, *Wuest's Word Studies from the Greek New Testament: For the English Reader 6th Edition*, (Grand Rapids: Erdmans, 1997).

3. David Kinnaman and Gabe Lyons, *Unchristian—What a New Generation Really Thinks About Christianity and Why it Matters*, (Grand Rapids: Baker Books, 2007), 50-51.

4. Jack W. Hayford, *Rebuilding the Real You—The Definitive Guide to the Holy Spirit's Work in Your Life*, (LakeMary: Charisma House, 2009), 58.

5. Earl D. Radmacher, Gen. ed., *The Nelson Study Bible— New Kings James Version*, (Nashville: Thomas Nelson Publishers, 1997), 900.

6. New International Version, (Nashville: Holman Bible Publishers, 1986).

7. Jane Willard, John Ortberg, and Dallas Willard Center, *Living In Christ's Presence—Final Words on Heaven and the Kingdom of God*, (Downers Grove: InterVarsity Press, 2014), 119.

8. George Barna, *Barna Study of Religious Change Since 1991 Shows Significant Changes by Faith Group*, (Ventura: GeorgeBarna.org, 2011).

9. Dallas Willard, *Renovation of the Heart—Putting on the Character of Christ*, (Colorado Springs: NavPress, 2002), 143.

10. J. P. Louw, and E. A. Nida, *Greek-English Lexicon of the New Testament: Based on Semantic Domains (Electronic ed, of the 2nd edition)*, (New York: United Bible Societies, 1996).

About the Author

John Leon has been involved in some form of ministry for over twenty years. He has served as a public-school principal, worked in the state legislature, and is now privileged to be the executive director of a 105-bed homeless shelter, providing over seven thousand meals a month 24-7.

John's greatest passion is studying, writing, and sharing the reality of Jesus Christ. His very pulse of ministry is mentoring people to become students of Jesus.

Pursuit is John's first major written work and is currently involved in several other writing projects. He has earned a bachelor of theology and master of divinity at The King's University in Southland, Texas.

Ministry Contact:

john@johnleonministries.org

CPSIA information can be obtained
at www.ICGtesting.com
Printed in the USA
LVHW110301010720
659431LV00001B/174